To

Katherine Isobel Henderson.

From

Jim

"In the face of the whole room Tom knelt down to pray."

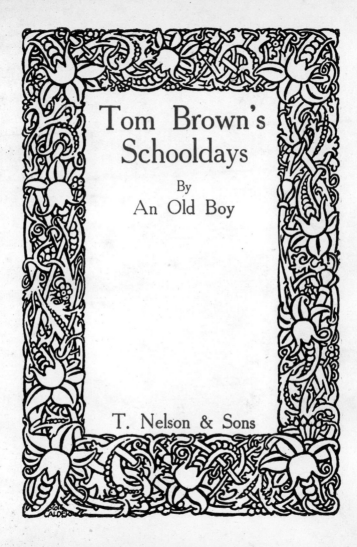

Tom Brown's Schooldays

By
An Old Boy

T. Nelson & Sons

CONTENTS.

PART I.

PART II.

CONTENTS

TOM BROWN'S SCHOOL DAYS.

CHAPTER I.

THE BROWN FAMILY.

> " I'm the Poet of White Horse Vale, sir,
>   With liberal notions under my cap."—*Ballad.*

THE Browns have become illustrious by the pen of Thackeray and the pencil of Doyle, within the memory of the young gentlemen who are now matriculating at the universities. Notwithstanding the well-merited but late fame which has now fallen upon them, any one at all acquainted with the family must feel that much has yet to be written and said before the British nation will be properly sensible of how much of its greatness it owes to the Browns. For centuries, in their quiet, dogged, homespun way, they have been sub-duing the earth in most English counties, and leaving their mark in American forests and Australian uplands. Wherever the fleets and armies of England have won renown, there stalwart sons of the Browns have done yeomen's work. With the yew bow and cloth-yard shaft at Cressy and Agincourt—with the brown bill and pike under the brave Lord Willoughby—with culverin and demi-culverin against Spaniards and Dutchmen—with hand-grenade and sabre, and musket and bayonet, under Rodney and St. Vincent, Wolfe and Moore, Nelson and Wellington, they have carried their lives in their hands, getting hard knocks and hard work in plenty—which was on the whole what they looked for, and the best thing for them—and little praise or pudding, which indeed they, and most of us, are better without. Talbots and Stanleys, St. Maurs, and such-like folk, have led armies and made laws time out of mind ; but those noble families would be somewhat astounded—if the accounts ever came to be fairly taken—to find how small their work for England has been by the side of that of the Browns.

These latter, indeed, have, until the present generation, rarely been sung by poet, or chronicled by sage. They have wanted their *sacer vates*, having been too solid to rise to the top by themselves, and not having been largely gifted with the talent of catching hold of, and holding on tight to, whatever good things happened to be going—the foundation of the fortunes of so many noble families. But the world goes on its way, and the wheel turns, and the wrongs of the Browns, like other wrongs, seem in a fair way to get righted. And this present writer, having for many years of his life been a devout Brown-worshipper, and, moreover, having the honour of being nearly connected with an eminently respectable branch of the great Brown family, is anxious, so far as in him lies, to help the wheel over, and throw his stone on to the pile.

However, gentle reader, or simple reader, whichever you may be, lest you should be led to waste your precious time upon these pages, I make so bold as at once to tell you the sort of folk you'll have to meet and put up with, if you and I are to jog on comfortably together. You shall hear at once what sort of folk the Browns are—at least my branch of them; and then, if you don't like the sort, why, cut the concern at once, and let you and I cry quits before either of us can grumble at the other.

In the first place, the Browns are a fighting family. One may question their wisdom, or wit, or beauty, but about their fight there can be no question. Wherever hard knocks of any kind, visible or invisible, are going, there the Brown who is nearest must shove in his carcass. And these carcasses, for the most part, answer very well to the characteristic propensity: they are a square-headed and snake-necked generation, broad in the shoulder, deep in the chest, and thin in the flank, carrying no lumber. Then for clanship, they are as bad as Highlanders; it is amazing the belief they have in one another. With them there is nothing like the Browns, to the third and fourth generation. "Blood is thicker than water," is one of their pet sayings. They can't be happy unless they are always meeting one another. Never were such people for family gatherings, which, were you a stranger, or sensitive, you might think had better not have been gathered together. For during the whole time of their being together they luxuriate in telling one another their minds on whatever subject turns up; and their minds are wonderfully antago-nistic, and all their opinions are downright beliefs. Till you've been among them some time and understand them, you can't think but that they are quarrelling. Not a bit of it. They love and respect one another ten times the more after a good set family arguing bout, and go back, one to his curacy, another to his chambers, and another to his regiment, freshened for work, and more than ever convinced that the Browns are the height of company.

This family training, too, combined with their turn for combativeness, makes them eminently quixotic. They can't let anything alone which they think going wrong. They must speak their mind about it, annoying all easy-going folk, and spend their time and money in having a tinker at it, however hopeless the job. It is an impossibility to a Brown to leave the most disreputable lame dog on the other side of a stile. Most other folk get tired of such work. The old Browns, with red faces, white whiskers, and bald heads, go on believing and fighting to a green old age. They have always a crotchet going, till the old man with the scythe reaps and garners them away for troublesome old boys as they are.

And the most provoking thing is, that no failures knock them up, or make them hold their hands, or think you, or me, or other sane people in the right. Failures slide off them like July rain off a duck's back feathers. Jem and his whole family turn out bad, and cheat them one week, and the next they are doing the same thing for Jack; and when he goes to the treadmill, and his wife and children to the workhouse, they will be on the lookout for Bill to take his place.

However, it is time for us to get from the general to the particular; so, leaving the great army of Browns, who are scattered over the whole empire on which the sun never sets, and whose general diffusion I take to be the chief cause of that empire's stability, let us at once fix our attention upon the small nest of Browns in which our hero was hatched, and which dwelt in that portion of the royal county of Berks which is called the Vale of White Horse.

Most of you have probably travelled down the Great

Western Railway as far as Swindon. Those of you who did so with their eyes open have been aware, soon after leaving the Didcot station, of a fine range of chalk hills running parallel with the railway on the left-hand side as you go down, and distant some two or three miles, more or less, from the line. The highest point in the range is the White Horse Hill, which you come in front of just before you stop at the Shrivenham station. If you love English scenery, and have a few hours to spare, you can't do better, the next time you pass, than stop at the Farringdon Road or Shrivenham station, and make your way to that highest point. And those who care for the vague old stories that haunt country-sides all about England, will not, if they are wise, be content with only a few hours' stay; for, glorious as the view is, the neighbourhood is yet more interesting for its relics of bygone times. I only know two English neighbourhoods thoroughly, and in each, within a circle of five miles, there is enough of interest and beauty to last any reasonable man his life. I believe this to be the case almost throughout the country, but each has a special attraction, and none can be richer than the one I am speaking of and going to introduce you to very particularly, for on this subject I must be prosy; so those that don't care for England in detail may skip the chapter.

O young England! young England! you who are born into these racing railroad times, when there's a Great Exhibition, or some monster sight, every year, and you can get over a couple of thousand miles of ground for three pound ten in a five-weeks' holiday, why don't you know more of your own birthplaces? You're all in the ends of the earth, it seems to me, as soon as you get your necks out of the educational collar, for midsummer holidays, long vacations, or what not—going round Ireland, with a return ticket, in a fortnight ; dropping your copies of Tennyson on the tops of Swiss mountains ; or pulling down the Danube in Oxford racing boats. And when you get home for a quiet fortnight, you turn the steam off, and lie on your backs in the paternal garden, surrounded by the last batch of books from Mudie's library, and half bored to death. Well, well ! I know it has its good side. You all patter French more or less, and perhaps German ; you have seen men and cities, no doubt, and have your opinions, such as they are, about schools of painting, high art, and all that ; have seen the pictures of Dresden and the Louvre, and know the taste of sour krout. All I say is, you don't know your own lanes and woods and fields. Though you may be choke-full of science, not one in twenty of you knows where to find the wood-sorrel, or bee-orchis, which grow in the next wood, or on the down three miles off, or what the bog-bean and wood-sage are good for. And as for the country legends, the stories of the old gable-ended farmhouses, the place where the last skirmish was fought in the civil wars, where the parish butts stood, where the last highwayman turned to bay, where the last ghost was laid by the parson, they're gone out of date altogether.

Now, in my time, when we got home by the old coach, which put us down at the cross-roads with our boxes, the first day of the holidays, and had been driven off by the family coachman, singing " Dulce Domum " at the top of our voices, there we were, fixtures, till black Monday came round. We had to cut out our own amusements within a walk or a ride of home. And so we got to know all the country folk and their ways and songs and stories by heart, and went over the fields and woods and hills, again and again, till we made friends of them all. We were Berkshire, or Gloucestershire, or

their eyrie. The ground falls away rapidly on all sides. Was there ever such turf in the whole world ? You sink up to your ankles at every step, and yet the spring of it is delicious. There is always a breeze in the " camp," as it is called ; and here it lies, just as the Romans left it, except that cairn on the east side, left by her Majesty's corps of sappers and miners the other day, when they and the engineer officer had finished their sojourn there, and their surveys for the ordnance map of Berkshire. It is altogether a place that you won't forget, a place to open a man's soul, and make him prophesy, as he looks down on that great Vale spread out as the garden of the Lord before him, and wave on wave of the mysterious downs behind, and to the right and left the chalk hills running away into the distance, along which he can trace for miles the old Roman road, " the Ridgeway " (" the Rudge," as the country folk call it), keeping straight along the highest back of the hills—such a place as Balak brought Balaam to, and told him to prophesy against the people in the valley beneath. And he could not, neither shall you, for they are a people of the Lord who abide there.

And now we leave the camp, and descend towards the west, and are on the Ashdown. We are treading on heroes. It is sacred ground for Englishmen—more sacred than all but one or two fields where their bones lie whitening. For this is the actual place where our Alfred won his great battle, the battle of Ashdown (" Æscendum " in the chroniclers), which broke the Danish power, and made England a Christian land. The Danes held the camp and the slope where we are standing—the whole crown of the hill, in fact. " The heathen had beforehand seized the higher ground," as old Asser says, having wasted everything behind them from London, and being just ready to burst down on the fair Vale, Alfred's own birthplace and heritage. And up the heights came the Saxons, as they did at the Alma. " The Christians led up their line from the lower ground. There stood also on that same spot a single thorn-tree, marvellous stumpy (which we ourselves with our very own eyes have seen)." Bless the old chronicler ! Does he think nobody ever saw the " single thorn-tree " but himself ? Why, there it stands to this very day, just on the edge of the slope, and I saw it not three weeks since—an old single thorn-tree, " marvellous stumpy." At least, if it isn't the same tree it ought to have been, for it's just in the place where the battle must have been won or lost—" around which, as I was saying, the two lines of foemen came together in battle with a huge shout. And in this place one of the two kings of the heathen and five of his earls fell down and died, and many thousands of the heathen side in the same place."* After which crowning mercy, the pious king, that there might never be wanting a sign and a memorial to the country-side, carved out on the northern side of the chalk hill, under the camp, where it is almost precipitous, the great Saxon White Horse, which he who will may see from the railway, and which gives its name to the Vale, over which it has looked these thousand years and more.

* " Pagani editiorem locum præoccupaverant. Christiani ab inferiori loco aciem dirigebant. Erat quoque in eodem loco unica spinosa arbor, brevis admodum (quam nos ipsi nostris propriis oculis vidimus). Circa quam ergo hostiles inter se acies cum ingenti clamore hostiliter conveniunt. Quo in loco alter de duobus Paganorum regibus et quinque comites occisi occubuerunt, et multa millia Paganæ partis in eodem loco. Cecidit illic ergo Bœgsceg Rex, et Sidroc ille senex comes, et Sidroc Junior comes, et Obsbern comes," etc.—*Annales Rerum Gestarum Ælfredi Magni, Auctore Asserio. Recensuit Franciscus Wise.* Oxford, 1722, p. 23.

Right down below the White Horse is a curious deep and broad gully called " the Manger," into one side of which the hills fall with a series of the most lovely sweeping curves, known as " the Giant's Stairs."   They are not a bit like stairs, but I never saw anything like them anywhere else, with their short green turf, and tender bluebells, and gossamer and thistle-down gleaming in the sun and the sheep-paths running along their sides like ruled lines.

The other side of the Manger is formed by the Dragon's Hill, a curious little round self-confident fellow, thrown forward from the range, utterly unlike everything round him. On this hill some deliverer of mankind— St. George, the country folk used to tell me—killed a dragon. Whether it were St. George, I cannot say ; but surely a dragon was killed there, for you may see the marks yet where his blood ran down, and more by token the place where it ran down is the easiest way up the hillside.

Passing along the Ridgeway to the west for about a mile, we come to a little clump of young beech and firs, with a growth of thorn and privet underwood. Here you may find nests of the strong down partridge and peewit, but take care that the keeper isn't down upon you ; and in the middle of it is an old cromlech, a huge flat stone raised on seven or eight others, and led up to by a path, with large single stones set up on each side. This is Wayland Smith's cave, a place of classic fame now ; but as Sir Walter has touched it, I may as well let it alone, and refer you to " Kenilworth " for the legend.

The thick, deep wood which you see in the hollow, about a mile off, surrounds Ashdown Park, built by Inigo Jones. Four broad alleys are cut through the wood from circumference to centre, and each leads to

one face of the house. The mystery of the downs hangs
about house and wood, as they stand there alone, so
unlike all around, with the green slopes studded with
great stones just about this part, stretching away on all
sides. It was a wise Lord Craven, I think, who pitched
his tent there.

Passing along the Ridgeway to the east, we soon come
to cultivated land. The downs, strictly so called, are no
more. Lincolnshire farmers have been imported, and
the long, fresh slopes are sheep-walks no more, but grow
famous turnips and barley. One of these improvers
lives over there at the " Seven Barrows " farm, another
mystery of the great downs. There are the barrows still,
solemn and silent, like ships in the calm sea, the sepul-
chres of some sons of men. But of whom ? It is three
miles from the White Horse—too far for the slain of Ashdown to be buried there. Who shall say what heroes are
waiting there ? But we must get down into the Vale
again, and so away by the Great Western Railway to
town, for time and the printer's devil press, and it is a
terrible long and slippery descent, and a shocking bad
road. At the bottom, however, there is a pleasant
public, whereat we must really take a modest quencher,
for the down air is provocative of thirst. So we pull up
under an old oak which stands before the door.

" What is the name of your hill, landlord ? "

" Blawing STWUN Hill, sir, to be sure."

[READER. " Sturm ? "

AUTHOR. " Stone, stupid—the Blowing Stone."]

" And of your house ? I can't make out the sign."

" Blawing Stwun, sir," says the landlord, pouring out
his old ale from a Toby Philpot jug, with a melodious
crash, into the long-necked glass.

" What queer names ! " say we, sighing at the end

of our draught, and holding out the glass to be replenished.

" Bean't queer at all, as I can see, sir," says mine host, handing back our glass, " seeing as this here is the Blawing Stwun, his self," putting his hand on a square lump of stone, some three feet and a half high, perforated with two or three queer holes, like petrified antediluvian rat-holes, which lies there close under the oak, under our very nose. We are more than ever puzzled, and drink our second glass of ale, wondering what will come next. " Like to hear un, sir ?" says mine host, setting down Toby Philpot on the tray, and resting both hands on the " Stwun." We are ready for anything ; and he, without waiting for a reply, applies his mouth to one of the ratholes. Something must come of it, if he doesn't burst. Good heavens ! I hope he has no apoplectic tendencies. Yes, here it comes, sure enough, a gruesome sound between a moan and a roar, and spreads itself away over the valley, and up the hillside, and into the woods at the back of the house, a ghost-like, awful voice. " Um do say, sir," says mine host, rising purple-faced, while the moan is still coming out of the Stwun, " as they used in old times to warn the country-side by blawing the Stwun when the enemy was a-comin', and as how folks could make un heered then for seven mile round ; leastways, so I've heered Lawyer Smith say, and he knows a smart sight about them old times." We can hardly swallow Lawyer Smith's seven miles ; but could the blowing of the stone have been a summons, a sort of sending the fiery cross round the neighbourhood in the old times ? What old times ? Who knows ? We pay for our beer, and are thankful.

" And what's the name of the village just below, landlord ?"

" Kingstone Lisle, sir."

" Fine plantations you've got here ? "

" Yes, sir; the Squire's 'mazing fond of trees and such like."

" No wonder. He's got some real beauties to be fond of. Good-day, landlord."

" Good-day, sir, and a pleasant ride to 'ee."

And now, my boys, you whom I want to get for readers, have you had enough ? Will you give in at once, and say you're convinced, and let me begin my story, or will you have more of it ? Remember, I've only been over a little bit of the hillside yet—what you could ride round easily on your ponies in an hour. I'm only just come down into the Vale, by Blowing Stone Hill; and if I once begin about the Vale, what's to stop me ? You'll have to hear all about Wantage, the birthplace of Alfred, and Farringdon, which held out so long for Charles the First (the Vale was near Oxford, and dreadfully malignant— full of Throgmortons, Puseys, and Pyes, and such like, and their brawny retainers). Did you ever read Thomas Ingoldsby's " Legend of Hamilton Tighe " ? If you haven't, you ought to have. Well, Farringdon is where he lived, before he went to sea ; his real name was Hamden Pye, and the Pyes were the great folk at Farringdon. Then there's Pusey. You've heard of the Pusey horn, which King Canute gave to the Puseys of that day, and which the gallant old squire, lately gone to his rest (whom Berkshire freeholders turned out of last Parliament, to their eternal disgrace, for voting according to his conscience), used to bring out on high days, holidays, and bonfire nights. And the splendid old cross church at Uffington, the Uffingas town. How the whole country-side teems with Saxon names and memories ! And the old moated grange at Compton, nestled close under the

country once in five years. A visit to Reading or Abing-
don twice a year, at assizes or quarter sessions, which
the Squire made on his horse with a pair of saddle-bags
containing his wardrobe, a stay of a day or two at some
country neighbour's, or an expedition to a county ball
or the yeomanry review, made up the sum of the Brown
locomotion in most years. A stray Brown from some
distant county dropped in every now and then ; or from
Oxford, on grave nag, an old don, contemporary of the
Squire ; and were looked upon by the Brown household
and the villagers with the same sort of feeling with which
we now regard a man who has crossed the Rocky Mountains, or launched a boat on the Great Lake in Central
Africa. The White Horse Vale, remember, was traversed
by no great road—nothing but country parish roads, and
these very bad. Only one coach ran there, and this one
only from Wantage to London, so that the western part
of the Vale was without regular means of moving on,
and certainly didn't seem to want them. There was the
canal, by the way, which supplied the country-side with
coal, and up and down which continually went the long
barges, with the big black men lounging by the side of the
horses along the towing-path, and the women in bright-
coloured handkerchiefs standing in the sterns steering.
Standing I say, but you could never see whether they
were standing or sitting, all but their heads and shoulders
being out of sight in the cozy little cabins which occupied some eight feet of the stern, and which Tom Brown
pictured to himself as the most desirable of residences.
His nurse told him that those good-natured-looking
women were in the constant habit of enticing children
into the barges, and taking them up to London and selling them, which Tom wouldn't believe, and which made
him resolve as soon as possible to accept the oft-proffered

invitation of these sirens to "young master" to come in and have a ride. But as yet the nurse was too much for Tom.

Yet why should I, after all, abuse the gadabout propensities of my countrymen? We are a vagabond nation now, that's certain, for better for worse. I am a vagabond; I have been away from home no less than five distinct times in the last year. The Queen sets us the example: we are moving on from top to bottom. Little dirty Jack, who abides in Clement's Inn gateway, and blacks my boots for a penny, takes his month's hoppicking every year as a matter of course. Why shouldn't he? I'm delighted at it. I love vagabonds, only I prefer poor to rich ones. Couriers and ladies'-maids, imperials and travelling carriages, are an abomination unto me; I cannot away with them. But for dirty Jack, and every good fellow who, in the words of the capital French song, moves about,

> " Comme le limaçon,
> Portant tout son bagage,
> Ses meubles, sa maison,"

on his own back, why, good luck to them, and many a merry roadside adventure, and steaming supper in the chimney corners of roadside inns, Swiss châlets, Hottentot kraals, or wherever else they like to go. So, having succeeded in contradicting myself in my first chapter (which gives me great hopes that you will all go on, and think me a good fellow notwithstanding my crotchets), I shall here shut up for the present, and consider my ways; having resolved to "sar' it out," as we say in the Vale, "holus bolus" just as it comes, and then you'll probably get the truth out of me.

CHAPTER II.

THE "VEAST."

"And the King commandeth and forbiddeth, that from henceforth neither fairs nor markets be kept in Churchyards, for the honour of the Church."—STATUTES: 13 *Edw. I.* Stat. II. cap. vi.

As that venerable and learned poet (whose voluminous works we all think it the correct thing to admire and talk about, but don't read often) most truly says, "The child is father to the man;" *à fortiori*, therefore, he must be father to the boy. So as we are going at any rate to see Tom Brown through his boyhood, supposing we never get any farther (which, if you show a proper sense of the value of this history, there is no knowing but what we may), let us have a look at the life and environments of the child in the quiet country village to which we were introduced in the last chapter.

Tom, as has been already said, was a robust and combative urchin, and at the age of four began to struggle against the yoke and authority of his nurse. That functionary was a good-hearted, tearful, scatter-brained girl, lately taken by Tom's mother, Madam Brown, as she was called, from the village school to be trained as nursery-maid. Madam Brown was a rare trainer of servants, and spent herself freely in the profession; for profession it was, and gave her more trouble by half than many people take to earn a good income. Her servants were known and sought after for miles round. Almost all the girls who attained a certain place in the village school were taken by her, one or two at a time, as housemaids, laundrymaids, nurserymaids, or kitchenmaids, and after a year or two's training were started in life amongst the neighbouring families, with good principles and wardrobes. One of the results of this system was the perpetual despair of Mrs. Brown's cook and own maid, who no sooner had a notable girl made to their hands than missus was sure to find a good place for her and send her off, taking in fresh importations from the school. Another was, that the house was always full of young girls, with clean, shining faces, who broke plates and scorched linen, but made an atmosphere of cheerful, homely life about the place, good for every one who came within its influence. Mrs. Brown loved young people, and in fact human creatures in general, above plates and linen. They were more like a lot of elder children than servants, and felt to her more as a mother or aunt than as a mistress.

Tom's nurse was one who took in her instruction very slowly—she seemed to have two left hands and no head; and so Mrs. Brown kept her on longer than usual, that she might expend her awkwardness and forgetfulness upon those who would not judge and punish her too strictly for them.

Charity Lamb was her name. It had been the immemorial habit of the village to christen children either by Bible names, or by those of the cardinal and other virtues; so that one was for ever hearing in the village street or on the green, shrill sounds of " Prudence! Prudence! thee cum' out o' the gutter; " or, " Mercy! drat the girl, what bist thee a-doin' wi' little Faith?" and there were Ruths, Rachels, Keziahs, in every corner. The same with the boys : they were Benjamins, Jacobs, Noahs, Enochs. I suppose the custom has come down from Puritan times. There it is, at any rate, very strong still in the Vale.

Well, from early morning till dewy eve, when she had it out of him in the cold tub before putting him to bed, Charity and Tom were pitted against one another.

Physical power was as yet on the side of Charity, but she hadn't a chance with him wherever headwork was wanted. This war of independence began every morning before breakfast, when Charity escorted her charge to a neighbouring farmhouse, which supplied the Browns, and where, by his mother's wish, Master Tom went to drink whey before breakfast. Tom had no sort of objection to whey, but he had a decided liking for curds, which were forbidden as unwholesome; and there was seldom a morning that he did not manage to secure a handful of hard curds, in defiance of Charity and of the farmer's wife. The latter good soul was a gaunt, angular woman, who, with an old black bonnet on the top of her head, the strings dangling about her shoulders, and her gown tucked through her pocket-holes, went clattering about the dairy, cheese-room, and yard, in high pattens. Charity was some sort of niece of the old lady's, and was consequently free of the farmhouse and garden, into which she could not resist going for the purposes of gossip and flirtation with the heir-apparent, who was a dawdling fellow, never out at work as he ought to have been. The moment Charity had found her cousin, or any other occupation, Tom would slip away; and in a minute shrill cries would be heard from the dairy, "Charity, Charity, thee lazy huzzy, where bist?" and Tom would break cover, hands and mouth full of curds, and take refuge on the shaky surface of the great muck reservoir in the middle of the yard, disturbing the repose of the great pigs. Here he was in safety, as no grown person could follow without getting over their knees; and the luckless Charity, while her aunt scolded her from the dairy door, for being "allus hankering about arter our Willum, instead of minding Master Tom," would descend from threats to coaxing, to lure Tom out of the muck, which was rising over his shoes, and would soon tell a tale on his stockings, for which she would be sure to catch it from missus's maid.

Tom had two abettors, in the shape of a couple of old boys, Noah and Benjamin by name, who defended him from Charity, and expended much time upon his education. They were both of them retired servants of former generations of the Browns. Noah Crooke was a keen, dry old man of almost ninety, but still able to totter about. He talked to Tom quite as if he were one of his own family, and indeed had long completely identified the Browns with himself. In some remote age he had been the attendant of a Miss Brown, and had conveyed her about the country on a pillion. He had a little round picture of the identical gray horse, caparisoned with the identical pillion, before which he used to do a sort of fetish worship, and abuse turnpike-roads and carriages. He wore an old full-bottomed wig, the gift of some dandy old Brown whom he had valeted in the middle of last century, which habiliment Master Tom looked upon with considerable respect, not to say fear ; and indeed his whole feeling towards Noah was strongly tainted with awe. And when the old gentleman was gathered to his fathers, Tom's lamentation over him was not unaccompanied by a certain joy at having seen the last of the wig. "Poor old Noah, dead and gone," said he ; "Tom Brown so sorry. Put him in the coffin, wig and all."

But old Benjy was young master's real delight and refuge. He was a youth by the side of Noah, scarce seventy years old—a cheery, humorous, kind-hearted old man, full of sixty years of Vale gossip, and of all sorts of helpful ways for young and old, but above all for children. It was he who bent the first pin with which Tom extracted his first stickleback out of "Pebbly

Brook," the little stream which ran through the village. The first stickleback was a splendid fellow, with fabulous red and blue gills. Tom kept him in a small basin till the day of his death, and became a fisherman from that day. Within a month from the taking of the first stickleback, Benjy had carried off our hero to the canal, in defiance of Charity; and between them, after a whole afternoon's popjoying, they had caught three or four small, coarse fish and a perch, averaging perhaps two and a half ounces each, which Tom bore home in rapture to his mother as a precious gift, and which she received like a true mother with equal rapture, instructing the cook nevertheless, in a private interview, not to prepare the same for the Squire's dinner. Charity had appealed against old Benjy in the meantime, representing the dangers of the canal banks; but Mrs. Brown, seeing the boy's inaptitude for female guidance, had decided in Benjy's favour, and from thenceforth the old man was Tom's dry nurse. And as they sat by the canal watching their little green-and-white float, Benjy would instruct him in the doings of deceased Browns. How his grandfather, in the early days of the great war, when there was much distress and crime in the Vale, and the magistrates had been threatened by the mob, had ridden in with a big stick in his hand, and held the petty sessions by himself. How his great-uncle, the rector, had encountered and laid the last ghost, who had frightened the old women, male and female, of the parish out of their senses, and who turned out to be the blacksmith's apprentice disguised in drink and a white sheet. It was Benjy, too, who saddled Tom's first pony, and instructed him in the mysteries of horsemanship, teaching him to throw his weight back and keep his hand low, and who stood chuckling outside the door of the girls' school when

Tom rode his little Shetland into the cottage and round the table, where the old dame and her pupils were seated at their work.

Benjy himself was come of a family distinguished in the Vale for their prowess in all athletic games. Some half-dozen of his brothers and kinsmen had gone to the wars, of whom only one had survived to come home, with a small pension, and three bullets in different parts of his body ; he had shared Benjy's cottage till his death, and had left him his old dragoon's sword and pistol, which hung over the mantelpiece, flanked by a pair of heavy single-sticks with which Benjy himself had won renown long ago as an old gamester, against the picked men of Wiltshire and Somersetshire, in many a good bout at the revels and pastimes of the country-side. For he had been a famous back-swordman in his young days, and a good wrestler at elbow and collar.

Back-swording and wrestling were the most serious holiday pursuits of the Vale—those by which men attained fame—and each village had its champion. I suppose that, on the whole, people were less worked then than they are now ; at any rate, they seemed to have more time and energy for the old pastimes. The great times for back-swording came round once a year in each village, at the feast. The Vale " veasts " were not the common statute feasts, but much more ancient business. They are literally, so far as one can ascertain, feasts of the dedication—that is, they were first established in the churchyard on the day on which the village church was opened for public worship, which was on the wake or festival of the patron saint, and have been held on the same day in every year since that time.

There was no longer any remembrance of why the " veast " had been instituted, but nevertheless it had a pleasant and almost sacred character of its own; for it was then that all the children of the village, wherever they were scattered, tried to get home for a holiday to visit their fathers and mothers and friends, bringing with them their wages or some little gift from up the country for the old folk. Perhaps for a day or two before, but at any rate on "veast day" and the day after, in our village, you might see strapping, healthy young men and women from all parts of the country going round from house to house in their best clothes, and finishing up with a call on Madam Brown, whom they would consult as to putting out their earnings to the best advantage, or how best to expend the same for the benefit of the old folk. Every household, however poor, managed to raise a "feast-cake" and a bottle of ginger or raisin wine, which stood on the cottage table ready for all comers, and not unlikely to make them remember feast-time, for feast-cake is very solid, and full of huge raisins. Moreover, feast-time was the day of reconciliation for the parish. If Job Higgins and Noah Freeman hadn't spoken for the last six months, their "old women" would be sure to get it patched up by that day. And though there was a good deal of drinking and low vice in the booths of an evening, it was pretty well confined to those who would have been doing the like, "veast or no veast;" and on the whole, the effect was humanizing and Christian. In fact, the only reason why this is not the case still is that gentlefolk and farmers have taken to other amusements, and have, as usual, forgotten the poor. They don't attend the feasts themselves, and call them disreputable; whereupon the steadiest of the poor leave them also, and they become what they are called. Class amusements, be they for dukes or plough-boys, always become nuisances and curses to a country.

The true charm of cricket and hunting is that they are still more or less sociable and universal; there's a place for every man who will come and take his part.

No one in the village enjoyed the approach of "veast day" more than Tom, in the year in which he was taken under old Benjy's tutelage. The feast was held in a large green field at the lower end of the village. The road to Farringdon ran along one side of it, and the brook by the side of the road; and above the brook was another large, gentle, sloping pasture-land, with a footpath running down it from the churchyard; and the old church, the originator of all the mirth, towered up with its gray walls and lancet windows, overlooking and sanctioning the whole, though its own share therein had been forgotten. At the point where the footpath crossed the brook and road, and entered on the field where the feast was held, was a long, low roadside inn; and on the opposite side of the field was a large white thatched farmhouse, where dwelt an old sporting farmer, a great promoter of the revels.

Past the old church, and down the footpath, pottered the old man and the child hand-in-hand early on the afternoon of the day before the feast, and wandered all round the ground, which was already being occupied by the "cheap Jacks," with their green-covered carts and marvellous assortment of wares; and the booths of more legitimate small traders, with their tempting arrays of fairings and eatables; and penny peep-shows and other shows, containing pink-eyed ladies, and dwarfs, and boa-constrictors, and wild Indians. But the object of most interest to Benjy, and of course to his pupil also, was the stage of rough planks some four feet high, which was being put up by the village carpenter for the back-swording and wrestling. And after surveying the whole tenderly, old Benjy led his charge away to the roadside inn, where he ordered a glass of ale and a long pipe for himself, and discussed these unwonted luxuries on the bench outside in the soft autumn evening with mine host, another old servant of the Browns, and speculated with him on the likelihood of a good show of old gamesters to contend for the morrow's prizes, and told tales of the gallant bouts of forty years back, to which Tom listened with all his ears and eyes.

But who shall tell the joy of the next morning, when the church bells were ringing a merry peal, and old Benjy appeared in the servants' hall, resplendent in a long blue coat and brass buttons, and a pair of old yellow buck-skins and top-boots which he had cleaned for and in-herited from Tom's grandfather, a stout thorn stick in his hand, and a nosegay of pinks and lavender in his buttonhole, and led away Tom in his best clothes, and two new shillings in his breeches-pockets? Those two, at any rate, look like enjoying the day's revel.

They quicken their pace when they get into the church-yard, for already they see the field thronged with country folk, the men in clean, white smocks or velveteen or fustian coats, with rough plush waistcoats of many colours, and the women in the beautiful, long scarlet cloak—the usual out-door dress of west-country women in those days, and which often descended in families from mother to daughter—or in new-fashioned stuff shawls, which, if they would but believe it, don't become them half so well. The air resounds with the pipe and tabor, and the drums and trumpets of the showmen shouting at the doors of their caravans, over which tremendous pictures of the wonders to be seen within hang temptingly; while through all rises the shrill " root-too-too-too " of Mr. Punch, and the unceasing pan-pipe of his satellite.

"Lawk a' massey, Mr. Benjamin," cries a stout, motherly woman in a red cloak, as they enter the field, "be that you? Well, I never! You do look purely. And how's the Squire, and madam, and the family?"

Benjy graciously shakes hands with the speaker, who has left our village for some years, but has come over for "veast" day on a visit to an old gossip, and gently indicates the heir-apparent of the Browns.

"Bless his little heart! I must gi' un a kiss.—Here, Susannah, Susannah!" cries she, raising herself from the embrace, "come and see Mr. Benjamin and young Master Tom.—You minds our Sukey, Mr. Benjamin; she be growed a rare slip of a wench since you seen her, though her'll be sixteen come Martinmas. I do aim to take her to see madam to get her a place."

And Sukey comes bouncing away from a knot of old school-fellows, and drops a curtsey to Mr. Benjamin. And elders come up from all parts to salute Benjy, and girls who have been madam's pupils to kiss Master Tom. And they carry him off to load him with fairings; and he returns to Benjy, his hat and coat covered with ribbons, and his pockets crammed with wonderful boxes which open upon ever new boxes, and popguns, and trumpets, and apples, and gilt gingerbread from the stall of Angel Heavens, sole vender thereof, whose booth groans with kings and queens, and elephants and prancing steeds, all gleaming with gold. There was more gold on Angel's cakes than there is ginger in those of this degenerate age. Skilled diggers might yet make a fortune in the churchyards of the Vale, by carefully washing the dust of the consumers of Angel's gingerbread. Alas! he is with his namesakes, and his receipts have, I fear, died with him.

And then they inspect the penny peep-show—at least

Tom does—while old Benjy stands outside and gossips and walks up the steps, and enters the mysterious doors of the pink-eyed lady and the Irish giant, who do not by any means come up to their pictures; and the boa will not swallow his rabbit, but there the rabbit is waiting to be swallowed; and what can you expect for tuppence? We are easily pleased in the Vale. Now there is a rush of the crowd, and a tinkling bell is heard, and shouts of laughter; and Master Tom mounts on Benjy's shoulders, and beholds a jingling match in all its glory. The games are begun, and this is the opening of them. It is a quaint game, immensely amusing to look at; and as I don't know whether it is used in your counties, I had better describe it. A large roped ring is made, into which are introduced a dozen or so of big boys and young men who mean to play; these are carefully blinded and turned loose into the ring, and then a man is introduced not blindfolded, with a bell hung round his neck, and his two hands tied behind him. Of course every time he moves the bell must ring, as he has no hand to hold it; and so the dozen blindfolded men have to catch him. This they cannot always manage if he is a lively fellow, but half of them always rush into the arms of the other half, or drive their heads together, or tumble over; and then the crowd laughs vehemently, and invents nicknames for them on the spur of the moment; and they, if they be choleric, tear off the handkerchiefs which blind them, and not unfrequently pitch into one another, each thinking that the other must have run against him on purpose. It is great fun to look at a jingling match certainly, and Tom shouts and jumps on old Benjy's shoulders at the sight, until the old man feels weary, and shifts him to the strong young shoulders of the groom, who has just got down to the fun.

And now, while they are climbing the pole in another part of the field, and muzzling in a flour-tub in another, the old farmer whose house, as has been said, overlooks the field, and who is master of the revels, gets up the steps on to the stage, and announces to all whom it may concern that a half-sovereign in money will be forthcoming to the old gamester who breaks most heads ; to which the Squire and he have added a new hat.

The amount of the prize is sufficient to stimulate the men of the immediate neighbourhood, but not enough to bring any very high talent from a distance ; so, after a glance or two round, a tall fellow, who is a down shepherd, chucks his hat on to the stage and climbs up the steps, looking rather sheepish. The crowd, of course, first cheer, and then chaff as usual, as he picks up his hat and begins handling the sticks to see which will suit him.

"Wooy, Willum Smith, thee canst plaay wi' he arra daay," says his companion to the blacksmith's apprentice, a stout young fellow of nineteen or twenty. Willum's sweetheart is in the " veast " somewhere, and has strictly enjoined him not to get his head broke at back-swording, on pain of her highest displeasure ; but as she is not to be seen (the women pretend not to like to see the back-sword play, and keep away from the stage), and as his hat is decidedly getting old, he chucks it on to the stage, and follows himself, hoping that he will only have to break other people's heads, or that, after all, Rachel won't really mind.

Then follows the greasy cap lined with fur of a half-gipsy, poaching, loafing fellow, who travels the Vale not for much good, I fancy :

" For twenty times was Peter feared
For once that Peter was respected,"

in fact.   And then three or four other hats, including the

glossy castor of Joe Willis, the self-elected and would-be champion of the neighbourhood, a well-to-do young butcher of twenty-eight or thereabouts, and a great strapping fellow, with his full allowance of bluster. This is a capital show of gamesters, considering the amount of the prize; so, while they are picking their sticks and drawing their lots, I think I must tell you, as shortly as I can, how the noble old game of back-sword is played; for it is sadly gone out of late, even in the Vale, and maybe you have never seen it.

The weapon is a good stout ash stick with a large basket handle, heavier and somewhat shorter than a common single-stick. The players are called "old game-sters"—why, I can't tell you—and their object is simply to break one another's heads; for the moment that blood runs an inch anywhere above the eyebrow, the old game-ster to whom it belongs is beaten, and has to stop. A very slight blow with the sticks will fetch blood, so that it is by no means a punishing pastime, if the men don't play on purpose and savagely at the body and arms of their adversaries. The old gamester going into action only takes off his hat and coat, and arms himself with a stick; he then loops the fingers of his left hand in a handkerchief or strap, which he fastens round his left leg, measuring the length, so that when he draws it tight with his left elbow in the air, that elbow shall just reach as high as his crown. Thus you see, so long as he chooses to keep his left elbow up, regardless of cuts, he has a perfect guard for the left side of his head. Then he advances his right hand above and in front of his head, holding his stick across, so that its point projects an inch or two over his left elbow; and thus his whole head is completely guarded, and he faces his man armed in like manner; and they stand some three feet apart, often nearer, and feint, and strike, and return at one another's heads, until one cries "hold," or blood flows. In the first case they are allowed a minute's time, and go on again ; in the latter another pair of gamesters are called on. If good men are playing, the quickness of the returns is marvellous : you hear the rattle like that a boy makes drawing his stick along palings, only heavier ; and the closeness of the men in action to one another gives it a strange interest, and makes a spell at back-swording a very noble sight.

They are all suited now with sticks, and Joe Willis and the gipsy man have drawn the first lot. So the rest lean against the rails of the stage, and Joe and the dark man meet in the middle, the boards having been strewed with sawdust, Joe's white shirt and spotless drab breeches and boots contrasting with the gipsy's coarse blue shirt and dirty green velveteen breeches and leather gaiters. Joe is evidently turning up his nose at the other, and half insulted at having to break his head.

The gipsy is a tough, active fellow, but not very skilful with his weapon, so that Joe's weight and strength tell in a minute ; he is too heavy metal for him. Whack, whack, whack, come his blows, breaking down the gipsy's guard, and threatening to reach his head every moment. There it is at last. "Blood, blood !" shout the spectators, as a thin stream oozes out slowly from the roots of his hair, and the umpire calls to them to stop. The gipsy scowls at Joe under his brows in no pleasant manner, while Master Joe swaggers about, and makes attitudes, and thinks himself, and shows that he thinks himself, the greatest man in the field.

Then follow several stout sets-to between the other candidates for the new hat, and at last come the shepherd and Willum Smith. This is the crack set-to of the day. They are both in famous wind, and there is no crying "hold." The shepherd is an old hand, and up to all the dodges. He tries them one after another, and very nearly gets at Willum's head by coming in near, and playing over his guard at the half-stick; but somehow Willum blunders through, catching the stick on his shoulders, neck, sides, every now and then, anywhere but on his head, and his returns are heavy and straight, and he is the youngest gamester and a favourite in the parish, and his gallant stand brings down shouts and cheers, and the knowing ones think he'll win if he keeps steady; and Tom, on the groom's shoulder, holds his hands together, and can hardly breathe for excitement.

Alas for Willum! His sweetheart, getting tired of female companionship, has been hunting the booths to see where he can have got to, and now catches sight of him on the stage in full combat. She flushes and turns pale; her old aunt catches hold of her, saying, "Bless 'ee, child, doan't 'ee go a'nigst it;" but she breaks away and runs towards the stage calling his name. Willum keeps up his guard stoutly, but glances for a moment towards the voice. No guard will do it, Willum, without the eye. The shepherd steps round and strikes, and the point of his stick just grazes Willum's forehead, fetching off the skin, and the blood flows, and the umpire cries, "Hold!" and poor Willum's chance is up for the day. But he takes it very well, and puts on his old hat and coat, and goes down to be scolded by his sweetheart, and led away out of mischief. Tom hears him say coaxingly, as he walks off,—

"Now doan't 'ee, Rachel! I wouldn't ha' done it, only I wanted summut to buy 'ee a fairing wi', and I be as vlush o' money as a twod o' veathers."

"Thee mind what I tells 'ee," rejoins Rachel saucily, "and doan't 'ee kep blethering about fairings."

Tom resolves in his heart to give Willum the remainder of his two shillings after the back-swording.

Joe Willis has all the luck to-day. His next bout ends in an easy victory, while the shepherd has a tough job to break his second head; and when Joe and the shepherd meet, and the whole circle expect and hope to see him get a broken crown, the shepherd slips in the first round and falls against the rails, hurting himself so that the old farmer will not let him go on, much as he wishes to try; and that impostor Joe (for he is certainly not the best man) struts and swaggers about the stage the conquering gamester, though he hasn't had five minutes' really trying play.

Joe takes the new hat in his hand, and puts the money into it, and then, as if a thought strikes him, and he doesn't think his victory quite acknowledged down below, walks to each face of the stage, and looks down, shaking the money, and chaffing, as how he'll stake hat and money and another half-sovereign "agin any gamester as hasn't played already." Cunning Joe! he thus gets rid of Willum and the shepherd, who is quite fresh again.

No one seems to like the offer, and the umpire is just coming down, when a queer old hat, something like a doctor of divinity's shovel, is chucked on to the stage, and an elderly, quiet man steps out, who has been watching the play, saying he should like to cross a stick wi' the prodigalish young chap.

The crowd cheer, and begin to chaff Joe, who turns up his nose and swaggers across to the sticks. "Imp'dent old wosbird!" says he; "I'll break the bald head on un to the truth."

The old boy is very bald, certainly, and the blood will show fast enough if you can touch him, Joe.

He takes off his long-flapped coat, and stands up in a

long-flapped waistcoat, which Sir Roger de Coverley might have worn when it was new, picks out a stick, and is ready for Master Joe, who loses no time, but begins his old game, whack, whack, whack, trying to break down the old man's guard by sheer strength. But it won't do; he catches every blow close by the basket, and though he is rather stiff in his returns, after a minute walks Joe about the stage, and is clearly a stanch old gamester. Joe now comes in, and making the most of his height, tries to get over the old man's guard at half-stick, by which he takes a smart blow in the ribs and another on the elbow, and nothing more. And now he loses wind and begins to puff, and the crowd laugh. "Cry 'hold,' Joe; thee'st met thy match!" Instead of taking good advice and getting his wind, Joe loses his temper, and strikes at the old man's body.

"Blood, blood!" shout the crowd; "Joe's head's broke!"

Who'd have thought it? How did it come? That body-blow left Joe's head unguarded for a moment, and with one turn of the wrist the old gentleman has picked a neat little bit of skin off the middle of his forehead; and though he won't believe it, and hammers on for three more blows despite of the shouts, is then convinced by the blood trickling into his eye. Poor Joe is sadly crest-fallen, and fumbles in his pocket for the other half-sovereign, but the old gamester won't have it. "Keep thy money, man, and gi's thy hand," says he; and they shake hands. But the old gamester gives the new hat to the shepherd, and, soon after, the half-sovereign to Willum, who thereout decorates his sweetheart with ribbons to his heart's content.

"Who can a be?" "Wur do a cum from?" ask the crowd. And it soon flies about that the old west-country champion, who played a tie with Shaw the Life-guardsman at " Vizes " twenty years before, has broken Joe Willis's crown for him.

How my country fair is spinning out ! I see I must skip the wrestling ; and the boys jumping in sacks, and rolling wheelbarrows blindfolded ; and the donkey-race, and the fight which arose thereout, marring the other-wise peaceful " veast ; " and the frightened scurrying away of the female feast-goers, and descent of Squire Brown, summoned by the wife of one of the combatants to stop it ; which he wouldn't start to do till he had got on his top-boots. Tom is carried away by old Benjy, dog-tired and surfeited with pleasure, as the evening comes on and the dancing begins in the booths ; and though Willum, and Rachel in her new ribbons, and many another good lad and lass, don't come away just yet, but have a good step out, and enjoy it, and get no harm thereby, yet we, being sober folk, will just stroll away up through the churchyard, and by the old yew-tree, and get a quiet dish of tea and a parley with our gossips, as the steady ones of our village do, and so to bed.

That's the fair, true sketch, as far as it goes, of one of the larger village feasts in the Vale of Berks, when I was a little boy. They are much altered for the worse, I am told. I haven't been at one these twenty years, but I have been at the statute fairs in some west-country towns, where servants are hired, and greater abomina-tions cannot be found. What village feasts have come to, I fear, in many cases, may be read in the pages of " Yeast " (though I never saw one so bad—thank God !).

Do you want to know why ? It is because, as I said before, gentlefolk and farmers have left off joining or taking an interest in them. They don't either subscribe to the prizes, or go down and enjoy the fun.

Is this a good or a bad sign? I hardly know. Bad, sure enough, if it only arises from the further separation of classes consequent on twenty years of buying cheap and selling dear, and its accompanying overwork; or because our sons and daughters have their hearts in London club-life, or so-called "society," instead of in the old English home-duties; because farmers' sons are apeing fine gentlemen, and farmers' daughters caring more to make bad foreign music than good English cheeses. Good, perhaps, if it be that the time for the old "veast" has gone by; that it is no longer the healthy, sound expression of English country holiday-making; that, in fact, we, as a nation, have got beyond it, and are in a transition state, feeling for and soon likely to find some better substitute.

Only I have just got this to say before I quit the text. Don't let reformers of any sort think that they are going really to lay hold of the working boys and young men of England by any educational grapnel whatever, which hasn't some *bonâ fide* equivalent for the games of the old country "veast" in it; something to put in the place of the back-swording and wrestling and racing; something to try the muscles of men's bodies, and the endurance of their hearts, and to make them rejoice in their strength. In all the new-fangled comprehensive plans which I see, this is all left out; and the consequence is, that your great mechanics' institutes end in intellectual priggism, and your Christian young men's societies in religious Pharisaism.

Well, well, we must bide our time. Life isn't all beer and skittles; but beer and skittles, or something better of the same sort, must form a good part of every Englishman's education. If I could only drive this into the heads of you rising parliamentary lords, and young

swells who "have your ways made for you," as the saying is, you, who frequent palaver houses and West-end
clubs, waiting always ready to strap yourselves on to the
back of poor dear old John, as soon as the present used-
up lot (your fathers and uncles), who sit there on the
great parliamentary-majorities' pack-saddle, and make
believe they're guiding him with their red-tape bridle,
tumble, or have to be lifted off!

I don't think much of you yet—I wish I could—though
you do go talking and lecturing up and down the country
to crowded audiences, and are busy with all sorts of
philanthropic intellectualism, and circulating libraries
and museums, and Heaven only knows what besides, and
try to make us think, through newspaper reports, that
you are, even as we, of the working classes. But bless
your hearts, we "ain't so green," though lots of us of
all sorts toady you enough certainly, and try to make
you think so.

I'll tell you what to do now: instead of all this trum-
peting and fuss, which is only the old parliamentary-
majority dodge over again, just you go, each of you
(you've plenty of time for it, if you'll only give up t'other
line), and quietly make three or four friends—real friends
—among us. You'll find a little trouble in getting at the
right sort, because such birds don't come lightly to your
lure; but found they may be. Take, say, two out of the
professions, lawyer, parson, doctor—which you will; one
out of trade; and three or four out of the working classes
—tailors, engineers, carpenters, engravers. There's plenty
of choice. Let them be men of your own ages, mind, and
ask them to your homes; introduce them to your wives
and sisters, and get introduced to theirs; give them
good dinners, and talk to them about what is really at
the bottom of your hearts; and box, and run, and row

with them, when you have a chance. Do all this honestly as man to man, and by the time you come to ride old John, you'll be able to do something more than sit on his back, and may feel his mouth with some stronger bridle than a red-tape one.

Ah, if you only would! But you have got too far out of the right rut, I fear. Too much over-civilization, and the deceitfulness of riches. It is easier for a camel to go through the eye of a needle. More's the pity. I never came across but two of you who could value a man wholly and solely for what was in him—who thought themselves verily and indeed of the same flesh and blood as John Jones the attorney's clerk, and Bill Smith the costermonger, and could act as if they thought so.

CHAPTER III.

SUNDRY WARS AND ALLIANCES.

POOR old Benjy! The " rheumatiz " has much to answer for all through English country-sides, but it never played a scurvier trick than in laying thee by the heels, when thou wast yet in a green old age. The enemy, which had long been carrying on a sort of border warfare, and trying his strength against Benjy's on the battlefield of his hands and legs, now, mustering all his forces, began laying siege to the citadel, and overrunning the whole country. Benjy was seized in the back and loins; and though he made strong and brave fight, it was soon clear enough that all which could be beaten of poor old Benjy would have to give in before long.

It was as much as he could do now, with the help of his big stick and frequent stops, to hobble down to the canal with Master Tom, and bait his hook for him, and sit and watch his angling, telling him quaint old country stories; and when Tom had no sport, and detecting a rat some hundred yards or so off along the bank, would rush off with Toby the turnspit terrier, his other faithful companion, in bootless pursuit, he might have tumbled in and been drowned twenty times over before Benjy could have got near him.

Cheery and unmindful of himself, as Benjy was, this loss of locomotive power bothered him greatly. He had got a new object in his old age, and was just beginning to think himself useful again in the world. He feared much, too, lest Master Tom should fall back again into the hands of Charity and the women. So he tried everything he could think of to get set up. He even went an expedition to the dwelling of one of those queer mortals, who— say what we will, and reason how we will—do cure simple people of diseases of one kind or another without the aid of physic, and so get to themselves the reputation of using charms, and inspire for themselves and their dwellings great respect, not to say fear, amongst a simple folk such as the dwellers in the Vale of White Horse. Where this power, or whatever else it may be, descends upon the shoulders of a man whose ways are not straight, he becomes a nuisance to the neighbourhood—a receiver of stolen goods, giver of love-potions, and deceiver of silly women—the avowed enemy of law and order, of justices of the peace, head-boroughs, and gamekeepers,—such a man, in fact, as was recently caught tripping, and deservedly dealt with by the Leeds justices, for seducing a girl who had come to him to get back a faithless lover, and has been convicted of bigamy since then. Sometimes, however, they are of quite a different stamp—men who pretend to nothing, and are with difficulty persuaded to exercise their occult arts in the simplest cases.

Of this latter sort was old Farmer Ives, as he was called, the " wise man " to whom Benjy resorted (taking Tom with him as usual), in the early spring of the year next after the feast described in the last chapter. Why he was called " farmer " I cannot say, unless it be that he was the owner of a cow, a pig or two, and some poultry, which he maintained on about an acre of land inclosed from the middle of a wild common, on which probably his father had squatted before lords of manors looked as keenly after their rights as they do now. Here he had lived no one knew how long, a solitary man. It was often rumoured that he was to be turned out and his cottage pulled down, but somehow it never came to pass ; and his pigs and cow went grazing on the common, and his geese hissed at the passing children and at the heels of the horse of my lord's steward, who often rode by with a covetous eye on the inclosure still unmolested. His dwelling was some miles from our village ; so Benjy, who was half ashamed of his errand, and wholly unable to walk there, had to exercise much ingenuity to get the means of transporting himself and Tom thither without exciting suspicion. However, one fine May morning he managed to borrow the old blind pony of our friend the publican, and Tom persuaded Madam Brown to give him a holiday to spend with old Benjy, and to lend them the Squire's light cart, stored with bread and cold meat and a bottle of ale. And so the two in high glee started behind old Dobbin, and jogged along the deep-rutted plashy roads, which had not been mended after their winter's wear, towards the dwelling of the wizard. About noon they passed the gate which opened on to the large common, and old Dobbin toiled slowly up the hill, while Benjy pointed out a little deep dingle on the left, out of which welled a tiny stream. As they crept up the hill

the tops of a few birch-trees came in sight, and blue
smoke curling up through their delicate light boughs;
and then the little white thatched home and inclosed
ground of Farmer Ives, lying cradled in the dingle, with
the gay gorse common rising behind and on both sides;
while in front, after traversing a gentle slope, the eye
might travel for miles and miles over the rich vale.
They now left the main road and struck into a green
track over the common marked lightly with wheel and
horse-shoe, which led down into the dingle and stopped
at the rough gate of Farmer Ives. Here they found the
farmer, an iron-gray old man, with a bushy eyebrow and
strong aquiline nose, busied in one of his vocations. He
was a horse and cow doctor, and was tending a sick
beast which had been sent up to be cured. Benjy hailed
him as an old friend, and he returned the greeting cordi-
ally enough, looking however hard for a moment both at
Benjy and Tom, to see whether there was more in their
visit than appeared at first sight. It was a work of
some difficulty and danger for Benjy to reach the ground,
which, however, he managed to do without mishap; and
then he devoted himself to unharnessing Dobbin and
turning him out for a graze (" a run " one could not say
of that virtuous steed) on the common. This done, he
extricated the cold provisions from the cart, and they entered the farmer's wicket; and he, shutting up the knife
with which he was taking maggots out of the cow's back
and sides, accompanied them towards the cottage. A big
old lurcher got up slowly from the door-stone, stretching
first one hind leg and then the other, and taking Tom's
caresses and the presence of Toby, who kept, however,
at a respectful distance, with equal indifference.

" Us be cum to pay 'ee a visit. I've a been long
minded to do't for old sake's sake, only I vinds I dwon't

get about now as I'd used to't. I be so plaguy bad wi' th' rheumatiz in my back." Benjy paused, in hopes of drawing the farmer at once on the subject of his ailments without further direct application.

" Ah, I see as you bean't quite so lissom as you was," replied the farmer, with a grim smile, as he lifted the latch of his door ; " we bean't so young as we was, nother on us, wuss luck."

The farmer's cottage was very like those of the better class of peasantry in general. A snug chimney corner with two seats, and a small carpet on the hearth, an old flint gun and a pair of spurs over the fireplace, a dresser with shelves on which some bright pewter plates and crockeryware were arranged, an old walnut table, a few chairs and settles, some framed samplers, and an old print or two, and a bookcase with some dozen volumes on the walls, a rack with flitches of bacon, and other stores fastened to the ceiling, and you have the best part of the furniture. No sign of occult art is to be seen, unless the bundles of dried herbs hanging to the rack and in the ingle and the row of labelled phials on one of the shelves betoken it.

Tom played about with some kittens who occupied the hearth, and with a goat who walked demurely in at the open door—while their host and Benjy spread the table for dinner—and was soon engaged in conflict with the cold meat, to which he did much honour. The two old men's talk was of old comrades and their deeds, mute inglorious Miltons of the Vale, and of the doings thirty years back, which didn't interest him much, except when they spoke of the making of the canal ; and then indeed he began to listen with all his ears, and learned, to his no small wonder, that his dear and wonderful canal had not been there always—was not, in fact, so old as Benjy or Farmer Ives, which caused a strange commotion in his small brain.

After dinner Benjy called attention to a wart which Tom had on the knuckles of his hand, and which the family doctor had been trying his skill on without success, and begged the farmer to charm it away. Farmer Ives looked at it, muttered something or another over it, and cut some notches in a short stick, which he handed to Benjy, giving him instructions for cutting it down on certain days, and cautioning Tom not to meddle with the wart for a fortnight. And then they strolled out and sat on a bench in the sun with their pipes, and the pigs came up and grunted sociably and let Tom scratch them; and the farmer, seeing how he liked animals, stood up and held his arms in the air, and gave a call, which brought a flock of pigeons wheeling and dashing through the birch-trees. They settled down in clusters on the farmer's arms and shoulders, making love to him and scrambling over one another's backs to get to his face; and then he threw them all off, and they fluttered about close by, and lighted on him again and again when he held up his arms. All the creatures about the place were clean and fearless, quite unlike their relations elsewhere; and Tom begged to be taught how to make all the pigs and cows and poultry in our village tame, at which the farmer only gave one of his grim chuckles.

It wasn't till they were just ready to go, and old Dobbin was harnessed, that Benjy broached the subject of his rheumatism again, detailing his symptoms one by one. Poor old boy! He hoped the farmer could charm it away as easily as he could Tom's wart, and was ready with equal faith to put another notched stick into his other pocket, for the cure of his own ailments. The physician shook his head, but nevertheless produced a bottle, and handed it to Benjy, with instructions for use. "Not as 't'll do 'ee much good—leastways I be afeard not," shading his eyes with his hand, and looking up at them in the cart. "There's only one thing as I knows on as'll cure old folks like you and I o' th' rheumatiz."

"Wot be that then, farmer?" inquired Benjy.

"Churchyard mould," said the old iron-gray man, with another chuckle. And so they said their good-byes and went their ways home. Tom's wart was gone in a fortnight, but not so Benjy's rheumatism, which laid him by the heels more and more. And though Tom still spent many an hour with him, as he sat on a bench in the sunshine, or by the chimney corner when it was cold, he soon had to seek elsewhere for his regular companions.

Tom had been accustomed often to accompany his mother in her visits to the cottages, and had thereby made acquaintance with many of the village boys of his own age. There was Job Rudkin, son of widow Rudkin, the most bustling woman in the parish. How she could ever have had such a stolid boy as Job for a child must always remain a mystery. The first time Tom went to their cottage with his mother, Job was not indoors; but he entered soon after, and stood with both hands in his pockets, staring at Tom. Widow Rudkin, who would have had to cross madam to get at young Hopeful—a breach of good manners of which she was wholly incapable —began a series of pantomime signs, which only puzzled him; and at last, unable to contain herself longer, burst out with, "Job! Job! where's thy cap?"

"What! bean't 'ee on ma head, mother?" replied Job, slowly extricating one hand from a pocket, and feeling for the article in question; which he found on his head sure enough, and left there, to his mother's horror and Tom's great delight.

Then there was poor Jacob Dodson, the half-witted boy, who ambled about cheerfully, undertaking messages and little helpful odds and ends for every one, which, however, poor Jacob managed always hopelessly to imbrangle. Everything came to pieces in his hands, and nothing would stop in his head. They nicknamed him Jacob Doodle-calf.

But above all there was Harry Winburn, the quickest and best boy in the parish. He might be a year older than Tom, but was very little bigger, and he was the Crichton of our village boys. He could wrestle and climb and run better than all the rest, and learned all that the schoolmaster could teach him faster than that worthy at all liked. He was a boy to be proud of, with his curly brown hair, keen gray eye, straight active figure, and little ears and hands and feet, "as fine as a lord's," as Charity remarked to Tom one day, talking, as usual, great nonsense. Lords' hands and ears and feet are just as ugly as other folk's when they are children, as any one may convince himself if he likes to look. Tight boots and gloves, and doing nothing with them, I allow make a difference by the time they are twenty.

Now that Benjy was laid on the shelf, and his young brothers were still under petticoat government, Tom, in search of companions, began to cultivate the village boys generally more and more. Squire Brown, be it said, was a true-blue Tory to the backbone, and believed honestly that the powers which be were ordained of God, and that loyalty and steadfast obedience were men's first duties. Whether it were in consequence or in spite of his political creed, I do not mean to give an opinion, though I have one; but certain it is that he held therewith divers social principles not generally supposed to be true blue in colour. Foremost of these, and the one which the Squire loved to propound above all others, was the belief that a man is to be valued wholly and solely for that which he is in himself, for that which stands up in the four fleshly walls of him, apart from clothes, rank, fortune, and all externals whatsoever. Which belief I take to be a wholesome corrective of all political opinions, and, if held sincerely, to make all opinions equally harmless, whether they be blue, red, or green. As a necessary corollary to this belief, Squire Brown held further that it didn't matter a straw whether his son associated with lords' sons or ploughmen's sons, provided they were brave and honest. He himself had played football and gone bird-nesting with the farmers whom he met at vestry and the labourers who tilled their fields, and so had his father and grandfather, with their progenitors. So he encouraged Tom in his intimacy with the boys of the village, and forwarded it by all means in his power, and gave them the run of a close for a playground, and provided bats and balls and a football for their sports.

Our village was blessed amongst other things with a well-endowed school. The building stood by itself, apart from the master's house, on an angle of ground where three roads met—an old gray stone building with a steep roof and mullioned windows. On one of the opposite angles stood Squire Brown's stables and kennel, with their backs to the road, over which towered a great elm-tree; on the third stood the village carpenter and wheelwright's large open shop, and his house and the schoolmaster's, with long low eaves, under which the swallows built by scores.

The moment Tom's lessons were over, he would now get him down to this corner by the stables, and watch till the boys came out of school. He prevailed on the groom to cut notches for him in the bark of the elm, so

that he could climb into the lower branches; and there
he would sit watching the school door, and speculating
on the possibility of turning the elm into a dwelling-place
for himself and friends, after the manner of the Swiss
Family Robinson. But the school hours were long and
Tom's patience short, so that he soon began to descend
into the street, and go and peep in at the school door
and the wheelwright's shop, and look out for something
to while away the time. Now the wheelwright was a
choleric man, and one fine afternoon, returning from a
short absence, found Tom occupied with one of his pet
adzes, the edge of which was fast vanishing under our
hero's care. A speedy flight saved Tom from all but one
sound cuff on the ears; but he resented this unjustifiable
interruption of his first essays at carpentering, and still
more the further proceedings of the wheelwright, who cut
a switch, and hung it over the door of his workshop,
threatening to use it upon Tom if he came within twenty
yards of his gate. So Tom, to retaliate, commenced a
war upon the swallows who dwelt under the wheelwright's
eaves, whom he harassed with sticks and stones; and
being fleeter of foot than his enemy, escaped all punishment, and kept him in perpetual anger. Moreover, his
presence about the school door began to incense the
master, as the boys in that neighbourhood neglected
their lessons in consequence; and more than once he
issued into the porch, rod in hand, just as Tom beat a
hasty retreat. And he and the wheelwright, laying their
heads together, resolved to acquaint the Squire with Tom's
afternoon occupations; but in order to do it with effect,
determined to take him captive and lead him away to
judgment fresh from his evil doings. This they would
have found some difficulty in doing, had Tom continued
the war single-handed, or rather single-footed, for he

would have taken to the deepest part of Pebbly Brook to escape them ; but, like other active powers, he was ruined by his alliances. Poor Jacob Doodle-calf could not go to the school with the other boys, and one fine afternoon, about three o'clock (the school broke up at four), Tom found him ambling about the street, and pressed him into a visit to the school-porch. Jacob, always ready to do what he was asked, consented, and the two stole down to the school together. Tom first reconnoitred the wheelwright's shop, and seeing no signs of activity, thought all safe in that quarter, and ordered at once an advance of all his troops upon the school-porch. The door of the school was ajar, and the boys seated on the nearest bench at once recognized and opened a correspondence with the invaders. Tom, waxing bold, kept putting his head into the school and making faces at the master when his back was turned. Poor Jacob, not in the least comprehending the situation, and in high glee at finding himself so near the school, which he had never been allowed to enter, suddenly, in a fit of enthusiasm, pushed by Tom, and ambling three steps into the school, stood there, looking round him and nodding with a self-approving smile. The master, who was stooping over a boy's slate, with his back to the door, became aware of something unusual, and turned quickly round. Tom rushed at Jacob, and began dragging him back by his smock-frock, and the master made at them, scattering forms and boys in his career. Even now they might have escaped, but that in the porch, barring retreat, appeared the crafty wheelwright, who had been watching all their proceedings. So they were seized, the school dismissed, and Tom and Jacob led away to Squire Brown as lawful prize, the boys following to the gate in groups, and speculating on the result.

The Squire was very angry at first, but the interview, by Tom's pleading, ended in a compromise. Tom was not to go near the school till three o'clock, and only then if he had done his own lessons well, in which case he was to be the bearer of a note to the master from Squire Brown; and the master agreed in such case to release ten or twelve of the best boys an hour before the time of breaking up, to go off and play in the close. The wheel-wright's adzes and swallows were to be for ever respected; and that hero and the master withdrew to the servants' hall to drink the Squire's health, well satisfied with their day's work.

The second act of Tom's life may now be said to have begun. The war of independence had been over for some time: none of the women now—not even his mother's maid—dared offer to help him in dressing or washing. Between ourselves, he had often at first to run to Benjy in an unfinished state of toilet. Charity and the rest of them seemed to take a delight in putting impossible buttons and ties in the middle of his back; but he would have gone without nether integuments altogether, sooner than have had recourse to female valeting. He had a room to himself, and his father gave him sixpence a week pocket-money. All this he had achieved by Benjy's advice and assistance. But now he had conquered another step in life—the step which all real boys so long to make: he had got amongst his equals in age and strength, and could measure him-self with other boys; he lived with those whose pur-suits and wishes and ways were the same in kind as his own.

The little governess who had lately been installed in the house found her work grow wondrously easy, for Tom slaved at his lessons, in order to make sure of his note to the schoolmaster. So there were very few days in the week in which Tom and the village boys were not playing in their close by three o'clock. Prisoner's base, rounders, high-cock-a-lorum, cricket, football—he was soon initiated into the delights of them all; and though most of the boys were older than himself, he managed to hold his own very well. He was naturally active and strong, and quick of eye and hand, and had the advantage of light shoes and well-fitting dress, so that in a short time he could run and jump and climb with any of them.

They generally finished their regular games half an hour or so before tea-time, and then began trials of skill and strength in many ways. Some of them would catch the Shetland pony who was turned out in the field, and get two or three together on his back, and the little rogue, enjoying the fun, would gallop off for fifty yards, and then turn round, or stop short and shoot them on to the turf, and then graze quietly on till he felt another load; others played at peg-top or marbles, while a few of the bigger ones stood up for a bout at wrestling. Tom at first only looked on at this pastime, but it had peculiar attractions for him, and he could not long keep out of it. Elbow and collar wrestling, as practised in the western counties, was, next to back-swording, the way to fame for the youth of the Vale; and all the boys knew the rules of it, and were more or less expert. But Job Rudkin and Harry Winburn were the stars—the former stiff and sturdy, with legs like small towers; the latter pliant as indiarubber and quick as lightning. Day after day they stood foot to foot, and offered first one hand and then the other, and grappled and closed, and swayed and strained, till a well-aimed crook of the heel or thrust of the loin took effect, and a fair back-fall ended the matter. And Tom watched with all his eyes, and first challenged one of the less scientific, and threw him ; and so one by one wrestled his way up to the leaders.

Then indeed for months he had a poor time of it ; it was not long indeed before he could manage to keep his legs against Job, for that hero was slow of offence, and gained his victories chiefly by allowing others to throw themselves against his immovable legs and loins. But Harry Winburn was undeniably his master ; from the first clutch of hands when they stood up, down to the last trip which sent him on to his back on the turf, he felt that Harry knew more and could do more than he. Luckily Harry's bright unconsciousness and Tom's natural good temper kept them from quarrelling ; and so Tom worked on and on, and trod more and more nearly on Harry's heels, and at last mastered all the dodges and falls except one. This one was Harry's own particular invention and pet ; he scarcely ever used it except when hard pressed, but then out it came, and as sure as it did, over went poor Tom. He thought about that fall at his meals, in his walks, when he lay awake in bed, in his dreams, but all to no purpose, until Harry one day in his open way suggested to him how he thought it should be met ; and in a week from that time the boys were equal, save only the slight difference of strength in Harry's favour, which some extra ten months of age gave. Tom had often afterwards reason to be thankful for that early drilling, and above all, for having mastered Harry Winburn's fall.

Besides their home games, on Saturdays the boys would wander all over the neighbourhood ; sometimes to the downs, or up to the camp, where they cut their initials out in the springy turf, and watched the hawks soaring, and the " peert " bird, as Harry Winburn called the gray plover, gorgeous in his wedding feathers ; and so home, racing down the Manger with many a roll among the thistles, or through Uffington Wood to watch the fox cubs playing in the green rides ; sometimes to Rosy Brook, to cut long whispering reeds which grew there, to make pan-pipes of; sometimes to Moor Mills, where was a piece of old forest land, with short browsed turf and tufted brambly thickets stretching under the oaks, amongst which rumour declared that a raven, last of his race, still lingered ; or to the sand-hills, in vain quest of rabbits; and bird-nesting in the season, anywhere and everywhere.

The few neighbours of the Squire's own rank every now and then would shrug their shoulders as they drove or rode by a party of boys with Tom in the middle, carrying along bulrushes or whispering reeds, or great bundles of cowslip and meadow-sweet, or young starlings or magpies, or other spoil of wood, brook, or meadow ; and Lawyer Red-tape might mutter to Squire Straight-back at the Board that no good would come of the young Browns, if they were let run wild with all the dirty village boys, whom the best farmers' sons even would not play with. And the squire might reply with a shake of his head that *his* sons only mixed with their equals, and never went into the village without the governess or a footman. But, luckily, Squire Brown was full as stiff-backed as his neighbours, and so went on his own way ; and Tom and his younger brothers, as they grew up, went on playing with the village boys, without the idea of equality or inequality (except in wrestling, running, and climbing) ever entering their heads, as it doesn't till it's put there by Jack Nastys or fine ladies' maids.

I don't mean to say it would be the case in all villages, but it certainly was so in this one : the village boys were full as manly and honest, and certainly purer, than those

in a higher rank; and Tom got more harm from his
equals in his first fortnight at a private school, where
he went when he was nine years old, than he had from
his village friends from the day he left Charity's apron-
strings.

Great was the grief amongst the village school-boys
when Tom drove off with the Squire, one August morning, to meet the coach on his way to school. Each of
them had given him some little present of the best that
he had, and his small private box was full of peg-tops,
white marbles (called "alley-taws" in the Vale), screws,
birds' eggs, whip-cord, jews-harps, and other miscel-
laneous boys' wealth. Poor Jacob Doodle-calf, in floods
of tears, had pressed upon him with spluttering earnest-
ness his lame pet hedgehog (he had always some poor
broken-down beast or bird by him); but this Tom had
been obliged to refuse, by the Squire's order. He had
given them all a great tea under the big elm in their
playground, for which Madam Brown had supplied the
biggest cake ever seen in our village; and Tom was
really as sorry to leave them as they to lose him, but
his sorrow was not unmixed with the pride and excitement of making a new step in life.

And this feeling carried him through his first parting
with his mother better than could have been expected.
Their love was as fair and whole as human love can be
—perfect self-sacrifice on the one side meeting a young
and true heart on the other. It is not within the scope
of my book, however, to speak of family relations, or
I should have much to say on the subject of English
mothers—ay, and of English fathers, and sisters, and
brothers too. Neither have I room to speak of our
private schools. What I have to say is about public
schools—those much-abused and much-belauded insti-

tutions peculiar to England. So we must hurry through Master Tom's year at a private school as fast as we can.

It was a fair average specimen, kept by a gentleman, with another gentleman as second master ; but it was little enough of the real work they did—merely coming into school when lessons were prepared and all ready to be heard. The whole discipline of the school out of lesson hours was in the hands of the two ushers, one of whom was always with the boys in their playground, in the school, at meals—in fact, at all times and every where, till they were fairly in bed at night.

Now the theory of private schools is (or was) constant supervision out of school—therein differing fundamentally from that of public schools.

It may be right or wrong ; but if right, this supervision surely ought to be the especial work of the head-master, the responsible person. The object of all schools is not to ram Latin and Greek into boys, but to make them good English boys, good future citizens ; and by far the most important part of that work must be done, or not done, out of school hours. To leave it, therefore, in the hands of inferior men, is just giving up the highest and hardest part of the work of education. Were I a private school-master, I should say, Let who will hear the boys their lessons, but let me live with them when they are at play and rest.

The two ushers at Tom's first school were not gentlemen, and very poorly educated, and were only driving their poor trade of usher to get such living as they could out of it. They were not bad men, but had little heart for their work, and of course were bent on making it as easy as possible. One of the methods by which they endeavoured to accomplish this was by encouraging talebearing, which had become a frightfully common vice in the school in consequence, and had sapped all the foundations of school morality. Another was, by favouring grossly the biggest boys, who alone could have given them much trouble ; whereby those young gentlemen became most abominable tyrants, oppressing the little boys in all the small mean ways which prevail in private schools.

Poor little Tom was made dreadfully unhappy in his first week by a catastrophe which happened to his first letter home. With huge labour he had, on the very evening of his arrival, managed to fill two sides of a sheet of letter-paper with assurances of his love for dear mamma, his happiness at school, and his resolves to do all she would wish. This missive, with the help of the boy who sat at the desk next him, also a new arrival, he managed to fold successfully ; but this done, they were sadly put to it for means of sealing. Envelopes were then unknown ; they had no wax, and dared not disturb the stillness of the evening school-room by getting up and going to ask the usher for some. At length Tom's friend, being of an ingenious turn of mind, suggested sealing with ink ; and the letter was accordingly stuck down with a blob of ink, and duly handed by Tom, on his way to bed, to the housekeeper to be posted. It was not till four days afterwards that the good dame sent for him, and produced the precious letter and some wax, saying, " O Master Brown, I forgot to tell you before, but your letter isn't sealed." Poor Tom took the wax in silence and sealed his letter, with a huge lump rising in his throat during the process, and then ran away to a quiet corner of the playground, and burst into an agony of tears. The idea of his mother waiting day after day for the letter he had promised her at once, and perhaps thinking him forgetful of her, when he had done all in his power to make good his promise, was as bitter a grief as any which he had to undergo for many a long year. His wrath, then, was proportionately violent when he was aware of two boys, who stopped close by him, and one of whom, a fat gaby of a fellow, pointed at him and called him " Young mammy-sick ! " Whereupon Tom arose, and giving vent thus to his grief and shame and rage, smote his derider on the nose, and made it bleed; which sent that young worthy howling to the usher, who reported Tom for violent and unprovoked assault and battery. Hitting in the face was a felony punishable with flogging, other hitting only a misdemeanour—a distinction not altogether clear in principle. Tom, however, escaped the penalty by pleading *primum tempus ;* and having written a second letter to his mother, inclosing some forget-me-nots, which he picked on their first half-holiday walk, felt quite happy again, and began to enjoy vastly a good deal of his new life.

These half-holiday walks were the great events of the week. The whole fifty boys started after dinner with one of the ushers for Hazeldown, which was distant some mile or so from the school. Hazeldown measured some three miles round, and in the neighbourhood were several woods full of all manner of birds and butterflies. The usher walked slowly round the down with such boys as liked to accompany him ; the rest scattered in all directions, being only bound to appear again when the usher had completed his round, and accompany him home. They were forbidden, however, to go anywhere except on the down and into the woods ; the village had been especially prohibited, where huge bull's-eyes and unctuous toffy might be procured in exchange for coin of the realm.

Various were the amusements to which the boys then betook themselves. At the entrance of the down there was a steep hillock, like the barrows of Tom's own downs. This mound was the weekly scene of terrific combats, at a game called by the queer name of " mud-patties." The boys who played divided into sides under different leaders, and one side occupied the mound. Then, all parties having provided themselves with many sods of turf, cut with their bread-and-cheese knives, the side which remained at the bottom proceeded to assault the mound, advancing up on all sides under cover of a heavy fire of turfs, and then struggling for victory with the occupants, which was theirs as soon as they could, even for a moment, clear the summit, when they in turn became the besieged. It was a good, rough, dirty game, and of great use in counteracting the sneaking tendencies of the school. Then others of the boys spread over the downs, looking for the holes of humble-bees and mice, which they dug up without mercy, often (I regret to say) killing and skinning the unlucky mice, and (I do not regret to say) getting well stung by the humble-bees. Others went after butterflies and birds' eggs in their seasons ; and Tom found on Hazeldown, for the first time, the beautiful little blue butterfly with golden spots on his wings, which he had never seen on his own downs, and dug out his first sand-martin's nest. This latter achievement resulted in a flogging, for the sand-martins built in a high bank close to the village, consequently out of bounds ; but one of the bolder spirits of the school, who never could be happy unless he was doing something to which risk was attached, easily persuaded Tom to break bounds and visit the martins' bank. From whence it being only a step to the toffy shop, what could be more simple than to go on there and fill their pockets ; or what more certain than that on their return, a distribution of treasure having been made, the usher should shortly detect the forbidden smell of bull's-eyes, and, a search ensuing, discover the state of the breeches-pockets of Tom and his ally ?

This ally of Tom's was indeed a desperate hero in the sight of the boys, and feared as one who dealt in magic, or something approaching thereto. Which reputation came to him in this wise. The boys went to bed at eight, and, of course, consequently lay awake in the dark for an hour or two, telling ghost-stories by turns. One night when it came to his turn, and he had dried up their souls by his story, he suddenly declared that he would make a fiery hand appear on the door ; and to the astonishment and terror of the boys in his room, a hand, or something like it, in pale light, did then and there appear. The fame of this exploit having spread to the other rooms, and being discredited there, the young necromancer declared that the same wonder would appear in all the rooms in turn, which it accordingly did ; and the whole circumstances having been privately reported to one of the ushers as usual, that functionary, after listening about at the doors of the rooms, by a sudden descent caught the performer in his night-shirt, with a box of phosphorus in his guilty hand. Lucifer-matches and all the present facilities for getting acquainted with fire were then unknown—the very name of phosphorus had something diabolic in it to the boy-mind ; so Tom's ally, at the cost of a sound flogging, earned what many older folk covet much—the very decided fear of most of his companions.

He was a remarkable boy, and by no means a bad one. Tom stuck to him till he left, and got into many scrapes by so doing. But he was the great opponent of the tale-bearing habits of the school, and the open enemy of the ushers ; and so worthy of all support.

Tom imbibed a fair amount of Latin and Greek at the school, but somehow, on the whole, it didn't suit him, or he it, and in the holidays he was constantly working the Squire to send him at once to a public school. Great was his joy then, when in the middle of his third half-year, in October 183–, a fever broke out in the village, and the master having himself slightly sickened of it, the whole of the boys were sent off at a day's notice to their respective homes.

The Squire was not quite so pleased as Master Tom to see that young gentleman's brown, merry face appear at home, some two months before the proper time, for the Christmas holidays ; and so, after putting on his thinking cap, he retired to his study and wrote several letters, the result of which was that, one morning at the breakfast-table, about a fortnight after Tom's return, he addressed his wife with—" My dear, I have arranged that Tom shall go to Rugby at once, for the last six weeks of this half-year, instead of wasting them in riding and loitering about home. It is very kind of the doctor to allow it. Will you see that his things are all ready by Friday, when I shall take him up to town, and send him down the next day by himself.

Mrs. Brown was prepared for the announcement, and merely suggested a doubt whether Tom were yet old enough to travel by himself. However, finding both father and son against her on this point, she gave in, like a wise woman, and proceeded to prepare Tom's kit for his launch into a public school.

CHAPTER IV.

THE STAGE COACH.

" Let the steam-pot hiss till it's hot ;
Give me the speed of the Tantivy trot."
Coaching Song, by R. E. E. Warburton, Esq.

" Now, sir, time to get up, if you please. Tally-ho coach for Leicester 'll be round in half an hour, and don't wait for nobody." So spake the boots of the Peacock Inn, Islington, at half-past two o'clock on the morning of a day in the early part of November 183–, giving Tom at the same time a shake by the shoulder, and then putting down a candle, and carrying off his shoes to clean.

Tom and his father arrived in town from Berkshire the day before, and finding, on inquiry, that the Birmingham coaches which ran from the city did not pass through Rugby, but deposited their passengers at Dunchurch, a village three miles distant on the main road, where said passengers had to wait for the Oxford and Leicester coach in the evening, or to take a post-chaise, had resolved that Tom should travel down by the Tally-ho, which diverged from the main road and passed through Rugby itself. And as the Tally-ho was an early coach, they had driven out to the Peacock to be on the road.

Tom had never been in London, and would have liked to have stopped at the Belle Savage, where they had been put down by the Star, just at dusk, that he might have gone roving about those endless, mysterious, gas-lit streets, which, with their glare and hum and moving crowds, excited him so that he couldn't talk even. But as soon as he found that the Peacock arrangement would get him to Rugby by twelve o'clock in the day, where-as otherwise he wouldn't be there till the evening, all other plans melted away, his one absorbing aim being to become a public school-boy as fast as possible, and six hours sooner or later seeming to him of the most alarming importance.

Tom and his father had alighted at the Peacock at about seven in the evening ; and having heard with unfeigned joy the paternal order, at the bar, of steaks and oyster-sauce for supper in half an hour, and seen his father seated cozily by the bright fire in the coffee-room with the paper in his hand, Tom had run out to see about him, had wondered at all the vehicles passing and repassing, and had fraternized with the boots and hostler, from whom he ascertained that the Tally-ho was a tip-top goer—ten miles an hour including stoppages— and so punctual that all the road set their clocks by her.

Then being summoned to supper, he had regaled himself in one of the bright little boxes of the Peacock coffee-room, on the beef-steak and unlimited oyster-sauce and brown stout (tasted then for the first time—a day to be marked for ever by Tom with a white stone) ; had at first attended to the excellent advice which his father was bestowing on him from over his glass of steaming brandy-and-water, and then began nodding, from the united effects of the stout, the fire, and the lecture ; till the Squire, observing Tom's state, and remembering that it was nearly nine o'clock, and that the Tally-ho left at three, sent the little fellow off to the chambermaid, with a shake of the hand (Tom having stipulated in the morning before starting that kissing should now cease between them), and a few parting words.

" And now, Tom, my boy," said the Squire, " remember you are going, at your own earnest request, to be chucked into this great school, like a young bear, with all your troubles before you—earlier than we should have sent you perhaps. If schools are what they were in my time, you'll see a great many cruel blackguard things done, and hear a deal of foul, bad talk. But never fear. You tell the truth, keep a brave and kind heart, and never listen to or say anything you wouldn't have your mother and sister hear, and you'll never feel ashamed to come home, or we to see you."

The allusion to his mother made Tom feel rather choky, and he would have liked to have hugged his father well, if it hadn't been for the recent stipulation.

As it was, he only squeezed his father's hand, and looked bravely up and said, " I'll try, father."

" I know you will, my boy. Is your money all safe ? "

" Yes," said Tom, diving into one pocket to make sure.

" And your keys ? " said the Squire.

" All right," said Tom, diving into the other pocket.

" Well, then, good-night. God bless you! I'll tell boots to call you, and be up to see you off."

Tom was carried off by the chambermaid in a brown study, from which he was roused in a clean little attic, by that buxom person calling him a little darling and kissing him as she left the room ; which indignity he was too much surprised to resent. And still thinking of his father's last words, and the look with which they were spoken, he knelt down and prayed that, come what might, he might never bring shame or sorrow on the dear folk at home.

Indeed, the Squire's last words deserved to have their effect, for they had been the result of much anxious thought. All the way up to London he had pondered what he should say to Tom by way of parting advice— something that the boy could keep in his head ready for use. By way of assisting meditation, he had even gone the length of taking out his flint and steel and tinder, and hammering away for a quarter of an hour till he had manufactured a light for a long Trichinopoli che-root, which he silently puffed, to the no small wonder of coachee, who was an old friend, and an institution on the Bath road, and who always expected a talk on the prospects and doings, agricultural and social, of the whole country, when he carried the Squire.

To condense the Squire's meditation, it was somewhat as follows : " I won't tell him to read his Bible, and love and serve God ; if he don't do that for his mother's sake and teaching, he won't for mine. Shall I go into the sort of temptations he'll meet with ? No, I can't do that. Never do for an old fellow to go into such things with a boy. He won't understand me. Do him more harm than good, ten to one. Shall I tell him to mind his work, and say he's sent to school to make himself a good scholar ? Well, but he isn't sent to school for that— at any rate, not for that mainly. I don't care a straw for Greek particles, or the digamma ; no more does his mother. What is he sent to school for ? Well, partly because he wanted so to go. If he'll only turn out a brave, helpful, truth-telling Englishman, and a gentle-man, and a Christian, that's all I want," thought the Squire ; and upon this view of the case he framed his last words of advice to Tom, which were well enough suited to his purpose.

For they were Tom's first thoughts as he tumbled out of bed at the summons of boots, and proceeded rapidly to wash and dress himself. At ten minutes to three he was down in the coffee-room in his stockings, carrying his hat-box, coat, and comforter in his hand ; and there he found his father nursing a bright fire, and a cup of hot coffee and a hard biscuit on the table.

" Now, then, Tom, give us your things here, and drink this. There's nothing like starting warm, old fellow."

Tom addressed himself to the coffee, and prattled away while he worked himself into his shoes and his great-coat, well warmed through—a Petersham coat with velvet collar, made tight after the abominable fashion of those days. And just as he is swallowing his last mouthful, winding his comforter round his throat, and tucking the ends into the breast of his coat, the horn sounds; boots looks in and says, "Tally-ho, sir;" and they hear the ring and the rattle of the four fast trotters and the town-made drag, as it dashes up to the Peacock.

"Anything for us, Bob?" says the burly guard, dropping down from behind, and slapping himself across the chest.

"Young gen'lm'n, Rugby; three parcels, Leicester; hamper o' game, Rugby," answers hostler.

"Tell young gent to look alive," says guard, opening the hind-boot and shooting in the parcels after examining them by the lamps. "Here, shove the portmanteau up a-top. I'll fasten him presently.—Now then, sir, jump up behind."

"Good-bye, father—my love at home." A last shake of the hand. Up goes Tom, the guard catching his hat-box and holding on with one hand, while with the other he claps the horn to his mouth. Toot, toot, toot! the hostlers let go their heads, the four bays plunge at the collar, and away goes the Tally-ho into the darkness, forty-five seconds from the time they pulled up. Hostler, boots, and the Squire stand looking after them under the Peacock lamp.

"Sharp work!" says the Squire, and goes in again to his bed, the coach being well out of sight and hearing.

Tom stands up on the coach and looks back at his father's figure as long as he can see it; and then the guard, having disposed of his luggage, comes to an anchor, and

finishes his buttonings and other preparations for facing
the three hours before dawn—no joke for those who
minded cold, on a fast coach in November, in the reign
of his late Majesty.

I sometimes think that you boys of this generation are
a deal tenderer fellows than we used to be. At any rate
you're much more comfortable travellers, for I see every
one of you with his rug or plaid, and other dodges for
preserving the caloric, and most of you going in those
fuzzy, dusty, padded first-class carriages. It was another affair altogether, a dark ride on the top of the Tally-
ho, I can tell you, in a tight Petersham coat, and your
feet dangling six inches from the floor. Then you knew
what cold was, and what it was to be without legs, for
not a bit of feeling had you in them after the first half-
hour. But it had its pleasures, the old dark ride. First
there was the consciousness of silent endurance, so dear
to every Englishman—of standing out against something,
and not giving in. Then there was the music of the
rattling harness, and the ring of the horses' feet on the
hard road, and the glare of the two bright lamps through
the steaming hoar frost, over the leaders' ears, into the
darkness; and the cheery toot of the guard's horn, to warn
some drowsy pikeman or the hostler at the next change;
and the looking forward to daylight; and last, but not
least, the delight of returning sensation in your toes.

Then the break of dawn and the sunrise, where can they
be ever seen in perfection but from a coach roof? You
want motion and change and music to see them in their
glory—not the music of singing men and singing women,
but good, silent music, which sets itself in your own head,
the accompaniment of work and getting over the ground.

The Tally-ho is past St. Albans, and Tom is enjoying
the ride, though half-frozen. The guard, who is alone

with him on the back of the coach, is silent, but has muffled Tom's feet up in straw, and put the end of an oat-sack over his knees. The darkness has driven him inwards, and he has gone over his little past life, and thought of all his doings and promises, and of his mother and sister, and his father's last words; and has made fifty good resolutions, and means to bear himself like a brave Brown as he is, though a young one. Then he has been forward into the mysterious boy-future, speculating as to what sort of place Rugby is, and what they do there, and calling up all the stories of public schools which he has heard from big boys in the holidays. He is choke-full of hope and life, notwithstanding the cold, and kicks his heels against the back-board, and would like to sing, only he doesn't know how his friend the silent guard might take it.

And now the dawn breaks at the end of the fourth stage, and the coach pulls up at a little roadside inn with huge stables behind. There is a bright fire gleaming through the red curtains of the bar window, and the door is open. The coachman catches his whip into a double thong, and throws it to the hostler; the steam of the horses rises straight up into the air. He has put them along over the last two miles, and is two minutes before his time. He rolls down from the box and into the inn. The guard rolls off behind. "Now, sir," says he to Tom, "you just jump down, and I'll give you a drop of something to keep the cold out."

Tom finds a difficulty in jumping, or indeed in finding the top of the wheel with his feet, which may be in the next world for all he feels; so the guard picks him off the coach top, and sets him on his legs, and they stump off into the bar, and join the coachman and the other outside passengers.

Here a fresh-looking barmaid serves them each with a glass of early purl as they stand before the fire, coachman and guard exchanging business remarks. The purl warms the cockles of Tom's heart, and makes him cough.

"Rare tackle that, sir, of a cold morning," says the coachman, smiling. "Time's up." They are out again and up; coachee the last, gathering the reins into his hands and talking to Jem the hostler about the mare's shoulder, and then swinging himself up on to the box—the horses dashing off in a canter before he falls into his seat. Toot-toot-tootle-too goes the horn, and away they are again, five-and-thirty miles on their road (nearly half-way to Rugby, thinks Tom), and the prospect of breakfast at the end of the stage.

And now they begin to see, and the early life of the country-side comes out—a market cart or two; men in smock-frocks going to their work, pipe in mouth, a whiff of which is no bad smell this bright morning. The sun gets up, and the mist shines like silver gauze. They pass the hounds jogging along to a distant meet, at the heels of the huntsman's hack, whose face is about the colour of the tails of his old pink, as he exchanges greetings with coachman and guard. Now they pull up at a lodge, and take on board a well-muffled-up sportsman, with his gun-case and carpet-bag. An early up-coach meets them, and the coachmen gather up their horses, and pass one another with the accustomed lift of the elbow, each team doing eleven miles an hour, with a mile to spare behind if necessary. And here comes breakfast.

"Twenty minutes here, gentlemen," says the coachman, as they pull up at half-past seven at the inn-door.

Have we not endured nobly this morning? and is not this a worthy reward for much endurance? There is the low, dark wainscoted room hung with sporting prints;

the hat-stand (with a whip or two standing up in it belonging to bagmen who are still snug in bed) by the door;
the blazing fire, with the quaint old glass over the mantelpiece, in which is stuck a large card with the list of the
meets for the week of the county hounds; the table
covered with the whitest of cloths and of china, and bearing a pigeon-pie, ham, round of cold boiled beef cut from
a mammoth ox, and the great loaf of household bread
on a wooden trencher. And here comes in the stout
head waiter, puffing under a tray of hot viands—kidneys
and a steak, transparent rashers and poached eggs, buttered toast and muffins, coffee and tea, all smoking hot.
The table can never hold it all. The cold meats are removed to the sideboard—they were only put on for show
and to give us an appetite. And now fall on, gentlemen
all. It is a well-known sporting-house, and the breakfasts
are famous. Two or three men in pink, on their way to
the meet, drop in, and are very jovial and sharp-set, as
indeed we all are.

"Tea or coffee, sir?" says head waiter, coming round
to Tom.

"Coffee, please," says Tom, with his mouth full of
muffin and kidney. Coffee is a treat to him, tea is not.

Our coachman, I perceive, who breakfasts with us, is
a cold beef man. He also eschews hot potations, and
addicts himself to a tankard of ale, which is brought him
by the barmaid. Sportsman looks on approvingly, and
orders a ditto for himself.

Tom has eaten kidney and pigeon-pie, and imbibed
coffee, till his little skin is as tight as a drum; and then
has the further pleasure of paying head waiter out of his
own purse, in a dignified manner, and walks out before
the inn-door to see the horses put to. This is done
leisurely and in a highly-finished manner by the hostlers,

as if they enjoyed the not being hurried. Coachman comes out with his waybill, and puffing a fat cigar which the sportsman has given him. Guard emerges from the tap, where he prefers breakfasting, licking round a tough-looking doubtful cheroot, which you might tie round your finger, and three whiffs of which would knock any one else out of time.

The pinks stand about the inn-door lighting cigars and waiting to see us start, while their hacks are led up and down the market-place, on which the inn looks. They all know our sportsman, and we feel a reflected credit when we see him chatting and laughing with them.

"Now, sir, please," says the coachman. All the rest of the passengers are up; the guard is locking up the hind-boot.

"A good run to you!" says the sportsman to the pinks, and is by the coachman's side in no time.

"Let 'em go, Dick!" The hostlers fly back, drawing off the cloths from their glossy loins, and away we go through the market-place and down the High Street, looking in at the first-floor windows, and seeing several worthy burgesses shaving thereat; while all the shop-boys who are cleaning the windows, and housemaids who are doing the steps, stop and look pleased as we rattle past, as if we were a part of their legitimate morning's amusement. We clear the town, and are well out between the hedgerows again as the town clock strikes eight.

The sun shines almost warmly, and breakfast has oiled all springs and loosened all tongues. Tom is encouraged by a remark or two of the guard's between the puffs of his oily cheroot, and besides is getting tired of not talking. He is too full of his destination to talk about anything else, and so asks the guard if he knows Rugby.

"Goes through it every day of my life. Twenty minutes afore twelve down—ten o'clock up."

"What sort of place is it, please?" says Tom.

Guard looks at him with a comical expression. "Werry out-o'-the-way place, sir; no paving to streets, nor no lighting. 'Mazin' big horse and cattle fair in autumn —lasts a week—just over now. Takes town a week to get clean after it. Fairish hunting country. But slow place, sir, slow place—off the main road, you see—only three coaches a day, and one on 'em a two-oss wan, more like a hearse nor a coach—Regulator—comes from Oxford. Young genl'm'n at school calls her Pig and Whistle, and goes up to college by her (six miles an hour) when they goes to enter. Belong to school, sir?"

"Yes," says Tom, not unwilling for a moment that the guard should think him an old boy. But then, having some qualms as to the truth of the assertion, and seeing that if he were to assume the character of an old boy he couldn't go on asking the questions he wanted, added—"That is to say, I'm on my way there. I'm a new boy."

The guard looked as if he knew this quite as well as Tom.

"You're werry late, sir," says the guard; "only six weeks to-day to the end of the half." Tom assented. "We takes up fine loads this day six weeks, and Monday and Tuesday arter. Hopes we shall have the pleasure of carrying you back."

Tom said he hoped they would; but he thought within himself that his fate would probably be the Pig and Whistle.

"It pays uncommon cert'nly," continues the guard. "Werry free with their cash is the young genl'm'n. But, Lor' bless you, we gets into such rows all 'long the road, what wi' their pea-shooters, and long whips, and hollering, and upsetting every one as comes by, I'd a sight sooner carry one or two on 'em, sir, as I may be a-carryin' of you now, than a coach-load."

"What do they do with the pea-shooters?" inquires Tom.

"Do wi' 'em! Why, peppers every one's faces as we comes near, 'cept the young gals, and breaks windows wi' them too, some on 'em shoots so hard. Now 'twas just here last June, as we was a-driving up the first-day boys, they was mendin' a quarter-mile of road, and there was a lot of Irish chaps, reg'lar roughs, a-breaking stones. As we comes up, ' Now, boys,' says young gent on the box (smart young fellow and desper't reckless), ' here's fun! Let the Pats have it about the ears.' ' God's sake, sir!' says Bob (that's my mate the coachman), ' don't go for to shoot at 'em. They'll knock us off the coach.' ' Damme, coachee,' says young my lord, ' you ain't afraid.—Hoora, boys! let 'em have it.' ' Hoora!' sings out the others, and fill their mouths choke-full of peas to last the whole line. Bob, seeing as 'twas to come, knocks his hat over his eyes, hollers to his osses, and shakes 'em up; and away we goes up to the line on 'em, twenty miles an hour. The Pats begin to hoora too, thinking it was a runaway; and first lot on 'em stands grinnin' and wavin' their old hats as we comes abreast on 'em; and then you'd ha' laughed to see how took aback and choking savage they looked, when they gets the peas a-stinging all over 'em. But bless you, the laugh weren't all of our side, sir, by a long way. We was going so fast, and they was so took aback, that they didn't take what was up till we was half-way up the line. Then 'twas, ' Look out all!' surely. They howls all down the line fit to frighten you; some on 'em runs arter us and tries to clamber up behind, only we hits 'em over the fingers and pulls their hands off; one as had had it very sharp act'ly runs right at the leaders, as though he'd ketch 'em by the heads, only luck'ly for him he misses his tip and comes over a heap o' stones first. The rest picks up stones, and gives it us right away till we gets out of shot, the young gents holding out werry manful with the pea-shooters and such stones as lodged on us, and a pretty many there was too. Then Bob picks his-self up again, and looks at young gent on box werry solemn. Bob'd had a rum un in the ribs, which'd like to ha' knocked him off the box, or made him drop the reins. Young gent on box picks hisself up, and so does we all, and looks round to count damage. Box's head cut open and his hat gone; 'nother young gent's hat gone; mine knocked in at the side, and not one on us as wasn't black and blue somewheres or another, most on 'em all over. Two pound ten to pay for damage to paint, which they subscribed for there and then, and give Bob and me a extra half-sovereign each; but I wouldn't go down that line again not for twenty half-sovereigns." And the guard shook his head slowly, and got up and blew a clear, brisk toot-toot.

"What fun!" said Tom, who could scarcely contain his pride at this exploit of his future school-fellows. He longed already for the end of the half, that he might join them.

"'Taint such good fun, though, sir, for the folk as meets the coach, nor for we who has to go back with it next day. Them Irishers last summer had all got stones ready for us, and was all but letting drive, and we'd got two reverend gents aboard too. We pulled up at the beginning of the line, and pacified them, and we're never going to carry no more pea-shooters, unless they promises not to fire where there's a line of Irish chaps a-stone-breaking." The guard stopped and pulled away at his cheroot, regarding Tom benignantly the while.

" Oh, don't stop ! Tell us something more about the pea-shooting."

" Well, there'd like to have been a pretty piece of work over it at Bicester, a while back. We was six mile from the town, when we meets an old square-headed gray-haired yeoman chap, a-jogging along quite quiet. He looks up at the coach, and just then a pea hits him on the nose, and some catches his cob behind and makes him dance up on his hind legs. I see'd the old boy's face flush and look plaguy awkward, and I thought we was in for somethin' nasty.

" He turns his cob's head and rides quietly after us just out of shot. How that 'ere cob did step ! We never shook him off not a dozen yards in the six miles. At first the young gents was werry lively on him ; but afore we got in, seeing how steady the old chap come on, they was quite quiet, and laid their heads together what they should do. Some was for fighting, some for axing his pardon. He rides into the town close after us, comes up when we stops, and says the two as shot at him must come before a magistrate ; and a great crowd comes round, and we couldn't get the osses to. But the young uns they all stand by one another, and says all or none must go, and as how they'd fight it out, and have to be carried. Just as 'twas gettin' serious, and the old boy and the mob was going to pull 'em off the coach, one little fellow jumps up and says, ' Here—I'll stay. I'm only going three miles farther. My father's name's Davis ; he's known about here, and I'll go before the magistrate with this gentleman.' ' What ! be thee parson Davis's son ? ' says the old boy. ' Yes,' says the young un. 'Well, I be mortal sorry to meet thee in such company; but for thy father's sake and thine (for thee bist a brave young chap) I'll say no more about it.' Didn't the boys cheer him, and the mob cheered the young chap; and then one of the biggest gets down, and begs his pardon werry gentlemanly for all the rest, saying as they all had been plaguy vexed from the first, but didn't like to ax his pardon till then, 'cause they felt they hadn't ought to shirk the consequences of their joke. And then they all got down, and shook hands with the old boy, and asked him to all parts of the country, to their homes; and we drives off twenty minutes behind time, with cheering and hollering as if we was county members. But, Lor' bless you, sir," says the guard, smacking his hand down on his knee and looking full into Tom's face, " ten minutes arter they was all as bad as ever."

Tom showed such undisguised and open-mouthed interest in his narrations that the old guard rubbed up his memory, and launched out into a graphic history of all the performances of the boys on the roads for the last twenty years. Off the road he couldn't go; the exploit must have been connected with horses or vehicles to hang in the old fellow's head. Tom tried him off his own ground once or twice, but found he knew nothing beyond, and so let him have his head, and the rest of the road bowled easily away; for old Blow-hard (as the boys called him) was a dry old file, with much kindness and humour, and a capital spinner of a yarn when he had broken the neck of his day's work, and got plenty of ale under his belt.

What struck Tom's youthful imagination most was the desperate and lawless character of most of the stories. Was the guard hoaxing him? He couldn't help hoping that they were true. It's very odd how almost all English boys love danger. You can get ten to join a game, or climb a tree, or swim a stream, when there's a chance of breaking their limbs or getting drowned, for one who'll stay on level ground, or in his depth, or play quoits or bowls.

The guard had just finished an account of a desperate fight which had happened at one of the fairs between the drovers and the farmers with their whips, and the boys with cricket-bats and wickets, which arose out of a playful but objectionable practice of the boys going round to the public-houses and taking the linch-pins out of the wheels of the gigs, and was moralizing upon the way in which the Doctor, "a terrible stern man he'd heard tell," had come down upon several of the performers, "sending three on 'em off next morning in a po-shay with a parish constable," when they turned a corner and neared the milestone, the third from Rugby. By the stone two boys stood, their jackets buttoned tight, waiting for the coach.

"Look here, sir," says the guard, after giving a sharp toot-toot; "there's two on 'em; out-and-out runners they be. They comes out about twice or three times a week, and spirts a mile alongside of us."

And as they came up, sure enough, away went two boys along the footpath, keeping up with the horses—the first a light, clean-made fellow going on springs; the other stout and round-shouldered, labouring in his pace, but going as dogged as a bull-terrier.

Old Blow-hard looked on admiringly. "See how beautiful that there un holds hisself together, and goes from his hips, sir," said he; "he's a 'mazin' fine runner. Now many coachmen as drives a first-rate team'd put it on, and try and pass 'em. But Bob, sir, bless you, he's tender-hearted; he'd sooner pull in a bit if he see'd 'em

a-gettin' beat. I do b'lieve, too, as that there un'd sooner
break his heart than let us go by him afore next milestone."

At the second milestone the boys pulled up short, and
waved their hats to the guard, who had his watch out
and shouted "4.56," thereby indicating that the mile had
been done in four seconds under the five minutes. They
passed several more parties of boys, all of them objects
of the deepest interest to Tom, and came in sight of the
town at ten minutes before twelve. Tom fetched a long
breath, and thought he had never spent a pleasanter day.
Before he went to bed he had quite settled that it must
be the greatest day he should ever spend, and didn't
alter his opinion for many a long year—if he has yet.

CHAPTER V.

RUGBY AND FOOTBALL.

"Foot and eye opposed
In dubious strife."—SCOTT.

"AND so here's Rugby, sir, at last, and you'll be in
plenty of time for dinner at the School-house, as I told
you," said the old guard, pulling his horn out of its case
and tootle-tooing away, while the coachman shook up
his horses, and carried them along the side of the school
close, round Dead-man's corner, past the school-gates, and
down the High Street to the Spread Eagle, the wheelers
in a spanking trot, and leaders cantering, in a style which
would not have disgraced "Cherry Bob," "ramping,
stamping, tearing, swearing Billy Harwood," or any other
of the old coaching heroes.

Tom's heart beat quick as he passed the great school-
field or close, with its noble elms, in which several games
at football were going on, and tried to take in at once

the long line of gray buildings, beginning with the chapel, and ending with the School-house, the residence of the head-master, where the great flag was lazily waving from the highest round tower. And he began already to be proud of being a Rugby boy, as he passed the school-gates, with the oriel window above, and saw the boys standing there, looking as if the town belonged to them, and nodding in a familiar manner to the coachman, as if any one of them would be quite equal to getting on the box, and working the team down street as well as he.

One of the young heroes, however, ran out from the rest, and scrambled up behind ; where, having righted himself, and nodded to the guard, with " How do, Jem ? " he turned short round to Tom, and after looking him over for a minute, began,—

" I say, you fellow, is your name Brown ? "

" Yes," said Tom, in considerable astonishment, glad, however, to have lighted on some one already who seemed to know him.

" Ah, I thought so.   You know my old aunt, Miss East. She lives somewhere down your way in Berkshire.   She wrote to me that you were coming to-day, and asked me to give you a lift."

Tom was somewhat inclined to resent the patronizing air of his new friend, a boy of just about his own height and age, but gifted with the most transcendent coolness and assurance, which Tom felt to be aggravating and hard to bear, but couldn't for the life of him help admiring and envying—especially when young my lord begins hectoring two or three long loafing fellows, half porter, half stableman, with a strong touch of the black-guard, and in the end arranges with one of them, nicknamed Cooey, to carry Tom's luggage up to the School-house for sixpence.

"And hark 'ee, Cooey; it must be up in ten minutes, or no more jobs from me.—Come along, Brown." And away swaggers the young potentate, with his hands in his pockets, and Tom at his side.

"All right, sir," says Cooey, touching his hat, with a leer and a wink at his companions.

"Hullo though," says East, pulling up, and taking another look at Tom; "this'll never do. Haven't you got a hat? We never wear caps here. Only the louts wear caps. Bless you, if you were to go into the quadrangle with that thing on, I don't know what'd happen." The very idea was quite beyond young Master East, and he looked unutterable things.

Tom thought his cap a very knowing affair, but confessed that he had a hat in his hat-box; which was accordingly at once extracted from the hind-boot, and Tom equipped in his go-to-meeting roof, as his new friend called it. But this didn't quite suit his fastidious taste in another minute, being too shiny; so, as they walk up the town, they dive into Nixon's the hatter's, and Tom is arrayed, to his utter astonishment, and without paying for it, in a regulation cat-skin at seven-and-sixpence, Nixon undertaking to send the best hat up to the matron's room, School-house, in half an hour.

"You can send in a note for a tile on Monday, and make it all right, you know," said Mentor; "we're allowed two seven-and-sixers a half, besides what we bring from home."

Tom by this time began to be conscious of his new social position and dignities, and to luxuriate in the realized ambition of being a public school-boy at last, with a vested right of spoiling two seven-and-sixers in half a year.

"You see," said his friend, as they strolled up towards

the school-gates, in explanation of his conduct, " a great deal depends on how a fellow cuts up at first. If he's got nothing odd about him, and answers straightforward, and holds his head up, he gets on. Now, you'll do very well as to rig, all but that cap. You see I'm doing the handsome thing by you, because my father knows yours; besides, I want to please the old lady. She gave me half a sov. this half, and perhaps'll double it next, if I keep in her good books."

There's nothing for candour like a lower-school boy, and East was a genuine specimen—frank, hearty, and good-natured, well-satisfied with himself and his position, and choke-full of life and spirits, and all the Rugby prejudices and traditions which he had been able to get together in the long course of one half-year during which he had been at the School-house.

And Tom, notwithstanding his bumptiousness, felt friends with him at once, and began sucking in all his ways and prejudices, as fast as he could understand them.

East was great in the character of cicerone. He carried Tom through the great gates, where were only two or three boys. These satisfied themselves with the stock questions, "You fellow, what's your name? Where do you come from? How old are you? Where do you board?" and, "What form are you in?" And so they passed on through the quadrangle and a small courtyard, upon which looked down a lot of little windows (belonging, as his guide informed him, to some of the School-house studies), into the matron's room, where East introduced Tom to that dignitary; made him give up the key of his trunk, that the matron might unpack his linen, and told the story of the hat and of his own presence of mind : upon the relation whereof the matron laughingly scolded him for the coolest new boy in the house ; and East, indignant at the accusation of newness, marched Tom off into the quadrangle, and began showing him the schools, and examining him as to his literary attainments ; the result of which was a prophecy that they would be in the same form, and could do their lessons together.

"And now come in and see my study—we shall have just time before dinner ; and afterwards, before calling over, we'll do the close."

Tom followed his guide through the School-house hall, which opens into the quadrangle. It is a great room, thirty feet long and eighteen high, or thereabouts, with two great tables running the whole length, and two large fireplaces at the side, with blazing fires in them, at one of which some dozen boys were standing and lounging, some of whom shouted to East to stop ; but he shot through with his convoy, and landed him in the long, dark passages, with a large fire at the end of each, upon which the studies opened. Into one of these, in the bottom passage, East bolted with our hero, slamming and bolting the door behind them, in case of pursuit from the hall, and Tom was for the first time in a Rugby boy's citadel.

He hadn't been prepared for separate studies, and was not a little astonished and delighted with the palace in question.

It wasn't very large, certainly, being about six feet long by four broad. It couldn't be called light, as there were bars and a grating to the window ; which little precautions were necessary in the studies on the ground-floor looking out into the close, to prevent the exit of small boys after locking up, and the entrance of contraband articles. But it was uncommonly comfortable to look at, Tom thought. The space under the window at the farther end was occupied by a square table covered with a reasonably clean and whole red and blue check tablecloth ; a hard-seated sofa covered with red stuff occupied one side, running up to the end, and making a seat for one, or by sitting close, for two, at the table ; and a good stout wooden chair afforded a seat to another boy, so that three could sit and work together. The walls were wainscoted half-way up, the wainscot being covered with green baize, the remainder with a bright-patterned paper, on which hung three or four prints of dogs' heads; Grimaldi winning the Aylesbury steeple-chase ; Amy Robsart, the reigning Waverley beauty of the day; and Tom Crib, in a posture of defence, which did no credit to the science of that hero, if truly represented. Over the door were a row of hat-pegs, and on each side book-cases with cupboards at the bottom, shelves and cup-boards being filled indiscriminately with school-books, a cup or two, a mouse-trap and candlesticks, leather straps, a fustian bag, and some curious-looking articles which puzzled Tom not a little, until his friend explained that they were climbing-irons, and showed their use. A cricket-bat and small fishing-rod stood up in one corner.

This was the residence of East and another boy in the same form, and had more interest for Tom than Windsor Castle, or any other residence in the British Isles. For was he not about to become the joint owner of a similar home, the first place he could call his own ? One's own ! What a charm there is in the words ! How long it takes boy and man to find out their worth ! How fast most of us hold on to them—faster and more jealously, the nearer we are to that general home into which we can take nothing, but must go naked as we came into the world ! When shall we learn that he who multiplieth possessions multiplieth troubles, and that the one single

use of things which we call our own is that they may be
his who hath need of them ?

"And shall I have a study like this too ? " said Tom.

"Yes, of course ; you'll be chummed with some fellow
on Monday, and you can sit here till then."

"What nice places ! "

"They're well enough," answered East, patronizingly,
"only uncommon cold at nights sometimes. Gower—
that's my chum—and I make a fire with paper on the
floor after supper generally, only that makes it so smoky."

"But there's a big fire out in the passage," said Tom.

"Precious little we get out of that, though," said East.
"Jones the prepostor has the study at the fire end, and
he has rigged up an iron rod and green baize curtain
across the passage, which he draws at night, and sits
there with his door open ; so he gets all the fire, and
hears if we come out of our studies after eight, or make
a noise. However, he's taken to sitting in the fifth-form
room lately, so we do get a bit of fire now sometimes ;
only to keep a sharp lookout that he don't catch you
behind his curtain when he comes down—that's all."

A quarter past one now struck, and the bell began toll-
ing for dinner ; so they went into the hall and took their
places, Tom at the very bottom of the second table, next
to the prepostor (who sat at the end to keep order there),
and East a few paces higher. And now Tom for the first
time saw his future school-fellows in a body. In they
came, some hot and ruddy from football or long walks,
some pale and chilly from hard reading in their studies,
some from loitering over the fire at the pastrycook's,
dainty mortals, bringing with them pickles and sauce-
bottles to help them with their dinners. And a great
big-bearded man, whom Tom took for a master, began
calling over the names, while the great joints were being

rapidly carved on the third table in the corner by the old
verger and the housekeeper. Tom's turn came last, and
meanwhile he was all eyes, looking first with awe at the
great man, who sat close to him, and was helped first,
and who read a hard-looking book all the time he was
eating ; and when he got up and walked off to the fire,
at the small boys round him, some of whom were reading,
and the rest talking in whispers to one another, or stealing one another's bread, or shooting pellets, or digging
their forks through the tablecloth. However, notwithstanding his curiosity, he managed to make a capital
dinner by the time the big man called " Stand up ! " and
said grace.

As soon as dinner was over, and Tom had been ques-
tioned by such of his neighbours as were curious as to
his birth, parentage, education, and other like matters,
East, who evidently enjoyed his new dignity of patron
and mentor, proposed having a look at the close, which
Tom, athirst for knowledge, gladly assented to ; and they
went out through the quadrangle and past the big fives
court, into the great playground.

"That's the chapel, you see," said East ; "and there,
just behind it, is the place for fights. You see it's most
out of the way of the masters, who all live on the other
side, and don't come by here after first lesson or callings-
over. That's when the fights come off. And all this part
where we are is the little-side ground, right up to the
trees ; and on the other side of the trees is the big-side
ground, where the great matches are played. And there's
the island in the farthest corner ; you'll know that well
enough next half, when there's island fagging. I say, it's
horrid cold ; let's have a run across." And away went
East, Tom close behind him. East was evidently putting
his best foot foremost ; and Tom, who was mighty proud

of his running, and not a little anxious to show his friend that, although a new boy, he was no milksop, laid himself down to work in his very best style. Right across the close they went, each doing all he knew, and there wasn't a yard between them when they pulled up at the island moat.

" I say," said East, as soon as he got his wind, looking with much increased respect at Tom, "you ain't a bad scud, not by no means. Well, I'm as warm as a toast now."

" But why do you wear white trousers in November ? " said Tom. He had been struck by this peculiarity in the costume of almost all the School-house boys.

" Why, bless us, don't you know ? No; I forgot. Why, to-day's the School-house match. Our house plays the whole of the School at football. And we all wear white trousers, to show 'em we don't care for hacks. You're in luck to come to-day. You just will see a match ; and Brooke's going to let me play in quarters. That's more than he'll do for any other lower-school boy, except James, and he's fourteen."

" Who's Brooke ? "

" Why, that big fellow who called over at dinner, to be sure. He's cock of the school, and head of the School-house side, and the best kick and charger in Rugby."

" Oh, but do show me where they play. And tell me about it. I love football so, and have played all my life. Won't Brooke let me play ? "

" Not he," said East, with some indignation. " Why, you don't know the rules ; you'll be a month learning them. And then it's no joke playing-up in a match, I can tell you—quite another thing from your private school games. Why, there's been two collar-bones broken this half, and a dozen fellows lamed. And last year a fellow had his leg broken."

Tom listened with the profoundest respect to this chapter of accidents, and followed East across the level ground till they came to a sort of gigantic gallows of two poles, eighteen feet high, fixed upright in the ground some fourteen feet apart, with a cross-bar running from one to the other at the height of ten feet or thereabouts.

"This is one of the goals," said East, "and you see the other, across there, right opposite, under the Doctor's wall. Well, the match is for the best of three goals; whichever side kicks two goals wins: and it won't do, you see, just to kick the ball through these posts—it must go over the cross-bar; any height'll do, so long as it's between the posts. You'll have to stay in goal to touch the ball when it rolls behind the posts, because if the other side touch it they have a try at goal. Then we fellows in quarters, we play just about in front of goal here, and have to turn the ball and kick it back before the big fellows on the other side can follow it up. And in front of us all the big fellows play, and that's where the scrummages are mostly."

Tom's respect increased as he struggled to make out his friend's technicalities, and the other set to work to explain the mysteries of "off your side," "drop-kicks," "punts," "places," and the other intricacies of the great science of football.

"But how do you keep the ball between the goals?" said he; "I can't see why it mightn't go right down to the chapel."

"Why, that's out of play," answered East. "You see this gravel-walk running down all along this side of the playing-ground, and the line of elms opposite on the other? Well, they're the bounds. As soon as the ball gets past them, it's in touch, and out of play. And then whoever first touches it has to knock it straight out amongst the players-up, who make two lines with a space between them, every fellow going on his own side. Ain't there just fine scrummages then! And the three trees you see there which come out into the play, that's a tremendous place when the ball hangs there, for you get thrown against the trees, and that's worse than any hack."

Tom wondered within himself, as they strolled back again towards the fives court, whether the matches were really such break-neck affairs as East represented, and whether, if they were, he should ever get to like them and play up well.

He hadn't long to wonder, however, for next minute East cried out, "Hurrah! here's the punt-about; come along and try your hand at a kick." The punt-about is the practice-ball, which is just brought out and kicked about anyhow from one boy to another before callings-over and dinner, and at other odd times. They joined the boys who had brought it out, all small School-house fellows, friends of East; and Tom had the pleasure of trying his skill, and performed very creditably, after first driving his foot three inches into the ground, and then nearly kicking his leg into the air, in vigorous efforts to accomplish a drop-kick after the manner of East.

Presently more boys and bigger came out, and boys from other houses on their way to calling-over, and more balls were sent for. The crowd thickened as three o'clock approached; and when the hour struck, one hundred and fifty boys were hard at work. Then the balls were held, the master of the week came down in cap and gown to calling-over, and the whole school of three hundred boys swept into the big school to answer to their names.

"I may come in, mayn't I?" said Tom, catching East by the arm, and longing to feel one of them.

"Yes, come along; nobody'll say anything. You won't be so eager to get into calling-over after a month," replied his friend; and they marched into the big school together, and up to the farther end, where that illustrious form, the lower fourth, which had the honour of East's patronage for the time being, stood.

The master mounted into the high desk by the door, and one of the prepostors of the week stood by him on the steps, the other three marching up and down the middle of the school with their canes, calling out, "Silence, silence!" The sixth form stood close by the door on the left, some thirty in number, mostly great big grown men, as Tom thought, surveying them from a distance with awe; the fifth form behind them, twice their number, and not quite so big. These on the left; and on the right the lower fifth, shell, and all the junior forms in order; while up the middle marched the three prepostors.

Then the prepostor who stands by the master calls out the names, beginning with the sixth form; and as he calls each boy answers "here" to his name, and walks out. Some of the sixth stop at the door to turn the whole string of boys into the close. It is a great match-day, and every boy in the school, will he, nill he, must be there. The rest of the sixth go forwards into the close, to see that no one escapes by any of the side gates.

To-day, however, being the School-house match, none of the School-house prepostors stay by the door to watch for truants of their side; there is *carte blanche* to the School-house fags to go where they like. "They trust to our honour," as East proudly informs Tom; "they know very well that no School-house boy would cut the match. If he did, we'd very soon cut him, I can tell you."

The master of the week being short-sighted, and the prepostors of the week small and not well up to their work, the lower-school boys employ the ten minutes which elapse before their names are called in pelting one another vigorously with acorns, which fly about in all directions. The small prepostors dash in every now and then, and generally chastise some quiet, timid boy who is equally afraid of acorns and canes, while the principal performers get dexterously out of the way. And so calling-over rolls on somehow, much like the big world, punishments lighting on wrong shoulders, and matters going generally in a queer, cross-grained way, but the end coming somehow, which is, after all, the great point. And now the master of the week has finished, and locked up the big school; and the prepostors of the week come out, sweeping the last remnant of the school fags, who had been loafing about the corners by the fives court, in hopes of a chance of bolting, before them into the close.

"Hold the punt-about!" "To the goals!" are the cries; and all stray balls are impounded by the authorities, and the whole mass of boys moves up towards the two goals, dividing as they go into three bodies. That little band on the left, consisting of from fifteen to twenty boys, Tom amongst them, who are making for the goal under the School-house wall, are the School-house boys who are not to play up, and have to stay in goal. The larger body moving to the island goal are the School boys in a like predicament. The great mass in the middle are the players-up, both sides mingled together; they are hanging their jackets (and all who mean real work), their hats, waistcoats, neck-handkerchiefs, and braces, on the railings round the small trees; and there they go by twos and threes up to their respective grounds. There is none of the colour and tastiness of get-up, you will perceive, which lends such a life to the present game at Rugby, making the dullest and worst-fought match a pretty sight. Now each house has its own uniform of cap and jersey, of some lively colour; but at the time we are speaking of plush caps have not yet come in, or uniforms of any sort, except the School-house white trousers, which are abominably cold to-day. Let us get to work, bare-headed, and girded with our plain leather straps. But we mean business, gentlemen.

And now that the two sides have fairly sundered, and each occupies its own ground, and we get a good look at them, what absurdity is this? You don't mean to say that those fifty or sixty boys in white trousers, many of them quite small, are going to play that huge mass opposite? Indeed I do, gentlemen. They're going to try, at any rate, and won't make such a bad fight of it either, mark my word; for hasn't old Brooke won the toss, with his lucky halfpenny, and got choice of goals and kick-off? The new ball you may see lie there quite by itself, in the middle, pointing towards the School or island goal; in another minute it will be well on its way there. Use that minute in remarking how the School-house side is drilled. You will see, in the first place, that the sixth-form boy, who has the charge of goal, has spread his force (the goalkeepers) so as to occupy the whole space behind the goal-posts, at distances of about five yards apart. A safe and well-kept goal is the foundation of all good play. Old Brooke is talking to the captain of quarters; and now he moves away. See how that youngster spreads his men (the light brigade) carefully over the ground, half-way between their own goal and the body of their own players-up (the heavy brigade). These again play in several bodies. There is young Brooke

and the bull-dogs. Mark them well. They are the
" fighting brigade," the " die-hards," larking about at
leap-frog to keep themselves warm, and playing tricks
on one another. And on each side of old Brooke, who is
now standing in the middle of the ground and just going
to kick off, you see a separate wing of players-up, each
with a boy of acknowledged prowess to look to—here
Warner, and there Hedge ; but over all is old Brooke, ab-
solute as he of Russia, but wisely and bravely ruling over
willing and worshipping subjects, a true football king.
His face is earnest and careful as he glances a last time
over his array, but full of pluck and hope—the sort of
look I hope to see in my general when I go out to fight.

The School side is not organized in the same way. The
goal-keepers are all in lumps, anyhow and nohow ; you
can't distinguish between the players-up and the boys in
quarters, and there is divided leadership. But with such
odds in strength and weight it must take more than that
to hinder them from winning ; and so their leaders seem
to think, for they let the players-up manage themselves.

But now look ! there is a slight move forward of the
School-house wings, a shout of " Are you ready ? " and
loud affirmative reply. Old Brooke takes half a dozen
quick steps, and away goes the ball spinning towards
the School goal, seventy yards before it touches ground,
and at no point above twelve or fifteen feet high, a model
kick-off ; and the School-house cheer and rush on. The
ball is returned, and they meet it and drive it back
amongst the masses of the School already in motion.
Then the two sides close, and you can see nothing for
minutes but a swaying crowd of boys, at one point vio-
lently agitated. That is where the ball is, and there are
the keen players to be met, and the glory and the hard
knocks to be got. You hear the dull thud, thud of the

ball, and the shouts of "Off your side," "Down with him," "Put him over," "Bravo." This is what we call "a scrummage," gentlemen, and the first scrummage in a School-house match was no joke in the consulship of Plancus.

But see! it has broken; the ball is driven out on the School-house side, and a rush of the School carries it past the School-house players-up. "Look out in quarters," Brooke's and twenty other voices ring out. No need to call, though: the School-house captain of quarters has caught it on the bound, dodges the foremost School boys, who are heading the rush, and sends it back with a good drop-kick well into the enemy's country. And then follows rush upon rush, and scrummage upon scrummage, the ball now driven through into the School-house quarters, and now into the School goal; for the School-house have not lost the advantage which the kick-off and a slight wind gave them at the outset, and are slightly "penning" their adversaries. You say you don't see much in it all—nothing but a struggling mass of boys, and a leather ball which seems to excite them all to great fury, as a red rag does a bull. My dear sir, a battle would look much the same to you, except that the boys would be men, and the balls iron; but a battle would be worth your looking at for all that, and so is a football match. You can't be expected to appreciate the delicate strokes of play, the turns by which a game is lost and won—it takes an old player to do that; but the broad philosophy of football you can understand if you will. Come along with me a little nearer, and let us consider it together.

The ball has just fallen again where the two sides are thickest, and they close rapidly around it in a scrummage. It must be driven through now by force or skill, till it flies out on one side or the other. Look how differently the boys face it! Here come two of the bull-dogs, bursting through the outsiders; in they go, straight to the heart of the scrummage, bent on driving that ball out on the opposite side. That is what they mean to do. My sons, my sons! you are too hot; you have gone past the ball, and must struggle now right through the scrummage, and get round and back again to your own side, before you can be of any further use. Here comes young Brooke; he goes in as straight as you, but keeps his head, and backs and bends, holding himself still behind the ball, and driving it furiously when he gets the chance. Take a leaf out of his book, you young chargers. Here comes Speedicut, and Flashman the School-house bully, with shouts and great action. Won't you two come up to young Brooke, after locking-up, by the School-house fire, with "Old fellow, wasn't that just a splendid scrummage by the three trees?" But he knows you, and so do we. You don't really want to drive that ball through that scrummage, chancing all hurt for the glory of the School-house, but to make us think that's what you want—a vastly different thing; and fellows of your kidney will never go through more than the skirts of a scrummage, where it's all push and no kicking. We respect boys who keep out of it, and don't sham going in; but you—we had rather not say what we think of you.

Then the boys who are bending and watching on the outside, mark them: they are most useful players, the dodgers, who seize on the ball the moment it rolls out from amongst the chargers, and away with it across to the opposite goal. They seldom go into the scrummage, but must have more coolness than the chargers. As endless as are boys' characters, so are their ways of facing or not facing a scrummage at football.

Three-quarters of an hour are gone; first winds are failing, and weight and numbers beginning to tell. Yard by yard the School-house have been driven back, contesting every inch of ground. The bull-dogs are the colour of mother earth from shoulder to ankle, except young Brooke, who has a marvellous knack of keeping his legs. The School-house are being penned in their turn, and now the ball is behind their goal, under the Doctor's wall. The Doctor and some of his family are there looking on, and seem as anxious as any boy for the success of the School-house. We get a minute's breathing-time before old Brooke kicks out, and he gives the word to play strongly for toucn, by the three trees. Away goes the ball, and the bull-dogs after it, and in another minute there is shout of "In touch!" "Our ball!" Now's your time, old Brooke, while your men are still fresh. He stands with the ball in his hand, while the two sides form in deep lines opposite one another; he must strike it straight out between them. The lines are thickest close to him, but young Brooke and two or three of his men are shifting up farther, where the opposite line is weak. Old Brooke strikes it out straight and strong, and it falls opposite his brother. Hurrah! that rush has taken it right through the School line, and away past the three trees, far into their quarters, and young Brooke and the bull-dogs are close upon it. The School leaders rush back, shouting, "Look out in goal!" and strain every nerve to catch him, but they are after the fleetest foot in Rugby. There they go straight for the School goal-posts, quarters scattering before them. One after another the bull-dogs go down, but young Brooke holds on. "He is down." No! a long stagger, but the danger is past. That was the shock of Crew, the most dangerous of dodgers. And now he is close to the School goal, the ball not three yards before him. There is a hurried rush of the School fags to the spot, but no one throws himself on the ball, the only chance, and young Brooke has touched it right under the School goal-posts.

The School leaders come up furious, and administer toco to the wretched fags nearest at hand. They may well be angry, for it is all Lombard Street to a china orange that the School-house kick a goal with the ball touched in such a good place. Old Brooke, of course, will kick it out, but who shall catch and place it ? Call Crab Jones. Here he comes, sauntering along with a straw in his mouth, the queerest, coolest fish in Rugby. If he were tumbled into the moon this minute, he would just pick himself up without taking his hands out of his pockets or turning a hair. But it is a moment when the boldest charger's heart beats quick. Old Brooke stands with the ball under his arm motioning the School back ; he will not kick out till they are all in goal, behind the posts. They are all edging forwards, inch by inch, to get nearer for the rush at Crab Jones, who stands there in front of old Brooke to catch the ball. If they can reach and destroy him before he catches, the danger is over ; and with one and the same rush they will carry it right away to the School-house goal. Fond hope ! it is kicked out and caught beautifully. Crab strikes his heel into the ground, to mark the spot where the ball was caught, beyond which the school line may not advance ; but there they stand, five deep, ready to rush the moment the ball touches the ground. Take plenty of room. Don't give the rush a chance of reaching you. Place it true and steady. Trust Crab Jones. He has made a small hole with his heel for the ball to lie on, by which he is resting on one knee, with his eye on old Brooke. "Now !" Crab places the ball at the word, old Brooke kicks, and it rises slowly and truly as the School rush forward.

Then a moment's pause, while both sides look up at the spinning ball. There it flies, straight between the two posts, some five feet above the cross-bar, an unquestioned goal; and a shout of real, genuine joy rings out from the School-house players-up, and a faint echo of it comes over the close from the goal-keepers under the Doctor's wall. A goal in the first hour—such a thing hasn't been done in the School-house match these five years.

"Over!" is the cry. The two sides change goals, and the School-house goal-keepers come threading their way across through the masses of the School, the most openly triumphant of them—amongst whom is Tom, a School-house boy of two hours' standing—getting their ears boxed in the transit. Tom indeed is excited beyond measure, and it is all the sixth-form boy, kindest and safest of goal-keepers, has been able to do, to keep him from rushing out whenever the ball has been near their goal. So he holds him by his side, and instructs him in the science of touching.

At this moment Griffith, the itinerant vender of oranges from Hill Morton, enters the close with his heavy baskets. There is a rush of small boys upon the little pale-faced man, the two sides mingling together, subdued by the great goddess Thirst, like the English and French by the streams in the Pyrenees. The leaders are past oranges and apples, but some of them visit their coats, and apply innocent-looking ginger-beer bottles to their mouths. It is no ginger-beer though, I fear, and will do you no good. One short mad rush, and then a stitch in the side, and no more honest play. That's what comes of those bottles.

But now Griffith's baskets are empty, the ball is placed again midway, and the School are going to kick off. Their leaders have sent their lumber into goal, and rated the rest soundly, and one hundred and twenty picked players-up are there, bent on retrieving the game. They are to keep the ball in front of the School-house goal, and then to drive it in by sheer strength and weight. They mean heavy play and no mistake, and so old Brooke sees, and places Crab Jones in quarters just before the goal, with four or five picked players who are to keep the ball away to the sides, where a try at goal, if obtained, will be less dangerous than in front. He himself, and Warner and Hedge, who have saved themselves till now, will lead the charges.

"Are you ready?" "Yes." And away comes the ball, kicked high in the air, to give the School time to rush on and catch it as it falls. And here they are amongst us. Meet them like Englishmen, you School-house boys, and charge them home. Now is the time to show what mettle is in you; and there shall be a warm seat by the hall fire, and honour, and lots of bottled beer to-night for him who does his duty in the next half-hour. And they are well met. Again and again the cloud of their players-up gathers before our goal, and comes threatening on, and Warner or Hedge, with young Brooke and the relics of the bull-dogs, break through and carry the ball back; and old Brooke ranges the field like Job's war-horse. The thickest scrummage parts asunder before his rush, like the waves before a clipper's bows; his cheery voice rings out over the field, and his eye is everywhere. And if these miss the ball, and it rolls dangerously in front of our goal, Crab Jones and his men have seized it and sent it away towards the sides with the unerring drop-kick. This is worth living for—

the whole sum of school-boy existence gathered up into one straining, struggling half-hour, a half-hour worth a year of common life.

The quarter to five has struck, and the play slackens for a minute before goal; but there is Crew, the artful dodger, driving the ball in behind our goal, on the island side, where our quarters are weakest. Is there no one to meet him? Yes; look at little East! The ball is just at equal distances between the two, and they rush together, the young man of seventeen and the boy of twelve, and kick it at the same moment. Crew passes on without a stagger; East is hurled forward by the shock, and plunges on his shoulder, as if he would bury himself in the ground; but the ball rises straight into the air, and falls behind Crew's back, while the "bravoes" of the School-house attest the pluckiest charge of all that hard-fought day. Warner picks East up lame and half stunned, and he hobbles back into goal, conscious of having played the man.

And now the last minutes are come, and the School gather for their last rush, every boy of the hundred and twenty who has a run left in him. Reckless of the defence of their own goal, on they come across the level big-side ground, the ball well down amongst them, straight for our goal, like the column of the Old Guard up the slope at Waterloo. All former charges have been child's play to this. Warner and Hedge have met them, but still on they come. The bull-dogs rush in for the last time; they are hurled over or carried back, striving hand, foot, and eyelids. Old Brooke comes sweeping round the skirts of the play, and turning short round, picks out the very heart of the scrummage, and plunges in. It wavers for a moment; he has the ball. No, it has passed him, and his voice rings out clear over the advancing tide, "Look out in goal!" Crab Jones catches it for a moment; but before he can kick, the rush is upon him and passes over him; and he picks himself up behind them with his straw in his mouth, a little dirtier, but as cool as ever.

The ball rolls slowly in behind the School-house goal, not three yards in front of a dozen of the biggest School players-up.

There stands the School-house prepostor, safest of goal-keepers, and Tom Brown by his side, who has learned his trade by this time. Now is your time, Tom. The blood of all the Browns is up, and the two rush in together, and throw themselves on the ball, under the very feet of the advancing column—the prepostor on his hands and knees, arching his back, and Tom all along on his face. Over them topple the leaders of the rush, shooting over the back of the prepostor, but falling flat on Tom, and knocking all the wind out of his small carcass. "Our ball," says the prepostor, rising with his prize; "but get up there; there's a little fellow under you." They are hauled and roll off him, and Tom is discovered, a motionless body.

Old Brooke picks him up. "Stand back, give him air," he says; and then feeling his limbs, adds, "No bones broken.—How do you feel, young un?"

"Hah-hah!" gasps Tom, as his wind comes back; "pretty well, thank you—all right."

"Who is he?" says Brooke.

"Oh, it's Brown; he's a new boy; I know him," says East, coming up.

"Well, he is a plucky youngster, and will make a player," says Brooke.

And five o'clock strikes. "No side" is called, and the first day of the School-house match is over.

CHAPTER VI.

AFTER THE MATCH.

" Some food we had."—SHAKESPEARE.

ης ποτος αδυς.—THEOCR. *Id.*

As the boys scattered away from the ground, and East, leaning on Tom's arm, and limping along, was beginning to consider what luxury they should go and buy for tea to celebrate that glorious victory, the two Brookes came striding by. Old Brooke caught sight of East, and stopped; put his hand kindly on his shoulder, and said, " Bravo, youngster; you played famously. Not much the matter, I hope ? "

" No, nothing at all," said East—" only a little twist from that charge."

" Well, mind and get all right for next Saturday." And the leader passed on, leaving East better for those few words than all the opodeldoc in England would have made him, and Tom ready to give one of his ears for as much notice. Ah! light words of those whom we love and honour, what a power ye are, and how carelessly wielded by those who can use you! Surely for these things also God will ask an account.

" Tea's directly after locking-up, you see," said East, hobbling along as fast as he could, " so you come along down to Sally Harrowell's; that's our School-house tuck-shop. She bakes such stunning murphies, we'll have a penn'orth each for tea. Come along, or they'll all be gone."

Tom's new purse and money burnt in his pocket; he wondered, as they toddled through the quadrangle and along the street, whether East would be insulted if he suggested further extravagance, as he had not sufficient

faith in a pennyworth of potatoes. At last he blurted
out,—

"I say, East, can't we get something else besides
potatoes? I've got lots of money, you know."

"Bless us, yes; I forgot," said East, "you've only
just come. You see all my tin's been gone this twelve
weeks—it hardly ever lasts beyond the first fortnight;
and our allowances were all stopped this morning for
broken windows, so I haven't got a penny. I've got a
tick at Sally's, of course; but then I hate running it
high, you see, towards the end of the half, 'cause one
has to shell out for it all directly one comes back, and
that's a bore."

Tom didn't understand much of this talk, but seized
on the fact that East had no money, and was denying
himself some little pet luxury in consequence. "Well,
what shall I buy?" said he, "I'm uncommon hungry."

"I say," said East, stopping to look at him and rest
his leg, "you're a trump, Brown. I'll do the same by
you next half. Let's have a pound of sausages then.
That's the best grub for tea I know of."

"Very well," said Tom, as pleased as possible; "where
do they sell them?"

"Oh, over here, just opposite." And they crossed the
street and walked into the cleanest little front room of a
small house, half parlour, half shop, and bought a pound
of most particular sausages, East talking pleasantly to
Mrs. Porter while she put them in paper, and Tom doing
the paying part.

From Porter's they adjourned to Sally Harrowell's,
where they found a lot of School-house boys waiting
for the roast potatoes, and relating their own exploits in
the day's match at the top of their voices. The street
opened at once into Sally's kitchen, a low brick-floored

room, with large recess for fire, and chimney-corner seats. Poor little Sally, the most good-natured and much-enduring of womankind, was bustling about, with a napkin in her hand, from her own oven to those of the neighbours' cottages up the yard at the back of the house. Stumps, her husband, a short, easy-going shoemaker, with a beery, humorous eye and ponderous calves, who lived mostly on his wife's earnings, stood in a corner of the room, exchanging shots of the roughest description of repartee with every boy in turn. " Stumps, you lout, you've had too much beer again to-day." " 'Twasn't of your paying for, then." " Stumps's calves are running down into his ankles ; they want to get to grass." " Better be doing that than gone altogether like yours," etc. Very poor stuff it was, but it served to make time pass ; and every now and then Sally arrived in the middle with a smoking tin of potatoes, which was cleared off in a few seconds, each boy as he seized his lot running off to the house with "Put me down two-penn'orth, Sally ;" "Put down three-penn'orth between me and Davis," etc. How she ever kept the accounts so straight as she did, in her head and on her slate, was a perfect wonder.

East and Tom got served at last, and started back for the School-house, just as the locking-up bell began to ring, East on the way recounting the life and adventures of Stumps, who was a character. Amongst his other small avocations, he was the hind carrier of a sedan-chair, the last of its race, in which the Rugby ladies still went out to tea, and in which, when he was fairly harnessed and carrying a load, it was the delight of small and mischievous boys to follow him and whip his calves. This was too much for the temper even of Stumps, and he would pursue his tormentors in a vindictive and apoplectic manner when released, but was easily pacified by twopence to buy beer with.

The lower-school boys of the School-house, some fifteen in number, had tea in the lower-fifth school, and were presided over by the old verger or head-porter. Each boy had a quarter of a loaf of bread and pat of butter, and as much tea as he pleased; and there was scarcely one who didn't add to this some further luxury, such as baked potatoes, a herring, sprats, or something of the sort. But few at this period of the half-year could live up to a pound of Porter's sausages, and East was in great magnificence upon the strength of theirs. He had produced a toasting-fork from his study, and set Tom to toast the sausages, while he mounted guard over their butter and potatoes. "'Cause," as he explained, "you're a new boy, and they'll play you some trick and get our butter; but you can toast just as well as I." So Tom, in the midst of three or four more urchins similarly employed, toasted his face and the sausages at the same time before the huge fire, till the latter cracked; when East from his watch-tower shouted that they were done, and then the feast proceeded, and the festive cups of tea were filled and emptied, and Tom imparted of the sausages in small bits to many neighbours, and thought he had never tasted such good potatoes or seen such jolly boys. They on their parts waived all ceremony, and pegged away at the sausages and potatoes, and remembering Tom's performance in goal, voted East's new crony a brick. After tea, and while the things were being cleared away, they gathered round the fire, and the talk on the match still went on; and those who had them to show pulled up their trousers and showed the hacks they had received in the good cause.

They were soon, however, all turned out of the school;

and East conducted Tom up to his bedroom, that he might get on clean things, and wash himself before singing.

"What's singing ?" said Tom, taking his head out of his basin, where he had been plunging it in cold water.

"Well, you are jolly green," answered his friend, from a neighbouring basin. "Why, the last six Saturdays of every half we sing of course ; and this is the first of them. No first lesson to do, you know, and lie in bed to-morrow morning."

"But who sings ?"

"Why, everybody, of course ; you'll see soon enough. We begin directly after supper, and sing till bed-time. It ain't such good fun now, though, as in the summer half; 'cause then we sing in the little fives court, under the library, you know. We take out tables, and the big boys sit round and drink beer — double allowance on Saturday nights ; and we cut about the quadrangle between the songs, and it looks like a lot of robbers in a cave. And the louts come and pound at the great gates, and we pound back again, and shout at them. But this half we only sing in the hall. Come along down to my study."

Their principal employment in the study was to clear out East's table, removing the drawers and ornaments and tablecloth ; for he lived in the bottom passage, and his table was in requisition for the singing.

Supper came in due course at seven o'clock, consisting of bread and cheese and beer, which was all saved for the singing ; and directly afterwards the fags went to work to prepare the hall. The School-house hall, as has been said, is a great long high room, with two large fires on one side, and two large iron-bound tables, one running down the middle, and the other along the wall opposite the fireplaces. Around the upper fire the fags placed the tables in the form of a horse-shoe, and upon them the jugs with the Saturday night's allowance of beer. Then the big boys used to drop in and take their seats, bringing with them bottled beer and song books; for although they all knew the songs by heart, it was the thing to have an old manuscript book descended from some departed hero, in which they were all carefully written out.

The sixth-form boys had not yet appeared; so, to fill up the gap, an interesting and time-honoured ceremony was gone through. Each new boy was placed on the table in turn, and made to sing a solo, under the penalty of drinking a large mug of salt and water if he resisted or broke down. However, the new boys all sing like nightingales to-night, and the salt water is not in requisition—Tom, as his part, performing the old west-country song of "The Leather Bottèl" with considerable applause. And at the half-hour down come the sixth and fifth form boys, and take their places at the tables, which are filled up by the next biggest boys, the rest, for whom there is no room at the table, standing round outside.

The glasses and mugs are filled, and then the fugleman strikes up the old sea-song,

> " A wet sheet and a flowing sea,
> And a wind that follows fast," etc.,

which is the invariable first song in the School-house; and all the seventy voices join in, not mindful of harmony, but bent on noise, which they attain decidedly, but the general effect isn't bad. And then follow " The British Grenadiers," " Billy Taylor," " The Siege of Seringapatam," " Three Jolly Postboys," and other vociferous songs in rapid succession, including "The Chesapeake and Shannon," a song lately introduced in honour of old Brooke; and when they come to the words,

> " Brave Broke he waved his sword, crying, Now, my lads, aboard,
> And we'll stop their playing Yankee-doodle-dandy oh ! "

you expect the roof to come down. The sixth and fifth know that " brave Broke " of the *Shannon* was no sort of relation to our old Brooke. The fourth form are uncertain in their belief, but for the most part hold that old Brooke *was* a midshipman then on board his uncle's ship. And the lower school never doubt for a moment that it was our old Brooke who led the boarders, in what capacity they care not a straw. During the pauses the bottled-beer corks fly rapidly, and the talk is fast and merry, and the big boys—at least all of them who have a fellow-feeling for dry throats—hand their mugs over their shoulders to be emptied by the small ones who stand round behind.

Then Warner, the head of the house, gets up and wants to speak; but he can't, for every boy knows what's coming. And the big boys who sit at the tables pound them and cheer; and the small boys who stand behind pound one another, and cheer, and rush about the hall cheering. Then silence being made, Warner reminds them of the old School-house custom of drinking the healths, on the first night of singing, of those who are going to leave at the end of the half. "He sees that they know what he is going to say already" (loud cheers), "and so won't keep them, but only ask them to treat the toast as it deserves. It is the head of the eleven, the head of big-side football, their leader on this glorious day—Pater Brooke ! "

And away goes the pounding and cheering again,

becoming deafening when old Brooke gets on his legs;
till, a table having broken down, and a gallon or so of
beer been upset, and all throats getting dry, silence en-
sues, and the hero speaks, leaning his hands on the table,
and bending a little forwards. No action, no tricks of
oratory—plain, strong, and straight, like his play.

"Gentlemen of the School-house! I am very proud
of the way in which you have received my name, and I
wish I could say all I should like in return. But I know
I shan't. However, I'll do the best I can to say what
seems to me ought to be said by a fellow who's just
going to leave, and who has spent a good slice of his life
here. Eight years it is, and eight such years as I can
never hope to have again. So now I hope you'll all
listen to me" (loud cheers of "That we will"), "for I'm
going to talk seriously. You're bound to listen to me,
for what's the use of calling me 'pater,' and all that, if
you don't mind what I say? And I'm going to talk seriously, because I feel so. It's a jolly time, too, getting to
the end of the half, and a goal kicked by us first day"
(tremendous applause), "after one of the hardest and
fiercest day's play I can remember in eight years."
(Frantic shoutings.) "The School played splendidly, too,
I will say, and kept it up to the last. That last charge of
theirs would have carried away a house. I never thought
to see anything again of old Crab there, except little
pieces, when I saw him tumbled over by it." (Laughter
and shouting, and great slapping on the back of Jones
by the boys nearest him.) "Well, but we beat 'em."
(Cheers.) "Ay, but why did we beat 'em? Answer me
that." (Shouts of "Your play.") "Nonsense! 'Twasn't
the wind and kick-off either—that wouldn't do it.
'Twasn't because we've half a dozen of the best players
in the school, as we have. I wouldn't change Warner,

and Hedge, and Crab, and the young un, for any six on their side." (Violent cheers.) "But half a dozen fellows can't keep it up for two hours against two hundred. Why is it, then? I'll tell you what I think. It's because we've more reliance on one another, more of a house feeling, more fellowship than the School can have. Each of us knows and can depend on his next-hand man better. That's why we beat 'em to-day. We've union, they've division—there's the secret." (Cheers.) "But how's this to be kept up? How's it to be improved? That's the question. For I take it we're all in earnest about beating the School, whatever else we care about. I know I'd sooner win two School-house matches running than get the Balliol scholarship any day." (Frantic cheers.)

"Now, I'm as proud of the house as any one. I believe it's the best house in the school, out and out." (Cheers.) "But it's a long way from what I want to see it. First, there's a deal of bullying going on. I know it well. I don't pry about and interfere; that only makes it more underhand, and encourages the small boys to come to us with their fingers in their eyes telling tales, and so we should be worse off than ever.. It's very little kindness for the sixth to meddle generally—you youngsters mind that. You'll be all the better football players for learning to stand it, and to take your own parts, and fight it through. But depend on it, there's nothing breaks up a house like bullying. Bullies are cowards, and one coward makes many; so good-bye to the School-house match if bullying gets ahead here." (Loud applause from the small boys, who look meaningly at Flashman and other boys at the tables.) "Then there's fuddling about in the public-house, and drinking bad spirits, and punch, and such rot-gut stuff. That won't make good drop-kicks or chargers of you, take my word for it. You get plenty of good beer here, and that's enough for you; and drinking isn't fine or manly, whatever some of you may think of it.

"One other thing I must have a word about. A lot of you think and say, for I've heard you, 'There's this new Doctor hasn't been here so long as some of us, and he's changing all the old customs. Rugby, and the School-house especially, are going to the dogs. Stand up for the good old ways, and down with the Doctor!' Now I'm as fond of old Rugby customs and ways as any of you, and I've been here longer than any of you, and I'll give you a word of advice in time, for I shouldn't like to see any of you getting sacked. 'Down with the Doctor's' easier said than done. You'll find him pretty tight on his perch, I take it, and an awkwardish customer to handle in that line. Besides now, what customs has he put down? There was the good old custom of taking the linchpins out of the farmers' and bagmen's gigs at the fairs, and a cowardly, blackguard custom it was. We all know what came of it, and no wonder the Doctor objected to it. But come now, any of you, name a custom that he has put down."

"The hounds," calls out a fifth-form boy, clad in a green cutaway with brass buttons and cord trousers, the leader of the sporting interest, and reputed a great rider and keen hand generally.

"Well, we had six or seven mangy harriers and beagles belonging to the house, I'll allow, and had had them for years, and that the Doctor put them down. But what good ever came of them? Only rows with all the keepers for ten miles round; and big-side hare-and-hounds is better fun ten times over. What else?"

No answer.

"Well, I won't go on. Think it over for yourselves. You'll find, I believe, that he don't meddle with any one that's worth keeping. And mind now, I say again, look out for squalls if you will go your own way, and that way ain't the Doctor's, for it'll lead to grief. You all know that I'm not the fellow to back a master through thick and thin. If I saw him stopping football, or cricket, or bathing, or sparring, I'd be as ready as any fellow to stand up about it. But he don't; he encourages them. Didn't you see him out to-day for half an hour watching us?" (loud cheers for the Doctor); "and he's a strong, true man, and a wise one too, and a public-school man too" (cheers), "and so let's stick to him, and talk no more rot, and drink his health as the head of the house." (Loud cheers.) "And now I've done blowing up, and very glad I am to have done. But it's a solemn thing to be thinking of leaving a place which one has lived in and loved for eight years; and if one can say a word for the good of the old house at such a time, why, it should be said, whether bitter or sweet. If I hadn't been proud of the house and you—ay, no one knows how proud—I shouldn't be blowing you up. And now let's get to singing. But before I sit down I must give you a toast to be drunk with three-times-three and all the honours. It's a toast which I hope every one of us, wherever he may go hereafter, will never fail to drink when he thinks of the brave, bright days of his boyhood. It's a toast which should bind us all together, and to those who've gone before and who'll come after us here. It is the dear old School-house—the best house of the best school in England!"

My dear boys, old and young, you who have belonged, or do belong, to other schools and other houses, don't begin throwing my poor little book about the room, and abusing me and it, and vowing you'll read no more when you get to this point. I allow you've provocation for it. But come now—would you, any of you, give a fig for a fellow who didn't believe in and stand up for his own house and his own school? You know you wouldn't. Then don't object to me cracking up the old School-house, Rugby. Haven't I a right to do it, when I'm taking all the trouble of writing this true history for all of your benefits? If you ain't satisfied, go and write the history of your own houses in your own times, and say all you know for your own schools and houses, provided it's true, and I'll read it without abusing you.

The last few words hit the audience in their weakest place. They had been not altogether enthusiastic at several parts of old Brooke's speech; but " the best house of the best school in England " was too much for them all, and carried even the sporting and drinking interests off their legs into rapturous applause, and (it is to be hoped) resolutions to lead a new life and remember old Brooke's words—which, however, they didn't altogether do, as will appear hereafter.

But it required all old Brooke's popularity to carry down parts of his speech—especially that relating to the Doctor. For there are no such bigoted holders by established forms and customs, be they never so foolish or meaningless, as English school-boys—at least, as the school-boys of our generation. We magnified into heroes every boy who had left, and looked upon him with awe and reverence when he revisited the place a year or so afterwards, on his way to or from Oxford or Cambridge; and happy was the boy who remembered him, and sure of an audience as he expounded what he used to do and say, though it were sad enough stuff to make angels, not to say head-masters, weep.

We looked upon every trumpery little custom and habit which had obtained in the School as though it had been a law of the Medes and Persians, and regarded the infringement or variation of it as a sort of sacrilege. And the Doctor, than whom no man or boy had a stronger liking for old school customs which were good and sensible, had, as has already been hinted, come into most decided collision with several which were neither the one nor the other. And as old Brooke had said, when he came into collision with boys or customs, there was nothing for them but to give in or take themselves off ; because what he said had to be done, and no mistake about it. And this was beginning to be pretty clearly understood. The boys felt that there was a strong man over them, who would have things his own way, and hadn't yet learnt that he was a wise and loving man also. His personal character and influence had not had time to make itself felt, except by a very few of the bigger boys with whom he came more directly into contact ; and he was looked upon with great fear and dislike by the great majority even of his own house. For he had found School and School-house in a state of monstrous license and misrule, and was still employed in the necessary but unpopular work of setting up order with a strong hand.

However, as has been said, old Brooke triumphed, and the boys cheered him and then the Doctor. And then more songs came, and the healths of the other boys about to leave, who each made a speech, one flowery, another maudlin, a third prosy, and so on, which are not necessary to be here recorded.

Half-past nine struck in the middle of the performance of " Auld Lang Syne," a most obstreperous proceeding, during which there was an immense amount of standing with one foot on the table, knocking mugs together and shaking hands, without which accompaniments it seems impossible for the youths of Britain to take part in that famous old song. The under-porter of the School-house entered during the performance, bearing five or six long wooden candlesticks with lighted dips in them, which he proceeded to stick into their holes in such part of the great tables as he could get at; and then stood outside the ring till the end of the song, when he was hailed with shouts.

"Bill, you old muff, the half-hour hasn't struck." "Here, Bill, drink some cocktail." "Sing us a song, old boy." "Don't you wish you may get the table?" Bill drank the proffered cocktail not unwillingly, and putting down the empty glass, remonstrated. "Now, gentlemen, there's only ten minutes to prayers, and we must get the hall straight."

Shouts of "No, no!" and a violent effort to strike up "Billy Taylor" for the third time. Bill looked appealingly to old Brooke, who got up and stopped the noise. "Now then, lend a hand, you youngsters, and get the tables back; clear away the jugs and glasses. Bill's right.—Open the windows, Warner." The boy addressed, who sat by the long ropes, proceeded to pull up the great windows, and let in a clear, fresh rush of night air, which made the candles flicker and gutter, and the fires roar. The circle broke up, each collaring his own jug, glass, and song-book; Bill pounced on the big table, and began to rattle it away to its place outside the buttery door. The lower-passage boys carried off their small tables, aided by their friends; while above all, standing on the great hall-table, a knot of untiring sons of harmony made night doleful by a prolonged performance of "God save the King." His Majesty King William the Fourth then reigned over us, a monarch deservedly popular amongst the boys addicted to melody, to whom he was chiefly known from the beginning of that excellent if slightly vulgar song in which they much delighted,—

> " Come, neighbours all, both great and small,
>   Perform your duties here,
>   And loudly sing, ' Live Billy, our king,'
>   For bating the tax upon beer."

Others of the more learned in songs also celebrated his praises in a sort of ballad, which I take to have been written by some Irish loyalist. I have forgotten all but the chorus, which ran,—

> " God save our good King William, be his name for ever blest ;
>   He's the father of all his people, and the guardian of all the rest."

In troth we were loyal subjects in those days, in a rough way. I trust that our successors make as much of her present Majesty, and, having regard to the greater refinement of the times, have adopted or written other songs equally hearty, but more civilized, in her honour.

Then the quarter to ten struck, and the prayer-bell rang. The sixth and fifth form boys ranged themselves in their school order along the wall, on either side of the great fires, the middle-fifth and upper-school boys round the long table in the middle of the hall, and the lower-school boys round the upper part of the second long table, which ran down the side of the hall farthest from the fires. Here Tom found himself at the bottom of all, in a state of mind and body not at all fit for prayers, as he thought ; and so tried hard to make himself serious, but couldn't, for the life of him, do anything but repeat in his head the choruses of some of the songs, and stare at all the boys opposite, wondering at the brilliancy of their waistcoats, and speculating what sort of fellows they were. The steps of the head-porter are heard on the stairs, and a light gleams at the door. " Hush ! "

from the fifth-form boys who stand there, and then in strides the Doctor, cap on head, book in one hand, and gathering up his gown in the other. He walks up the middle, and takes his post by Warner, who begins calling over the names. The Doctor takes no notice of anything, but quietly turns over his book and finds the place, and then stands, cap in hand and finger in book, looking straight before his nose. He knows better than any one when to look, and when to see nothing. To-night is singing night, and there's been lots of noise and no harm done—nothing but beer drunk, and nobody the worse for it, though some of them do look hot and excited. So the Doctor sees nothing, but fascinates Tom in a horrible manner as he stands there, and reads out the psalm, in that deep, ringing, searching voice of his. Prayers are over, and Tom still stares open-mouthed after the Doctor's retiring figure, when he feels a pull at his sleeve, and turning round, sees East.

" I say, were you ever tossed in a blanket ? "

" No," said Tom ; " why ? "

" 'Cause there'll be tossing to-night, most likely, before the sixth come up to bed. So if you funk, you just come along and hide, or else they'll catch you and toss you."

"Were you ever tossed? Does it hurt?" inquired Tom.

" Oh yes, bless you, a dozen times," said East, as he hobbled along by Tom's side upstairs. " It don't hurt unless you fall on the floor. But most fellows don't like it."

They stopped at the fireplace in the top passage, where were a crowd of small boys whispering together, and evidently unwilling to go up into the bedrooms. In a minute, however, a study door opened, and a sixth-form boy came out, and off they all scuttled up the stairs, and then noiselessly dispersed to their different rooms.

Tom's heart beat rather quick as he and East reached their room, but he had made up his mind. "I shan't hide, East," said he.

"Very well, old fellow," replied East, evidently pleased; "no more shall I. They'll be here for us directly."

The room was a great big one, with a dozen beds in it, but not a boy that Tom could see except East and himself. East pulled off his coat and waistcoat, and then sat on the bottom of his bed whistling and pulling off his boots. Tom followed his example.

A noise and steps are heard in the passage, the door opens, and in rush four or five great fifth-form boys, headed by Flashman in his glory.

Tom and East slept in the farther corner of the room, and were not seen at first.

"Gone to ground, eh?" roared Flashman. "Push 'em out then, boys; look under the beds." And he pulled up the little white curtain of the one nearest him. "Who-o-op!" he roared, pulling away at the leg of a small boy, who held on tight to the leg of the bed, and sang out lustily for mercy.

"Here, lend a hand, one of you, and help me pull out this young howling brute.—Hold your tongue, sir, or I'll kill you."

"Oh, please, Flashman, please, Walker, don't toss me! I'll fag for you—I'll do anything—only don't toss me."

"You be hanged," said Flashman, lugging the wretched boy along; "'twon't hurt you, —— you!—Come along, boys; here he is."

"I say, Flashey," sang out another of the big boys, "drop that; you heard what old Pater Brooke said to-night. I'll be hanged if we'll toss any one against their will. No more bullying. Let him go, I say."

Flashman, with an oath and a kick, released his prey, who rushed headlong under his bed again, for fear they should change their minds, and crept along underneath the other beds, till he got under that of the sixth-form boy, which he knew they daren't disturb.

"There's plenty of youngsters don't care about it," said Walker. "Here, here's Scud East—you'll be tossed, won't you, young un?" Scud was East's nickname, or Black, as we called it, gained by his fleetness of foot.

"Yes," said East, "if you like, only mind my foot."

"And here's another who didn't hide.—Hullo! new boy; what's your name, sir?"

"Brown."

"Well, Whitey Brown, you don't mind being tossed?"

"No," said Tom, setting his teeth.

"Come along then, boys," sang out Walker; and away they all went, carrying along Tom and East, to the intense relief of four or five other small boys, who crept out from under the beds and behind them.

"What a trump Scud is!" said one. "They won't come back here now."

"And that new boy, too; he must be a good-plucked one."

"Ah! wait till he has been tossed on to the floor; see how he'll like it then!"

Meantime the procession went down the passage to Number 7, the largest room, and the scene of the tossing, in the middle of which was a great open space. Here they joined other parties of the bigger boys, each with a captive or two, some willing to be tossed, some sullen, and some frightened to death. At Walker's suggestion all who were afraid were let off, in honour of Pater Brooke's speech.

Then a dozen big boys seized hold of a blanket, dragged

from one of the beds. "In with Scud; quick! there's no time to lose." East was chucked into the blanket. "Once, twice, thrice, and away!" Up he went like a shuttlecock, but not quite up to the ceiling.

"Now, boys, with a will," cried Walker; "once, twice, thrice, and away!" This time he went clean up, and kept himself from touching the ceiling with his hand, and so again a third time, when he was turned out, and up went another boy. And then came Tom's turn. He lay quite still, by East's advice, and didn't dislike the "once, twice, thrice;" but the "away" wasn't so pleasant. They were in good wind now, and sent him slap up to the ceiling first time, against which his knees came rather sharply. But the moment's pause before descending was the rub—the feeling of utter helplessness and of leaving his whole inside behind him sticking to the ceiling. Tom was very near shouting to be set down when he found himself back in the blanket, but thought of East, and didn't; and so took his three tosses without a kick or a cry, and was called a young trump for his pains.

He and East, having earned it, stood now looking on. No catastrophe happened, as all the captives were cool hands, and didn't struggle. This didn't suit Flashman. What your real bully likes in tossing is when the boys kick and struggle, or hold on to one side of the blanket, and so get pitched bodily on to the floor; it's no fun to him when no one is hurt or frightened.

"Let's toss two of them together, Walker," suggested he.

"What a cursed bully you are, Flashey!" rejoined the other. "Up with another one."

And so no two boys were tossed together, the peculiar hardship of which is, that it's too much for human nature to lie still then and share troubles ; and so the wretched pair of small boys struggle in the air which shall fall a-top in the descent, to the no small risk of both falling out of the blanket, and the huge delight of brutes like Flashman.

But now there's a cry that the prepostor of the room is coming ; so the tossing stops, and all scatter to their different rooms ; and Tom is left to turn in, with the first day's experience of a public school to meditate upon.

CHAPTER VII.

SETTLING TO THE COLLAR.

> " Says Giles, ' 'Tis mortal hard to go,
>   But if so be's I must,
> I means to follow arter he
>   As goes hisself the fust.' "—*Ballad.*

EVERYBODY, I suppose, knows the dreamy, delicious state in which one lies, half asleep, half awake, while consciousness begins to return after a sound night's rest in a new place which we are glad to be in, following upon a day of unwonted excitement and exertion. There are few pleasanter pieces of life. The worst of it is that they last such a short time ; for nurse them as you will, by lying perfectly passive in mind and body, you can't make more than five minutes or so of them. After which time the stupid, obtrusive, wakeful entity which we call " I," as impatient as he is stiff-necked, spite of our teeth will force himself back again, and take possession of us down to our very toes.

It was in this state that Master Tom lay at half-past seven on the morning following the day of his arrival, and from his clean little white bed watched the movements of Bogle (the generic name by which the successive shoeblacks of the School-house were known), as he marched round from bed to bed, collecting the dirty shoes and boots, and depositing clean ones in their places.

There he lay, half doubtful as to where exactly in the universe he was, but conscious that he had made a step in life which he had been anxious to make. It was only just light as he looked lazily out of the wide windows, and saw the tops of the great elms, and the rooks circling about and cawing remonstrances to the lazy ones of their commonwealth before starting in a body for the neighbouring ploughed fields. The noise of the room-door closing behind Bogle, as he made his exit with the shoe-basket under his arm, roused him thoroughly, and he sat up in bed and looked round the room. What in the world could be the matter with his shoulders and loins? He felt as if he had been severely beaten all down his back—the natural results of his performance at his first match. He drew up his knees and rested his chin on them, and went over all the events of yesterday, rejoicing in his new life, what he had seen of it, and all that was to come.

Presently one or two of the other boys roused themselves, and began to sit up and talk to one another in low tones. Then East, after a roll or two, came to an anchor also, and nodding to Tom, began examining his ankle.

"What a pull," said he, "that it's lie-in-bed, for I shall be as lame as a tree, I think."

It was Sunday morning, and Sunday lectures had not yet been established; so that nothing but breakfast intervened between bed and eleven o'clock chapel—a gap by no means easy to fill up : in fact, though received with the correct amount of grumbling, the first lecture instituted by the Doctor shortly afterwards was a great boon to the School. It was lie-in-bed, and no one was in a hurry to get up, especially in rooms where the sixth-form boy was a good-tempered fellow, as was the case in Tom's room, and allowed the small boys to talk and laugh and do pretty much what they pleased, so long as they didn't disturb him. His bed was a bigger one than the rest, standing in the corner by the fireplace, with a washing-stand and large basin by the side, where he lay in state with his white curtains tucked in so as to form a retiring place—an awful subject of contemplation to Tom, who slept nearly opposite, and watched the great man rouse himself and take a book from under his pillow, and begin reading, leaning his head on his hand, and turning his back to the room. Soon, however, a noise of striving urchins arose, and muttered encouragements from the neighbouring boys of " Go it, Tadpole ! " " Now, young Green ! " " Haul away his blanket ! " " Slipper him on the hands ! " Young Green and little Hall, commonly called Tadpole, from his great black head and thin legs, slept side by side far away by the door, and were for ever playing one another tricks, which usually ended, as on this morning, in open and violent collision ; and now, unmindful of all order and authority, there they were, each hauling away at the other's bedclothes with one hand, and with the other, armed with a slipper, belabouring whatever portion of the body of his adversary came within reach.

" Hold that noise up in the corner," called out the prepostor, sitting up and looking round his curtains ; and the Tadpole and young Green sank down into their disordered beds ; and then, looking at his watch, added, " Hullo ! past eight. Whose turn for hot water ? "

(Where the prepostor was particular in his ablutions, the fags in his room had to descend in turn to the kitchen, and beg or steal hot water for him ; and often the custom extended farther, and two boys went down every morning to get a supply for the whole room.)

"East's and Tadpole's," answered the senior fag, who kept the rota.

"I can't go," said East; "I'm dead lame."

"Well, be quick some of you, that's all," said the great man, as he turned out of bed, and putting on his slippers, went out into the great passage, which runs the whole length of the bedrooms, to get his Sunday habiliments out of his portmanteau.

"Let me go for you," said Tom to East; "I should like it."

"Well, thank 'ee, that's a good fellow. Just pull on your trousers, and take your jug and mine. Tadpole will show you the way."

And so Tom and the Tadpole, in nightshirts and trousers, started off downstairs, and through "Thos's hole," as the little buttery, where candles and beer and bread and cheese were served out at night, was called, across the School-house court, down a long passage, and into the kitchen ; where, after some parley with the stalwart, handsome cook, who declared that she had filled a dozen jugs already, they got their hot water, and returned with all speed and great caution. As it was, they narrowly escaped capture by some privateers from the fifth-form rooms, who were on the lookout for the hot-water convoys, and pursued them up to the very door of their room, making them spill half their load in the passage. "Better than going down again though," as Tadpole remarked, "as we should have had to do if those beggars had caught us."

By the time that the calling-over bell rang, Tom and his new comrades were all down, dressed in their best clothes, and he had the satisfaction of answering " here " to his name for the first time, the prepostor of the week having put it in at the bottom of his list. And then came breakfast and a saunter about the close and town with East, whose lameness only became severe when any fagging had to be done. And so they whiled away the time until morning chapel.

It was a fine November morning, and the close soon became alive with boys of all ages, who sauntered about on the grass, or walked round the gravel walk, in parties of two or three. East, still doing the cicerone, pointed out all the remarkable characters to Tom as they passed : Osbert, who could throw a cricket-ball from the little-side ground over the rook-trees to the Doctor's wall ; Gray, who had got the Balliol scholarship, and, what East evidently thought of much more importance, a half-holiday for the School by his success ; Thorne, who had run ten miles in two minutes over the hour ; Black, who had held his own against the cock of the town in the last row with the louts ; and many more heroes, who then and there walked about and were worshipped, all trace of whom has long since vanished from the scene of their fame. And the fourth-form boy who reads their names rudely cut on the old hall tables, or painted upon the big-side cupboard (if hall tables and big-side cupboards still exist), wonders what manner of boys they were. It will be the same with you who wonder, my sons, what-ever your prowess may be in cricket, or scholarship, or football. Two or three years, more or less, and then the steadily advancing, blessed wave will pass over your names as it has passed over ours. Nevertheless, play your games and do your work manfully—see only that that be done—and let the remembrance of it take care of itself.

The chapel-bell began to ring at a quarter to eleven, and Tom got in early and took his place in the lowest row, and watched all the other boys come in and take their places, filling row after row; and tried to construe the Greek text which was inscribed over the door with the slightest possible success, and wondered which of the masters, who walked down the chapel and took their seats in the exalted boxes at the end, would be his lord. And then came the closing of the doors, and the Doctor in his robes, and the service, which, however, didn't impress him much, for his feeling of wonder and curiosity was too strong. And the boy on one side of him was scratching his name on the oak panelling in front, and he couldn't help watching to see what the name was, and whether it was well scratched; and the boy on the other side went to sleep, and kept falling against him; and on the whole, though many boys even in that part of the school were serious and attentive, the general atmosphere was by no means devotional; and when he got out into the close again, he didn't feel at all comfortable, or as if he had been to church.

But at afternoon chapel it was quite another thing. He had spent the time after dinner in writing home to his mother, and so was in a better frame of mind; and his first curiosity was over, and he could attend more to the service. As the hymn after the prayers was being sung, and the chapel was getting a little dark, he was beginning to feel that he had been really worshipping. And then came that great event in his, as in every Rugby boy's life of that day—the first sermon from the Doctor.

More worthy pens than mine have described that scene—the oak pulpit standing out by itself above the School seats; the tall, gallant form, the kindling eye, the voice, now soft as the low notes of a flute, now clear and stirring as the call of the light-infantry bugle, of him who stood there Sunday after Sunday, witnessing and pleading for his Lord, the King of righteousness and love and glory, with whose Spirit he was filled, and in whose power he spoke; the long lines of young faces, rising tier above tier down the whole length of the chapel, from the little boy's who had just left his mother to the young man's who was going out next week into the great world, rejoicing in his strength. It was a great and solemn sight, and never more so than at this time of year, when the only lights in the chapel were in the pulpit and at the seats of the prepostors of the week, and the soft twilight stole over the rest of the chapel, deepening into darkness in the high gallery behind the organ.

But what was it, after all, which seized and held these three hundred boys, dragging them out of themselves, willing or unwilling, for twenty minutes, on Sunday afternoons? True, there always were boys scattered up and down the School, who in heart and head were worthy to hear and able to carry away the deepest and wisest words there spoken. But these were a minority always, generally a very small one, often so small a one as to be countable on the fingers of your hand. What was it that moved and held us, the rest of the three hundred reckless, childish boys, who feared the Doctor with all our hearts, and very little besides in heaven or earth; who thought more of our sets in the School than of the Church of Christ, and put the traditions of Rugby and the public opinion of boys in our daily life above the laws of God? We couldn't enter into half that we heard; we hadn't the knowledge of our own hearts or the knowledge of one another, and little enough of the faith, hope, and love needed to that end. But we listened, as all boys in their better moods will listen (ay, and men too for the

matter of that), to a man whom we felt to be, with all his
heart and soul and strength, striving against whatever
was mean and unmanly and unrighteous in our little
world. It was not the cold, clear voice of one giving
advice and warning from serene heights to those who
were struggling and sinning below, but the warm, living
voice of one who was fighting for us and by our sides,
and calling on us to help him and ourselves and one
another. And so, wearily and little by little, but surely
and steadily on the whole, was brought home to the
young boy, for the first time, the meaning of his life—
that it was no fool's or sluggard's paradise into which
he had wandered by chance, but a battlefield ordained
from of old, where there are no spectators, but the
youngest must take his side, and the stakes are life and
death. And he who roused this consciousness in them
showed them at the same time, by every word he spoke
in the pulpit, and by his whole daily life, how that battle
was to be fought, and stood there before them their
fellow-soldier and the captain of their band—the true
sort of captain, too, for a boy's army—one who had no
misgivings, and gave no uncertain word of command,
and, let who would yield or make truce, would fight the
fight out (so every boy felt) to the last gasp and the last
drop of blood. Other sides of his character might take
hold of and influence boys here and there; but it was
this thoroughness and undaunted courage which, more
than anything else, won his way to the hearts of the great
mass of those on whom he left his mark, and made them
believe first in him and then in his Master.

It was this quality above all others which moved such
boys as our hero, who had nothing whatever remarkable
about him except excess of boyishness—by which I mean
animal life in its fullest measure, good nature and honest

impulses, hatred of injustice and meanness, and thought-lessness enough to sink a three-decker. And so, during the next two years, in which it was more than doubtful whether he would get good or evil from the School, and before any steady purpose or principle grew up in him, whatever his week's sins and shortcomings might have been, he hardly ever left the chapel on Sunday evenings without a serious resolve to stand by and follow the Doctor, and a feeling that it was only cowardice (the incarnation of all other sins in such a boy's mind) which hindered him from doing so with all his heart.

The next day Tom was duly placed in the third form, and began his lessons in a corner of the big School. He found the work very easy, as he had been well grounded, and knew his grammar by heart; and, as he had no intimate companions to make him idle (East and his other School-house friends being in the lower fourth, the form above him), soon gained golden opinions from his master, who said he was placed too low, and should be put out at the end of the half-year. So all went well with him in School, and he wrote the most flourishing letters home to his mother, full of his own success and the unspeakable delights of a public school.

In the house, too, all went well. The end of the half-year was drawing near, which kept everybody in a good humour, and the house was ruled well and strongly by Warner and Brooke. True, the general system was rough and hard, and there was bullying in nooks and corners —bad signs for the future; but it never got farther, or dared show itself openly, stalking about the passages and hall and bedrooms, and making the life of the small boys a continual fear.

Tom, as a new boy, was of right excused fagging for the first month, but in his enthusiasm for his new life

5

this privilege hardly pleased him ; and East and others of his young friends, discovering this, kindly allowed him to indulge his fancy, and take their turns at night fagging and cleaning studies. These were the principal duties of the fags in the house. From supper until nine o'clock three fags taken in order stood in the passages, and answered any prepostor who called "Fag," racing to the door, the last comer having to do the work. This consisted generally of going to the buttery for beer and bread and cheese (for the great men did not sup with the rest, but had each his own allowance in his study or the fifth-form room), cleaning candlesticks and putting in new candles, toasting cheese, bottling beer, and carrying messages about the house ; and Tom, in the first blush of his hero-worship, felt it a high privilege to receive orders from and be the bearer of the supper of old Brooke. And besides this night-work, each prepostor had three or four fags specially allotted to him, of whom he was supposed to be the guide, philosopher, and friend, and who in return for these good offices had to clean out his study every morning by turns, directly after first lesson and before he returned from breakfast. And the pleasure of seeing the great men's studies, and looking at their pictures, and peeping into their books, made Tom a ready substitute for any boy who was too lazy to do his own work. And so he soon gained the character of a good-natured, willing fellow, who was ready to do a turn for any one.

In all the games, too, he joined with all his heart, and soon became well versed in all the mysteries of foot-ball, by continual practice at the School-house little-side, which played daily.

The only incident worth recording here, however, was his first run at hare-and-hounds. On the last Tuesday but one of the half-year he was passing through the hall after dinner, when he was hailed with shouts from Tadpole and several other fags seated at one of the long tables, the chorus of which was, " Come and help us tear up scent."

Tom approached the table in obedience to the mysterious summons, always ready to help, and found the party engaged in tearing up old newspapers, copy-books, and magazines, into small pieces, with which they were filling four large canvas bags.

" It's the turn of our house to find scent for big-side hare-and-hounds," exclaimed Tadpole. " Tear away; there's no time to lose before calling-over."

" I think it's a great shame," said another small boy, " to have such a hard run for the last day."

" Which run is it ? " said Tadpole.

" Oh, the Barby run, I hear," answered the other ; " nine miles at least, and hard ground ; no chance of getting in at the finish, unless you're a first-rate scud."

" Well, I'm going to have a try," said Tadpole ; " it's the last run of the half, and if a fellow gets in at the end big-side stands ale and bread and cheese and a bowl of punch ; and the Cock's such a famous place for ale."

" I should like to try too," said Tom.

" Well, then, leave your waistcoat behind, and listen at the door, after calling-over, and you'll hear where the meet is."

After calling-over, sure enough there were two boys at the door, calling out, " Big-side hare-and-hounds meet at White Hall ; " and Tom, having girded himself with leather strap, and left all superfluous clothing behind, set off for White Hall, an old gable-ended house some quarter of a mile from the town, with East, whom he had persuaded to join, notwithstanding his prophecy that they could never get in, as it was the hardest run of the year.

At the meet they found some forty or fifty boys, and Tom felt sure, from having seen many of them run at football, that he and East were more likely to get in than they.

After a few minutes' waiting, two well-known runners, chosen for the hares, buckled on the four bags filled with scent, compared their watches with those of young Brooke and Thorne, and started off at a long, slinging trot across the fields in the direction of Barby.

Then the hounds clustered round Thorne, who explained shortly, " They're to have six minutes' law. We run into the Cock, and every one who comes in within a quarter of an hour of the hares 'll be counted, if he has been round Barby church." Then came a minute's pause or so; and then the watches are pocketed, and the pack is led through the gateway into the field which the hares had first crossed. Here they break into a trot, scattering over the field to find the first traces of the scent which the hares throw out as they go along. The old hounds make straight for the likely points, and in a minute a cry of " Forward " comes from one of them, and the whole pack, quickening their pace, make for the spot, while the boy who hit the scent first, and the two or three nearest to him, are over the first fence, and making play along the hedgerow in the long grass-field beyond. The rest of the pack rush at the gap already made, and scramble through, jostling one another. " Forward " again, before they are half through. The pace quickens into a sharp run, the tail hounds all straining to get up to the lucky leaders. They are gallant hares, and the scent lies thick right across another meadow and into a ploughed field, where the pace begins to tell; then over a good wattle with a ditch on the other side, and down a large pasture studded with old thorns, which slopes down to the first brook. The great Leicestershire sheep charge away across the field as the pack comes racing down the slope. The brook is a small one, and the scent lies right ahead up the opposite slope, and as thick as ever—not a turn or a check to favour the tail hounds, who strain on, now trailing in a long line, many a youngster beginning to drag his legs heavily, and feel his heart beat like a hammer, and the bad-plucked ones thinking that after all it isn't worth while to keep it up.

Tom, East, and the Tadpole had a good start, and are well up for such young hands, and after rising the slope and crossing the next field, find themselves up with the leading hounds, who have overrun the scent, and are trying back. They have come a mile and a half in about eleven minutes, a pace which shows that it is the last day. About twenty-five of the original starters only show here, the rest having already given in ; the leaders are busy making casts into the fields on the left and right, and the others get their second winds.

Then comes the cry of "Forward" again from young Brooke, from the extreme left, and the pack settles down to work again steadily and doggedly, the whole keeping pretty well together. The scent, though still good, is not so thick ; there is no need of that, for in this part of the run every one knows the line which must be taken, and so there are no casts to be made, but good downright running and fencing to be done. All who are now up mean coming in, and they come to the foot of Barby Hill without losing more than two or three more of the pack. This last straight two miles and a half is always a vantage ground for the hounds, and the hares know it well ; they are generally viewed on the side of Barby Hill, and all eyes are on the lookout for them to-day. But not a sign of them appears, so now will be the hard work for the hounds, and there is nothing for it but to cast about for the scent, for it is now the hares' turn, and they may baffle the pack dreadfully in the next two miles.

Ill fares it now with our youngsters that they are School-house boys, and so follow young Brooke, for he takes the wide casts round to the left, conscious of his own powers, and loving the hard work. For if you would consider for a moment, you small boys, you would remember that the Cock, where the run ends and the good ale will be going, lies far out to the right on the Dunchurch road, so that every cast you take to the left is so much extra work. And at this stage of the run, when the evening is closing in already, no one remarks whether you run a little cunning or not ; so you should stick to those crafty hounds who keep edging away to the right, and not follow a prodigal like young Brooke, whose legs are twice as long as yours and of cast-iron, wholly indifferent to one or two miles more or less. However, they struggle after him, sobbing and plunging along, Tom and East pretty close, and Tadpole, whose big head begins to pull him down, some thirty yards behind.

Now comes a brook, with stiff clay banks, from which they can hardly drag their legs, and they hear faint cries for help from the wretched Tadpole, who has fairly stuck fast. But they have too little run left in themselves to pull up for their own brothers. Three fields more, and another check, and then "Forward" called away to the extreme right.

The two boys' souls die within them ; they can never do it. Young Brooke thinks so too, and says kindly, "You'll cross a lane after next field ; keep down it, and you'll hit the Dunchurch road below the Cock," and then steams away for the run in, in which he's sure to be first, as if he were just starting. They struggle on across the next field, the " forwards " getting fainter and fainter, and then ceasing. The whole hunt is out of ear-shot, and all hope of coming in is over.

" Hang it all ! " broke out East, as soon as he had got wind enough, pulling off his hat and mopping at his face, all spattered with dirt and lined with sweat, from which went up a thick steam into the still, cold air. " I told you how it would be. What a thick I was to come ! Here we are, dead beat, and yet I know we're close to the run in, if we knew the country."

" Well," said Tom, mopping away, and gulping down his disappointment, " it can't be helped. We did our best anyhow. Hadn't we better find this lane, and go down it, as young Brooke told us ? "

" I suppose so—nothing else for it," grunted East. "If ever I go out last day again." Growl, growl, growl.

So they tried back slowly and sorrowfully, and found the lane, and went limping down it, plashing in the cold puddly ruts, and beginning to feel how the run had taken it out of them. The evening closed in fast, and clouded over, dark, cold, and dreary.

" I say, it must be locking-up, I should think," remarked East, breaking the silence—" it's so dark."

" What if we're late ? " said Tom.

" No tea, and sent up to the Doctor," answered East.

The thought didn't add to their cheerfulness. Presently a faint halloo was heard from an adjoining field. They answered it and stopped, hoping for some competent rustic to guide them, when over a gate some twenty yards ahead crawled the wretched Tadpole, in a state of collapse. He had lost a shoe in the brook, and had been groping after it up to his elbows in the stiff, wet clay, and a more miserable creature in the shape of boy seldom has been seen.

The sight of him, notwithstanding, cheered them, for he was some degrees more wretched than they. They also cheered him, as he was no longer under the dread of passing his night alone in the fields. And so, in better heart, the three plashed painfully down the never-ending lane. At last it widened, just as utter darkness set in, and they came out on a turnpike road, and there paused, bewildered, for they had lost all bearings, and knew not whether to turn to the right or left.

Luckily for them they had not to decide, for lumbering along the road, with one lamp lighted and two spavined horses in the shafts, came a heavy coach, which after a moment's suspense they recognized as the Oxford coach, the redoubtable Pig and Whistle.

It lumbered slowly up, and the boys, mustering their last run, caught it as it passed, and began clambering up behind, in which exploit East missed his footing and fell flat on his nose along the road. Then the others hailed the old scarecrow of a coachman, who pulled up and agreed to take them in for a shilling ; so there they sat on the back seat, drubbing with their heels, and their teeth chattering with cold, and jogged into Rugby some forty minutes after locking-up.

Five minutes afterwards three small, limping, shivering figures steal along through the Doctor's garden, and into the house by the servants' entrance (all the other gates have been closed long since), where the first thing they light upon in the passage is old Thomas, ambling along, candle in one hand and keys in the other.

He stops and examines their condition with a grim smile. "Ah ! East, Hall, and Brown, late for locking-up. Must go up to the Doctor's study at once."

"Well but, Thomas, mayn't we go and wash first? You can put down the time, you know."

"Doctor's study d'rectly you come in—that's the orders," replied old Thomas, motioning towards the stairs at the end of the passage which led up into the Doctor's house; and the boys turned ruefully down it, not cheered by the old verger's muttered remark, "What a pickle they boys be in!" Thomas referred to their faces and habiliments, but they construed it as indicating the Doctor's state of mind. Upon the short flight of stairs they paused to hold counsel.

"Who'll go in first?" inquires Tadpole.

"You—you're the senior," answered East.

"Catch me. Look at the state I'm in," rejoined Hall, showing the arms of his jacket. "I must get behind you two."

"Well, but look at me," said East, indicating the mass of clay behind which he was standing; "I'm worse than you, two to one. You might grow cabbages on my trousers."

"That's all down below, and you can keep your legs behind the sofa," said Hall.

"Here, Brown; you're the show-figure. You must lead."

"But my face is all muddy," argued Tom.

"Oh, we're all in one boat for that matter; but come on; we're only making it worse, dawdling here."

"Well, just give us a brush then," said Tom. And they began trying to rub off the superfluous dirt from each other's jackets; but it was not dry enough, and the rubbing made them worse; so in despair they pushed through the swing-door at the head of the stairs, and found themselves in the Doctor's hall.

"That's the library door," said East in a whisper,

pushing Tom forwards. The sound of merry voices and laughter came from within, and his first hesitating knock was unanswered. But at the second, the Doctor's voice said, "Come in;" and Tom turned the handle, and he, with the others behind him, sidled into the room.

The Doctor looked up from his task; he was working away with a great chisel at the bottom of a boy's sailing boat, the lines of which he was no doubt fashioning on the model of one of Nicias's galleys. Round him stood three or four children; the candles burnt brightly on a large table at the farther end, covered with books and papers, and a great fire threw a ruddy glow over the rest of the room. All looked so kindly, and homely, and comfortable that the boys took heart in a moment, and Tom advanced from behind the shelter of the great sofa. The Doctor nodded to the children, who went out, casting curious and amused glances at the three young scarecrows.

"Well, my little fellows," began the Doctor, drawing himself up with his back to the fire, the chisel in one hand and his coat-tails in the other, and his eyes twinkling as he looked them over; "what makes you so late?"

"Please, sir, we've been out big-side hare-and-hounds, and lost our way."

"Hah! you couldn't keep up, I suppose?"

"Well, sir," said East, stepping out, and not liking that the Doctor should think lightly of his running powers, "we got round Barby all right; but then——"

"Why, what a state you're in, my boy!" interrupted the Doctor, as the pitiful condition of East's garments was fully revealed to him.

"That's the fall I got, sir, in the road," said East, looking down at himself; "the Old Pig came by——"

"The what?" said the Doctor.

"The Oxford coach, sir," explained Hall.

"Hah! yes, the Regulator," said the Doctor.

"And I tumbled on my face, trying to get up behind," went on East.

"You're not hurt, I hope?" said the Doctor.

"Oh no, sir."

"Well now, run upstairs, all three of you, and get clean things on, and then tell the housekeeper to give you some tea. You're too young to try such long runs. Let Warner know I've seen you. Good-night."

"Good-night, sir." And away scuttled the three boys in high glee.

"What a brick, not to give us even twenty lines to learn!" said the Tadpole, as they reached their bed-room; and in half an hour afterwards they were sitting by the fire in the housekeeper's room at a sumptuous tea, with cold meat—"Twice as good a grub as we should have got in the hall," as the Tadpole remarked with a grin, his mouth full of buttered toast. All their griev-ances were forgotten, and they were resolving to go out the first big side next half, and thinking hare-and-hounds the most delightful of games.

A day or two afterwards the great passage outside the bedrooms was cleared of the boxes and portmanteaus, which went down to be packed by the matron, and great games of chariot-racing, and cock-fighting, and bolster-ing went on in the vacant space, the sure sign of a closing half-year.

Then came the making up of parties for the journey home, and Tom joined a party who were to hire a coach, and post with four horses to Oxford.

Then the last Saturday, on which the Doctor came round to each form to give out the prizes, and hear the master's last reports of how they and their charges had been conducting themselves; and Tom, to his huge delight, was praised, and got his remove into the lower-fourth, in which all his School-house friends were.

On the next Tuesday morning at four o'clock hot coffee was going on in the housekeeper's and matron's rooms; boys wrapped in great-coats and mufflers were swallowing hasty mouthfuls, rushing about, tumbling over luggage, and asking questions all at once of the matron; outside the School-gates were drawn up several chaises and the four-horse coach which Tom's party had chartered, the postboys in their best jackets and breeches, and a cornopean player, hired for the occasion, blowing away "A southerly wind and a cloudy sky," waking all peaceful inhabitants half-way down the High Street.

Every minute the bustle and hubbub increased: porters staggered about with boxes and bags, the cornopean played louder. Old Thomas sat in his den with a great yellow bag by his side, out of which he was paying journey-money to each boy, comparing by the light of a solitary dip the dirty, crabbed little list in his own handwriting with the Doctor's list and the amount of his cash; his head was on one side, his mouth screwed up, and his spectacles dim from early toil. He had prudently locked the door, and carried on his operations solely through the window, or he would have been driven wild and lost all his money.

"Thomas, do be quick; we shall never catch the Highflyer at Dunchurch."

"That's your money all right, Green."

"Hullo, Thomas, the Doctor said I was to have two pound ten; you've only given me two pound." (I fear that Master Green is not confining himself strictly to truth.) Thomas turns his head more on one side than ever, and spells away at the dirty list. Green is forced away from the window.

"Here, Thomas—never mind him; mine's thirty shillings." "And mine too," "And mine," shouted others.

One way or another, the party to which Tom belonged all got packed and paid, and sallied out to the gates, the cornopean playing frantically "Drops of Brandy," in allusion, probably, to the slight potations in which the musician and postboys had been already indulging. All luggage was carefully stowed away inside the coach and in the front and hind boots, so that not a hat-box was visible outside. Five or six small boys, with pea-shooters, and the cornopean player, got up behind; in front the big boys, mostly smoking, not for pleasure, but because they are now gentlemen at large, and this is the most correct public method of notifying the fact.

"Robinson's coach will be down the road in a minute; it has gone up to Bird's to pick up. We'll wait till they're close, and make a race of it," says the leader. "Now, boys, half a sovereign apiece if you beat 'em into Dunchurch by one hundred yards."

"All right, sir," shouted the grinning postboys.

Down comes Robinson's coach in a minute or two, with a rival cornopean, and away go the two vehicles, horses galloping, boys cheering, horns playing loud. There is a special providence over school-boys as well as sailors, or they must have upset twenty times in the first five miles—sometimes actually abreast of one another, and the boys on the roofs exchanging volleys of peas; now nearly running over a post-chaise which had started before them; now half-way up a bank; now with a wheel and a half over a yawning ditch: and all this in a dark morning, with nothing but their own lamps to guide them. However, it's all over at last, and they have run over nothing but an old pig in Southam Street. The last peas are distributed in the Corn Market at Oxford, where they arrive between eleven and twelve, and sit down to a sumptuous breakfast at the Angel, which they are made to pay for accordingly. Here the party breaks up, all going now different ways; and Tom orders out a chaise and pair as grand as a lord, though he has scarcely five shillings left in his pocket, and more than twenty miles to get home.

" Where to, sir ? "

" Red Lion, Farringdon," says Tom, giving hostler a shilling.

" All right, sir.—Red Lion, Jem," to the postboy; and Tom rattles away towards home. At Farringdon, being known to the innkeeper, he gets that worthy to pay for the Oxford horses, and forward him in another chaise at once ; and so the gorgeous young gentleman arrives at the paternal mansion, and Squire Brown looks rather blue at having to pay two pound ten shillings for the posting expenses from Oxford. But the boy's intense joy at getting home, and the wonderful health he is in, and the good character he brings, and the brave stories he tells of Rugby, its doings and delights, soon mollify the Squire, and three happier people didn't sit down to dinner that day in England (it is the boy's first dinner at six o'clock at home—great promotion already) than the Squire and his wife and Tom Brown, at the end of his first half-year at Rugby.

CHAPTER VIII.

THE WAR OF INDEPENDENCE.

" They are slaves who will not choose
    Hatred, scoffing, and abuse,
    Rather than in silence shrink
    From the truth they needs must think ;
    They are slaves who dare not be
    In the right with two or three."
        LOWELL, *Stanzas on Freedom.*

THE lower-fourth form, in which Tom found himself at the beginning of the next half-year, was the largest form in the lower school, and numbered upwards of forty boys. Young gentlemen of all ages from nine to fifteen were to be found there, who expended such part of their energies as was devoted to Latin and Greek upon a book of Livy, the "Bucolics" of Virgil, and the "Hecuba" of Euripides, which were ground out in small daily portions. The driving of this unlucky lower-fourth must have been grievous work to the unfortunate master, for it was the most unhappily constituted of any in the school. Here stuck the great stupid boys, who, for the life of them, could never master the accidence—the objects alternately of mirth and terror to the youngsters, who were daily taking them up and laughing at them in lesson, and getting kicked by them for so doing in play-hours. There were no less than three unhappy fellows in tail coats, with incipient down on their chins, whom the Doctor and the master of the form were always endeavouring to hoist into the upper school, but whose parsing and construing resisted the most well-meant shoves. Then came the mass of the form, boys of eleven and twelve, the most mischievous and reckless age of British youth, of whom East and Tom Brown were fair specimens. As full of tricks as monkeys, and of excuses as

Irishwomen, making fun of their master, one another, and their lessons, Argus himself would have been puzzled to keep an eye on them; and as for making them steady or serious for half an hour together, it was simply hopeless. The remainder of the form consisted of young prodigies of nine and ten, who were going up the school at the rate of a form a half-year, all boys' hands and wits being against them in their progress. It would have been one man's work to see that the precocious youngsters had fair play; and as the master had a good deal besides to do, they hadn't, and were for ever being shoved down three or four places, their verses stolen, their books inked, their jackets whitened, and their lives otherwise made a burden to them.

The lower-fourth, and all the forms below it, were heard in the great school, and were not trusted to prepare their lessons before coming in, but were whipped into school three-quarters of an hour before the lesson began by their respective masters, and there, scattered about on the benches, with dictionary and grammar, hammered out their twenty lines of Virgil and Euripides in the midst of babel. The masters of the lower school walked up and down the great school together during this three-quarters of an hour, or sat in their desks reading or looking over copies, and keeping such order as was possible. But the lower-fourth was just now an overgrown form, too large for any one man to attend to properly, and consequently the elysium or ideal form of the young scapegraces who formed the staple of it.

Tom, as has been said, had come up from the third with a good character, but the temptations of the lower-fourth soon proved too strong for him, and he rapidly fell away, and became as unmanageable as the rest. For some weeks, indeed, he succeeded in maintaining the appearance of steadiness, and was looked upon favourably by his new master, whose eyes were first opened by the following little incident.

Besides the desk which the master himself occupied, there was another large unoccupied desk in the corner of the great school, which was untenanted. To rush and seize upon this desk, which was ascended by three steps and held four boys, was the great object of ambition of the lower-fourths; and the contentions for the occupation of it bred such disorder that at last the master forbade its use altogether. This, of course, was a challenge to the more adventurous spirits to occupy it; and as it was capacious enough for two boys to lie hid there completely, it was seldom that it remained empty, notwithstanding the veto. Small holes were cut in the front, through which the occupants watched the masters as they walked up and down; and as lesson time approached, one boy at a time stole out and down the steps, as the masters' backs were turned, and mingled with the general crowd on the forms below. Tom and East had successfully occupied the desk some half-dozen times, and were grown so reckless that they were in the habit of playing small games with fives balls inside when the masters were at the other end of the big school. One day, as ill-luck would have it, the game became more exciting than usual, and the ball slipped through East's fingers, and rolled slowly down the steps and out into the middle of the school, just as the masters turned in their walk and faced round upon the desk. The young delinquents watched their master, through the lookout holes, march slowly down the school straight upon their retreat, while all the boys in the neighbourhood, of course, stopped their work to look on; and not only were they ignominiously drawn out, and caned over the hand then and there, but their characters for steadiness were gone from that time. However, as they only shared the fate of some three-fourths of the rest of the form, this did not weigh heavily upon them.

In fact, the only occasions on which they cared about the matter were the monthly examinations, when the Doctor came round to examine their form, for one long, awful hour, in the work which they had done in the preceding month. The second monthly examination came round soon after Tom's fall, and it was with anything but lively anticipations that he and the other lower-fourth boys came in to prayers on the morning of the examination day.

Prayers and calling-over seemed twice as short as usual, and before they could get construes of a tithe of the hard passages marked in the margin of their books, they were all seated round, and the Doctor was standing in the middle, talking in whispers to the master. Tom couldn't hear a word which passed, and never lifted his eyes from his book; but he knew by a sort of magnetic instinct that the Doctor's under-lip was coming out, and his eye beginning to burn, and his gown getting gathered up more and more tightly in his left hand. The suspense was agonizing, and Tom knew that he was sure on such occasions to make an example of the School-house boys. "If he would only begin," thought Tom, "I shouldn't mind."

At last the whispering ceased, and the name which was called out was not Brown. He looked up for a moment, but the Doctor's face was too awful; Tom wouldn't have met his eye for all he was worth, and buried himself in his book again.

The boy who was called up first was a clever, merry School-house boy, one of their set; he was some connection of the Doctor's, and a great favourite, and ran in and out of his house as he liked, and so was selected for the first victim.

" Triste lupus stabulis," began the luckless youngster, and stammered through some eight or ten lines.

"There, that will do," said the Doctor; "now construe."

On common occasions the boy could have construed the passage well enough probably, but now his head was gone.

" Triste lupus, the sorrowful wolf," he began.

A shudder ran through the whole form, and the Doctor's wrath fairly boiled over. He made three steps up to the construer, and gave him a good box on the ear. The blow was not a hard one, but the boy was so taken by surprise that he started back; the form caught the back of his knees, and over he went on to the floor behind. There was a dead silence over the whole school. Never before and never again while Tom was at school did the Doctor strike a boy in lesson. The provocation must have been great. However, the victim had saved his form for that occasion, for the Doctor turned to the top bench, and put on the best boys for the rest of the hour; and though, at the end of the lesson, he gave them all such a rating as they did not forget, this terrible field-day passed over without any severe visitations in the shape of punishments or floggings. Forty young scape-graces expressed their thanks to the " sorrowful wolf " in their different ways before second lesson.

But a character for steadiness once gone is not easily recovered, as Tom found; and for years afterwards he went up the school without it, and the masters' hands were against him, and his against them. And he regarded them, as a matter of course, as his natural enemies.

Matters were not so comfortable, either, in the house as they had been; for old Brooke left at Christmas, and

one or two others of the sixth-form boys at the following
Easter. Their rule had been rough, but strong and
just in the main, and a higher standard was beginning
to be set up; in fact, there had been a short foretaste
of the good time which followed some years later. Just
now, however, all threatened to return into darkness
and chaos again. For the new prepostors were either
small young boys, whose cleverness had carried them up
to the top of the school, while in strength of body and
character they were not yet fit for a share in the government; or else big fellows of the wrong sort—boys whose
friendships and tastes had a downward tendency, who
had not caught the meaning of their position and work,
and felt none of its responsibilities. So under this no-
government the School-house began to see bad times.
The big fifth-form boys, who were a sporting and drinking set, soon began to usurp power, and to fag the little
boys as if they were prepostors, and to bully and oppress
any who showed signs of resistance. The bigger sort
of sixth-form boys just described soon made common
cause with the fifth, while the smaller sort, hampered
by their colleagues' desertion to the enemy, could not
make head against them. So the fags were without
their lawful masters and protectors, and ridden over
rough-shod by a set of boys whom they were not bound
to obey, and whose only right over them stood in their
bodily powers; and, as old Brooke had prophesied, the
house by degrees broke up into small sets and parties,
and lost the strong feeling of fellowship which he set so
much store by, and with it much of the prowess in games
and the lead in all school matters which he had done so
much to keep up.

In no place in the world has individual character more
weight than at a public school. Remember this, I be-

seech you, all you boys who are getting into the upper forms. Now is the time in all your lives, probably, when you may have more wide influence for good or evil on the society you live in than you ever can have again. Quit yourselves like men, then; speak up, and strike out if necessary, for whatsoever is true, and manly, and lovely, and of good report; never try to be popular, but only to do your duty and help others to do theirs, and you may leave the tone of feeling in the school higher than you found it, and so be doing good which no living soul can measure to generations of your countrymen yet unborn. For boys follow one another in herds like sheep, for good or evil; they hate thinking, and have rarely any settled principles. Every school, indeed, has its own traditionary standard of right and wrong, which cannot be transgressed with impunity, marking certain things as low and blackguard, and certain others as lawful and right. This standard is ever varying, though it changes only slowly and little by little; and, subject only to such standard, it is the leading boys for the time being who give the tone to all the rest, and make the School either a noble institution for the training of Christian Englishmen, or a place where a young boy will get more evil than he would if he were turned out to make his way in London streets, or anything between these two extremes.

The change for the worse in the School-house, however, didn't press very heavily on our youngsters for some time. They were in a good bedroom, where slept the only prepostor left who was able to keep thorough order, and their study was in his passage. So, though they were fagged more or less, and occasionally kicked or cuffed by the bullies, they were, on the whole, well off; and the fresh, brave school-life, so full of games, adventures, and good-fellowship, so ready at forgetting, so capacious at enjoying, so bright at forecasting, out-weighed a thousand-fold their troubles with the master of their form, and the occasional ill-usage of the big boys in the house. It wasn't till some year or so after the events recorded above that the prepostor of their room and passage left. None of the other sixth-form boys would move into their passage, and, to the disgust and indignation of Tom and East, one morning after breakfast they were seized upon by Flashman, and made to carry down his books and furniture into the unoccupied study, which he had taken. From this time they began to feel the weight of the tyranny of Flashman and his friends, and, now that trouble had come home to their own doors, began to look out for sympathizers and partners amongst the rest of the fags; and meetings of the oppressed began to be held, and murmurs to arise, and plots to be laid as to how they should free themselves and be avenged on their enemies.

While matters were in this state, East and Tom were one evening sitting in their study. They had done their work for first lesson, and Tom was in a brown study, brooding, like a young William Tell, upon the wrongs of fags in general, and his own in particular.

" I say, Scud," said he at last, rousing himself to snuff the candle, " what right have the fifth-form boys to fag us as they do ? "

" No more right than you have to fag them," answered East, without looking up from an early number of " Pick-wick," which was just coming out, and which he was luxuriously devouring, stretched on his back on the sofa.

Tom relapsed into his brown study, and East went on reading and chuckling. The contrast of the boys' faces would have given infinite amusement to a looker-on—the one so solemn and big with mighty purpose, the other radiant and bubbling over with fun.

"Do you know, old fellow, I've been thinking it over a good deal," began Tom again.

"Oh yes, I know—fagging you are thinking of. Hang it all! But listen here, Tom—here's fun. Mr. Winkle's horse——"

"And I've made up my mind," broke in Tom, "that I won't fag except for the sixth."

"Quite right too, my boy," cried East, putting his finger on the place and looking up; "but a pretty peck of troubles you'll get into, if you're going to play that game. However, I'm all for a strike myself, if we can get others to join. It's getting too bad."

"Can't we get some sixth-form fellow to take it up?" asked Tom.

"Well, perhaps we might. Morgan would interfere, I think. Only," added East, after a moment's pause, "you see, we should have to tell him about it, and that's against School principles. Don't you remember what old Brooke said about learning to take our own parts?"

"Ah, I wish old Brooke were back again. It was all right in his time."

"Why, yes, you see, then the strongest and best fellows were in the sixth, and the fifth-form fellows were afraid of them, and they kept good order; but now our sixth-form fellows are too small, and the fifth don't care for them, and do what they like in the house."

"And so we get a double set of masters," cried Tom indignantly—"the lawful ones, who are responsible to the Doctor at any rate, and the unlawful, the tyrants, who are responsible to nobody."

"Down with the tyrants!" cried East; "I'm all for law and order, and hurrah for a revolution."

"I shouldn't mind if it were only for young Brooke now," said Tom; "he's such a good-hearted, gentlemanly fellow, and ought to be in the sixth. I'd do anything for him. But that blackguard Flashman, who never speaks to one without a kick or an oath——"

"The cowardly brute," broke in East—"how I hate him! And he knows it too; he knows that you and I think him a coward. What a bore that he's got a study in this passage! Don't you hear them now at supper in his den? Brandy-punch going, I'll bet. I wish the Doctor would come out and catch him. We must change our study as soon as we can."

"Change or no change, I'll never fag for him again," said Tom, thumping the table.

"Fa-a-a-ag!" sounded along the passage from Flashman's study. The two boys looked at one another in silence. It had struck nine, so the regular night-fags had left duty, and they were the nearest to the supper-party. East sat up, and began to look comical, as he always did under difficulties.

"Fa-a-a-ag!" again. No answer.

"Here, Brown! East! you cursed young skulks," roared out Flashman, coming to his open door; "I know you're in; no shirking."

Tom stole to their door, and drew the bolts as noiselessly as he could; East blew out the candle.

"Barricade the first," whispered he. "Now, Tom, mind, no surrender."

"Trust me for that," said Tom between his teeth.

In another minute they heard the supper-party turn out and come down the passage to their door. They held their breaths, and heard whispering, of which they only made out Flashman's words, "I know the young brutes are in."

Then came summonses to open, which being un-answered, the assault commenced. Luckily the door was a good strong oak one, and resisted the united weight of Flashman's party. A pause followed, and they heard a besieger remark, "They're in safe enough. Don't you see how the door holds at top and bottom? So the bolts must be drawn. We should have forced the lock long ago." East gave Tom a nudge, to call attention to this scientific remark.

Then came attacks on particular panels, one of which at last gave way to the repeated kicks; but it broke inwards, and the broken pieces got jammed across (the door being lined with green baize), and couldn't easily be removed from outside: and the besieged, scorning further concealment, strengthened their defences by pressing the end of their sofa against the door. So, after one or two more ineffectual efforts, Flashman and Company retired, vowing vengeance in no mild terms.

The first danger over, it only remained for the besieged to effect a safe retreat, as it was now near bed-time. They listened intently, and heard the supper-party re-settle themselves, and then gently drew back first one bolt and then the other. Presently the convivial noises began again steadily. "Now then, stand by for a run," said East, throwing the door wide open and rushing into the passage, closely followed by Tom. They were too quick to be caught; but Flashman was on the lookout, and sent an empty pickle-jar whizzing after them, which narrowly missed Tom's head, and broke into twenty pieces at the end of the passage. "He wouldn't mind killing one, if he wasn't caught," said East, as they turned the corner.

There was no pursuit, so the two turned into the hall, where they found a knot of small boys round the fire.

Their story was told. The war of independence had broken out. Who would join the revolutionary forces? Several others present bound themselves not to fag for the fifth form at once. One or two only edged off, and left the rebels. What else could they do? "I've a good mind to go to the Doctor straight," said Tom.

"That'll never do. Don't you remember the levy of the school last half?" put in another.

In fact, the solemn assembly, a levy of the School, had been held, at which the captain of the School had got up, and after premising that several instances had occurred of matters having been reported to the masters; that this was against public morality and School tradition; that a levy of the sixth had been held on the subject, and they had resolved that the practice must be stopped at once; and given out that any boy, in whatever form, who should thenceforth appeal to a master, without having first gone to some prepostor and laid the case before him, should be thrashed publicly, and sent to Coventry.

"Well, then, let's try the sixth. Try Morgan," suggested another. "No use"—"Blabbing won't do," was the general feeling.

"I'll give you fellows a piece of advice," said a voice from the end of the hall. They all turned round with a start, and the speaker got up from a bench on which he had been lying unobserved, and gave himself a shake. He was a big, loose-made fellow, with huge limbs which had grown too far through his jacket and trousers. "Don't you go to anybody at all—you just stand out; say you won't fag. They'll soon get tired of licking you. I've tried it on years ago with their forerunners."

"No! Did you? Tell us how it was?" cried a chorus of voices, as they clustered round him.

"Well, just as it is with you. The fifth form would fag us, and I and some more struck, and we beat 'em. The good fellows left off directly, and the bullies who kept on soon got afraid."

"Was Flashman here then?"

"Yes; and a dirty, little, snivelling, sneaking fellow he was too. He never dared join us, and used to toady the bullies by offering to fag for them, and peaching against the rest of us."

"Why wasn't he cut, then?" said East.

"Oh, toadies never get cut; they're too useful. Besides, he has no end of great hampers from home, with wine and game in them; so he toadied and fed himself into favour."

The quarter-to-ten bell now rang, and the small boys went off upstairs, still consulting together, and praising their new counsellor, who stretched himself out on the bench before the hall fire again. There he lay, a very queer specimen of boyhood, by name Diggs, and familiarly called "the Mucker." He was young for his size, and a very clever fellow, nearly at the top of the fifth. His friends at home, having regard, I suppose, to his age, and not to his size and place in the school, hadn't put him into tails; and even his jackets were always too small; and he had a talent for destroying clothes and making himself look shabby. He wasn't on terms with Flashman's set, who sneered at his dress and ways behind his back; which he knew, and revenged himself by asking Flashman the most disagreeable questions, and treating him familiarly whenever a crowd of boys were round him. Neither was he intimate with any of the other bigger boys, who were warned off by his oddnesses, for he was a very queer fellow; besides, amongst other failings, he had that of impecuniosity in a remarkable degree. He brought as much money as other boys to school, but got rid of it in no time, no one knew how; and then, being also reckless, borrowed from any one; and when his debts accumulated and creditors pressed, would have an auction in the hall of everything he possessed in the world, selling even his school-books, candlestick, and study table. For weeks after one of these auctions, having rendered his study uninhabitable, he would live about in the fifth-form room and hall, doing his verses on old letter-backs and odd scraps of paper, and learning his lessons no one knew how. He never meddled with any little boy, and was popular with them, though they all looked on him with a sort of compassion, and called him "Poor Diggs," not being able to resist appearances, or to disregard wholly even the sneers of their enemy Flashman. However, he seemed equally indifferent to the sneers of big boys and the pity of small ones, and lived his own queer life with much apparent enjoyment to himself. It is necessary to introduce Diggs thus particularly, as he not only did Tom and East good service in their present warfare, as is about to be told, but soon afterwards, when he got into the sixth, chose them for his fags, and excused them from study-fagging, thereby earning unto himself eternal gratitude from them and all who are interested in their history.

And seldom had small boys more need of a friend, for the morning after the siege the storm burst upon the rebels in all its violence. Flashman laid wait, and caught Tom before second lesson, and receiving a point-blank "No" when told to fetch his hat, seized him and twisted his arm, and went through the other methods of torture in use. "He couldn't make me cry, though," as Tom said triumphantly to the rest of the rebels; "and

I kicked his shins well, I know." And soon it crept out that a lot of the fags were in league, and Flashman excited his associates to join him in bringing the young vagabonds to their senses; and the house was filled with constant chasings, and sieges, and lickings of all sorts; and in return, the bullies' beds were pulled to pieces and drenched with water, and their names written up on the walls with every insulting epithet which the fag invention could furnish. The war, in short, raged fiercely; but soon, as Diggs had told them, all the better fellows in the fifth gave up trying to fag them, and public feeling began to set against Flashman and his two or three intimates, and they were obliged to keep their doings more secret, but being thorough bad fellows, missed no opportunity of torturing in private. Flashman was an adept in all ways, but above all in the power of saying cutting and cruel things, and could often bring tears to the eyes of boys in this way, which all the thrashings in the world wouldn't have wrung from them.

And as his operations were being cut short in other directions, he now devoted himself chiefly to Tom and East, who lived at his own door, and would force himself into their study whenever he found a chance, and sit there, sometimes alone, and sometimes with a companion, interrupting all their work, and exulting in the evident pain which every now and then he could see he was inflicting on one or the other.

The storm had cleared the air for the rest of the house, and a better state of things now began than there had been since old Brooke had left; but an angry, dark spot of thunder-cloud still hung over the end of the passage where Flashman's study and that of East and Tom lay.

He felt that they had been the first rebels, and that

the rebellion had been to a great extent successful; but what above all stirred the hatred and bitterness of his heart against them was that in the frequent collisions which there had been of late they had openly called him coward and sneak. The taunts were too true to be forgiven. While he was in the act of thrashing them, they would roar out instances of his funking at football, or shirking some encounter with a lout of half his own size. These things were all well enough known in the house, but to have his own disgrace shouted out by small boys, to feel that they despised him, to be unable to silence them by any amount of torture, and to see the open laugh and sneer of his own associates (who were looking on, and took no trouble to hide their scorn from him, though they neither interfered with his bullying nor lived a bit the less intimately with him), made him beside himself. Come what might, he would make those boys' lives miserable. So the strife settled down into a personal affair between Flashman and our youngsters—a war to the knife, to be fought out in the little cockpit at the end of the bottom passage.

Flashman, be it said, was about seventeen years old, and big and strong of his age. He played well at all games where pluck wasn't much wanted, and managed generally to keep up appearances where it was; and having a bluff, off-hand manner, which passed for heartiness, and considerable powers of being pleasant when he liked, went down with the school in general for a good fellow enough. Even in the School-house, by dint of his command of money, the constant supply of good things which he kept up, and his adroit toadyism, he had managed to make himself not only tolerated, but rather popular amongst his own contemporaries; although young Brooke scarcely spoke to him, and one or two others of the right sort showed their opinions of him whenever a chance offered. But the wrong sort happened to be in the ascendant just now, and so Flashman was a formidable enemy for small boys. This soon became plain enough. Flashman left no slander unspoken, and no deed undone, which could in any way hurt his victims, or isolate them from the rest of the house. One by one most of the other rebels fell away from them, while Flashman's cause prospered, and several other fifth-form boys began to look black at them and ill-treat them as they passed about the house. By keeping out of bounds, or at all events out of the house and quadrangle, all day, and carefully barring themselves in at night, East and Tom managed to hold on without feeling very miserable; but it was as much as they could do. Greatly were they drawn then towards old Diggs, who, in an uncouth way, began to take a good deal of notice of them, and once or twice came to their study when Flashman was there, who immediately decamped in consequence. The boys thought that Diggs must have been watching.

When therefore, about this time, an auction was one night announced to take place in the hall, at which, amongst the superfluities of other boys, all Diggs's *penates* for the time being were going to the hammer, East and Tom laid their heads together, and resolved to devote their ready cash (some four shillings sterling) to redeem such articles as that sum would cover. Accordingly, they duly attended to bid, and Tom became the owner of two lots of Diggs's things:—Lot 1, price one-and-threepence, consisting (as the auctioneer remarked) of a "valuable assortment of old metals," in the shape of a mouse-trap, a cheese-toaster without a handle, and a saucepan: Lot 2, of a villainous dirty table-cloth and green-baize curtain; while East, for one-and-sixpence, purchased a leather paper-case, with a lock but no key, once handsome, but now much the worse for wear. But they had still the point to settle of how to get Diggs to take the things without hurting his feelings. This they solved by leaving them in his study, which was never locked when he was out. Diggs, who had attended the auction, remembered who had bought the lots, and came to their study soon after, and sat silent for some time, cracking his great red finger-joints. Then he laid hold of their verses, and began looking over and altering them, and at last got up, and turning his back to them, said, " You're uncommon good-hearted little beggars, you two. I value that paper-case; my sister gave it to me last holidays. I won't forget." And so he tumbled out into the passage, leaving them somewhat embarrassed, but not sorry that he knew what they had done.

The next morning was Saturday, the day on which the allowances of one shilling a week were paid—an important event to spendthrift youngsters; and great was the disgust amongst the small fry to hear that all the allowances had been impounded for the Derby lottery. That great event in the English year, the Derby, was celebrated at Rugby in those days by many lotteries. It was not an improving custom, I own, gentle reader, and led to making books, and betting, and other objectionable results; but when our great Houses of Palaver think it right to stop the nation's business on that day, and many of the members bet heavily themselves, can you blame us boys for following the example of our betters ? At any rate we did follow it. First there was the great school lottery, where the first prize was six or seven pounds; then each house had one or more separate lotteries. These were all nominally voluntary,

no boy being compelled to put in his shilling who didn't
choose to do so. But besides Flashman, there were three
or four other fast, sporting young gentlemen in the School-
house, who considered subscription a matter of duty and
necessity; and so, to make their duty come easy to the
small boys, quietly secured the allowances in a lump
when given out for distribution, and kept them. It was
no use grumbling—so many fewer tartlets and apples
were eaten and fives balls bought on that Saturday;
and after locking-up, when the money would otherwise
have been spent, consolation was carried to many a small
boy by the sound of the night-fags shouting along the
passages, " Gentlemen sportsmen of the School-house,
the lottery's going to be drawn in the hall."   It was
pleasant to be called a gentleman sportsman, also to
have a chance of drawing a favourite horse.

The hall was full of boys, and at the head of one of
the long tables stood the sporting interest, with a hat
before them, in which were the tickets folded up. One of
them then began calling out the list of the house. Each
boy as his name was called drew a ticket from the hat,
and opened it ; and most of the bigger boys, after drawing, left the hall directly to go back to their studies
or the fifth-form room. The sporting interest had all
drawn blanks, and they were sulky accordingly ; neither
of the favourites had yet been drawn, and it had come
down to the upper-fourth. So now, as each small boy
came up and drew his ticket, it was seized and opened
by Flashman, or some other of the standers-by. But no
great favourite is drawn until it comes to the Tadpole's
turn, and he shuffles up and draws, and tries to make
off, but is caught, and his ticket is opened like the rest.

" Here you are !   Wanderer—the third favourite!"
shouts the opener.

"I say, just give me my ticket, please," remonstrates Tadpole.

"Hullo! don't be in a hurry," breaks in Flashman; "what'll you sell Wanderer for now?"

"I don't want to sell," rejoins Tadpole.

"Oh, don't you! Now listen, you young fool: you don't know anything about it; the horse is no use to you. He won't win, but I want him as a hedge. Now, I'll give you half a crown for him." Tadpole holds out, but between threats and cajoleries at length sells half for one shilling and sixpence—about a fifth of its fair market value; however, he is glad to realize anything, and, as he wisely remarks, "Wanderer mayn't win, and the tizzy is safe anyhow."

East presently comes up and draws a blank. Soon after comes Tom's turn. His ticket, like the others, is seized and opened. "Here you are then," shouts the opener, holding it up—"Harkaway!—By Jove, Flashey, your young friend's in luck."

"Give me the ticket," says Flashman, with an oath, leaning across the table with open hand and his face black with rage.

"Wouldn't you like it?" replies the opener, not a bad fellow at the bottom, and no admirer of Flashman.— "Here, Brown, catch hold." And he hands the ticket to Tom, who pockets it. Whereupon Flashman makes for the door at once, that Tom and the ticket may not escape, and there keeps watch until the drawing is over and all the boys are gone, except the sporting set of five or six, who stay to compare books, make bets, and so on; Tom, who doesn't choose to move while Flashman is at the door; and East, who stays by his friend, anticipating trouble. The sporting set now gathered round Tom. Public opinion wouldn't allow them actually to rob him of his ticket, but any humbug or intimidation by which he could be driven to sell the whole or part at an under-value was lawful.

"Now, young Brown, come, what'll you sell me Harkaway for? I hear he isn't going to start. I'll give you five shillings for him," begins the boy who had opened the ticket. Tom, remembering his good deed, and moreover in his forlorn state wishing to make a friend, is about to accept the offer, when another cries out, "I'll give you seven shillings." Tom hesitated, and looked from one to the other.

"No, no!" said Flashman, pushing in, "leave me to deal with him; we'll draw lots for it afterwards. Now, sir, you know me: you'll sell Harkaway to us for five shillings, or you'll repent it."

"I won't sell a bit of him," answered Tom shortly.

"You hear that now!" said Flashman, turning to the others. "He's the coxiest young blackguard in the house. I always told you so. We're to have all the trouble and risk of getting up the lotteries for the benefit of such fellows as he."

Flashman forgets to explain what risk they ran, but he speaks to willing ears. Gambling makes boys selfish and cruel as well as men.

"That's true. We always draw blanks," cried one.
—"Now, sir, you shall sell half, at any rate."

"I won't," said Tom, flushing up to his hair, and lumping them all in his mind with his sworn enemy.

"Very well then; let's roast him," cried Flashman, and catches hold of Tom by the collar. One or two boys hesitate, but the rest join in. East seizes Tom's arm, and tries to pull him away, but is knocked back by one of the boys, and Tom is dragged along struggling. His shoulders are pushed against the mantelpiece, and

he is held by main force before the fire, Flashman drawing his trousers tight by way of extra torture. Poor
East, in more pain even than Tom, suddenly thinks of
Diggs, and darts off to find him. " Will you sell now
for ten shillings ? " says one boy who is relenting.

Tom only answers by groans and struggles.

" I say, Flashey, he has had enough," says the same
boy, dropping the arm he holds.

" No, no ; another turn'll do it," answers Flashman.

But poor Tom is done already, turns deadly pale, and
his head falls forward on his breast, just as Diggs, in
frantic excitement, rushes into the hall with East at his
heels.

" You cowardly brutes ! " is all he can say, as he
catches Tom from them and supports him to the hall
table. " Good God ! he's dying. Here, get some cold
water—run for the housekeeper."

Flashman and one or two others slink away; the
rest, ashamed and sorry, bend over Tom or run for
water, while East darts off for the housekeeper. Water
comes, and they throw it on his hands and face, and he
begins to come to. " Mother ! "—the words came feebly
and slowly—" it's very cold to-night." Poor old Diggs
is blubbering like a child. " Where am I ? " goes on
Tom, opening his eyes. " Ah ! I remember now."
And he shut his eyes again and groaned.

" I say," is whispered, " we can't do any good, and
the housekeeper will be here in a minute." And all but
one steal away. He stays with Diggs, silent and sorrowful, and fans Tom's face.

The housekeeper comes in with strong salts, and Tom
soon recovers enough to sit up. There is a smell of
burning. She examines his clothes, and looks up inquiringly. The boys are silent.

"How did he come so?" No answer. "There's been some bad work here," she adds, looking very serious, "and I shall speak to the Doctor about it." Still no answer.

"Hadn't we better carry him to the sick-room?" suggests Diggs.

"Oh, I can walk now," says Tom; and, supported by East and the housekeeper, goes to the sick-room.

The boy who held his ground is soon amongst the rest, who are all in fear of their lives. "Did he peach?" "Does she know about it?"

"Not a word; he's a stanch little fellow." And pausing a moment, he adds, "I'm sick of this work; what brutes we've been!"

Meantime Tom is stretched on the sofa in the housekeeper's room, with East by his side, while she gets wine and water and other restoratives.

"Are you much hurt, dear old boy?" whispers East.

"Only the back of my legs," answers Tom. They are indeed badly scorched, and part of his trousers burnt through. But soon he is in bed with cold bandages. At first he feels broken, and thinks of writing home and getting taken away; and the verse of a hymn he had learned years ago sings through his head, and he goes to sleep, murmuring,—

> "Where the wicked cease from troubling,
> And the weary are at rest."

But after a sound night's rest, the old boy-spirit comes back again. East comes in, reporting that the whole house is with him; and he forgets everything, except their old resolve never to be beaten by that bully Flashman.

Not a word could the housekeeper extract from either of them, and though the Doctor knew all that she knew that morning, he never knew any more.

I trust and believe that such scenes are not possible now at school, and that lotteries and betting-books have gone out; but I am writing of schools as they were in our time, and must give the evil with the good.

CHAPTER IX.

A CHAPTER OF ACCIDENTS.

" Wherein I [speak] of most disastrous chances,
Of moving accidents by flood and field,
Of hair-breadth 'scapes."—SHAKESPEARE.

WHEN Tom came back into school after a couple of days in the sick-room, he found matters much changed for the better, as East had led him to expect. Flashman's brutality had disgusted most even of his intimate friends, and his cowardice had once more been made plain to the house; for Diggs had encountered him on the morning after the lottery, and after high words on both sides, had struck him, and the blow was not returned. However, Flashey was not unused to this sort of thing, and had lived through as awkward affairs before, and, as Diggs had said, fed and toadied himself back into favour again. Two or three of the boys who had helped to roast Tom came up and begged his pardon, and thanked him for not telling anything. Morgan sent for him, and was inclined to take the matter up warmly, but Tom begged him not to do it; to which he agreed, on Tom's promising to come to him at once in future—a promise which, I regret to say, he didn't keep. Tom kept Harkaway all to himself, and won the second prize in the lottery, some thirty shillings, which he and East contrived to spend in about three days in the purchase of pictures for their study, two new bats and a cricket-ball—all the best that could be got—and a supper of sausages, kidneys, and beef-steak pies to all the rebels. Light come, light go; they wouldn't have been comfortable with money in their pockets in the middle of the half.

The embers of Flashman's wrath, however, were still smouldering, and burst out every now and then in sly blows and taunts, and they both felt that they hadn't quite done with him yet. It wasn't long, however, before the last act of that drama came, and with it the end of bullying for Tom and East at Rugby. They now often stole out into the hall at nights, incited thereto partly by the hope of finding Diggs there and having a talk with him, partly by the excitement of doing something which was against rules; for, sad to say, both of our youngsters, since their loss of character for steadiness in their form, had got into the habit of doing things which were forbidden, as a matter of adventure,—just in the same way, I should fancy, as men fall into smuggling, and for the same sort of reasons—thoughtlessness in the first place. It never occurred to them to consider why such and such rules were laid down: the reason was nothing to them, and they only looked upon rules as a sort of challenge from the rule-makers, which it would be rather bad pluck in them not to accept; and then again, in the lower parts of the school they hadn't enough to do. The work of the form they could manage to get through pretty easily, keeping a good enough place to get their regular yearly remove; and not having much ambition beyond this, their whole superfluous steam was available for games and scrapes. Now, one rule of the house which it was a daily pleasure of all such boys to break was that after supper all fags, except the three on duty in the passages, should remain in their own studies until nine o'clock; and if caught about the

passages or hall, or in one another's studies, they were
liable to punishments or caning.   The rule was stricter
than its observance ; for most of the sixth spent their
evenings in the fifth-form room, where the library was,
and the lessons were learnt in common.   Every now and
then, however, a prepostor would be seized with a fit of
district visiting, and would make a tour of the passages
and hall and the fags' studies.   Then, if the owner were
entertaining a friend or two, the first kick at the door
and ominous " Open here " had the effect of the shadow
of a hawk over a chicken-yard : every one cut to cover
—one small boy diving under the sofa, another under
the table, while the owner would hastily pull down a
book or two and open them, and cry out in a meek voice,
" Hullo, who's there ? " casting an anxious eye round
to see that no protruding leg or elbow could betray the
hidden boys.   " Open, sir, directly ; it's Snooks."   " Oh,
I'm very sorry ; I didn't know it was you, Snooks."
And then with well-feigned zeal the door would be opened,
young hopeful praying that that beast Snooks mightn't
have heard the scuffle caused by his coming.   If a study
was empty, Snooks proceeded to draw the passages and
hall to find the truants.

Well, one evening, in forbidden hours, Tom and East
were in the hall.   They occupied the seats before the
fire nearest the door, while Diggs sprawled as usual before the farther fire.   He was busy with a copy of verses,
and East and Tom were chatting together in whispers
by the light of the fire, and splicing a favourite old fives
bat which had sprung.   Presently a step came down the
bottom passage.   They listened a moment, assured themselves that it wasn't a prepostor, and then went on with
their work, and the door swung open, and in walked Flashman.   He didn't see Diggs, and thought it a good chance

to keep his hand in; and as the boys didn't move for him, struck one of them, to make them get out of his way.

" What's that for ? " growled the assaulted one.

" Because I choose. You've no business here. Go to your study."

" You can't send us."

" Can't I ? Then I'll thrash you if you stay," said Flashman savagely.

" I say, you two," said Diggs, from the end of the hall, rousing up and resting himself on his elbow—" you'll never get rid of that fellow till you lick him. Go in at him, both of you. I'll see fair play."

Flashman was taken aback, and retreated two steps. East looked at Tom. " Shall we try ! " said he. " Yes," said Tom desperately. So the two advanced on Flashman, with clenched fists and beating hearts. They were about up to his shoulder, but tough boys of their age, and in perfect training ; while he, though strong and big, was in poor condition from his monstrous habit of stuffing and want of exercise. Coward as he was, however, Flashman couldn't swallow such an insult as this ; besides, he was confident of having easy work, and so faced the boys, saying, " You impudent young black-guards ! " Before he could finish his abuse, they rushed in on him, and began pummelling at all of him which they could reach. He hit out wildly and savagely ; but the full force of his blows didn't tell—they were too near to him. It was long odds, though, in point of strength ; and in another minute Tom went spinning backwards over a form, and Flashman turned to demolish East with a savage grin. But now Diggs jumped down from the table on which he had seated himself. " Stop there," shouted he ; " the round's over—half-minute time al-lowed."

"What the —— is it to you?" faltered Flashman, who began to lose heart.

"I'm going to see fair, I tell you," said Diggs, with a grin, and snapping his great red fingers; "'taint fair for you to be fighting one of them at a time.—Are you ready, Brown? Time's up."

The small boys rushed in again. Closing, they saw, was their best chance, and Flashman was wilder and more flurried than ever: he caught East by the throat, and tried to force him back on the iron-bound table. Tom grasped his waist, and remembering the old throw he had learned in the Vale from Harry Winburn, crooked his leg inside Flashman's, and threw his whole weight forward. The three tottered for a moment, and then over they went on to the floor, Flashman striking his head against a form in the hall.

The two youngsters sprang to their legs, but he lay there still. They began to be frightened. Tom stooped down, and then cried out, scared out of his wits, "He's bleeding awfully. Come here, East! Diggs, he's dying!"

"Not he," said Diggs, getting leisurely off the table; "it's all sham; he's only afraid to fight it out."

East was as frightened as Tom. Diggs lifted Flashman's head, and he groaned.

"What's the matter?" shouted Diggs.

"My skull's fractured," sobbed Flashman.

"Oh, let me run for the housekeeper!" cried Tom. "What shall we do?"

"Fiddlesticks! It's nothing but the skin broken," said the relentless Diggs, feeling his head. "Cold water and a bit of rag's all he'll want."

"Let me go," said Flashman surlily, sitting up; "I don't want your help."

"We're really very sorry——" began East.

"Hang your sorrow!" answered Flashman, holding his handkerchief to the place; "you shall pay for this, I can tell you, both of you." And he walked out of the hall.

"He can't be very bad," said Tom, with a deep sigh, much relieved to see his enemy march so well.

"Not he," said Diggs; "and you'll see you won't be troubled with him any more. But, I say, your head's broken too; your collar is covered with blood."

"Is it though?" said Tom, putting up his hand; "I didn't know it."

"Well, mop it up, or you'll have your jacket spoilt.— And you have got a nasty eye, Scud. You'd better go and bathe it well in cold water."

"Cheap enough too, if we're done with our old friend Flashey," said East, as they made off upstairs to bathe their wounds.

They had done with Flashman in one sense, for he never laid finger on either of them again; but whatever harm a spiteful heart and venomous tongue could do them, he took care should be done. Only throw dirt enough, and some of it is sure to stick; and so it was with the fifth form and the bigger boys in general, with whom he associated more or less, and they not at all. Flashman managed to get Tom and East into disfavour, which did not wear off for some time after the author of it had disappeared from the School world. This event, much prayed for by the small fry in general, took place a few months after the above encounter. One fine summer evening Flashman had been regaling himself on gin-punch, at Brownsover; and, having exceeded his usual limits, started home uproarious. He fell in with a friend or two coming back from bathing, proposed a glass of beer, to which they assented, the weather being hot, and they thirsty souls, and unaware of the quantity of drink which Flashman had already on board. The short result was, that Flashey became beastly drunk. They tried to get him along, but couldn't; so they chartered a hurdle and two men to carry him. One of the masters came upon them, and they naturally enough fled. The flight of the rest raised the master's suspicions, and the good angel of the fags incited him to examine the freight, and, after examination, to convoy the hurdle himself up to the School-house; and the Doctor, who had long had his eye on Flashman, arranged for his withdrawal next morning.

The evil that men and boys too do lives after them: Flashman was gone, but our boys, as hinted above, still felt the effects of his hate. Besides, they had been the movers of the strike against unlawful fagging. The cause was righteous—the result had been triumphant to a great extent; but the best of the fifth—even those who had never fagged the small boys, or had given up the practice cheerfully—couldn't help feeling a small grudge against the first rebels. After all, their form had been defied, on just grounds, no doubt—so just, indeed, that they had at once acknowledged the wrong, and remained passive in the strife. Had they sided with Flashman and his set, the rebels must have given way at once. They couldn't help, on the whole, being glad that they had so acted, and that the resistance had been successful against such of their own form as had shown fight; they felt that law and order had gained thereby, but the ringleaders they couldn't quite pardon at once. "Confoundedly coxy those young rascals will get, if we don't mind," was the general feeling.

So it is, and must be always, my dear boys. If the angel Gabriel were to come down from heaven, and head a successful rise against the most abominable and unrighteous vested interest which this poor old world groans under, he would most certainly lose his character for many years, probably for centuries, not only with the upholders of said vested interest, but with the respectable mass of the people whom he had delivered. They wouldn't ask him to dinner, or let their names appear with his in the papers; they would be very careful how they spoke of him in the Palaver, or at their clubs. What can we expect, then, when we have only poor gallant blundering men like Kossuth, Garibaldi, Mazzini, and righteous causes which do not triumph in their hands — men who have holes enough in their armour, God knows, easy to be hit by respectabilities sitting in their lounging chairs, and having large balances at their bankers'? But you are brave, gallant boys, who hate easy-chairs, and have no balances or bankers. You only want to have your heads set straight, to take the right side; so bear in mind that majorities, especially respectable ones, are nine times out of ten in the wrong; and that if you see a man or boy striving earnestly on the weak side, however wrong-headed or blundering he may be, you are not to go and join the cry against him. If you can't join him and help him, and make him wiser, at any rate remember that he has found something in the world which he will fight and suffer for, which is just what you have got to do for yourselves; and so think and speak of him tenderly.

So East and Tom, the Tadpole, and one or two more, became a sort of young Ishmaelites, their hands against every one, and every one's hand against them. It has been already told how they got to war with the masters and the fifth form, and with the sixth it was much the same. They saw the prepostors cowed by or joining with the fifth and shirking their own duties; so they didn't respect them, and rendered no willing obedience. It had been one thing to clean out studies for sons of heroes like old Brooke, but was quite another to do the like for Snooks and Green, who had never faced a good scrummage at football, and couldn't keep the passages in order at night. So they only slurred through their fagging just well enough to escape a licking, and not always that, and got the character of sulky, unwilling fags. In the fifth-form room, after supper, when such matters were often discussed and arranged, their names were for ever coming up.

'I say, Green," Snooks began one night, "isn't that new boy, Harrison, your fag?"

" Yes; why?"

" Oh, I know something of him at home, and should like to excuse him. Will you swop?"

" Who will you give me?"

" Well, let's see. There's Willis, Johnson. No, that won't do. Yes, I have it. There's young East; I'll give you him."

" Don't you wish you may get it?" replied Green. " I'll give you two for Willis, if you like."

" Who, then?" asked Snooks.

" Hall and Brown."

" Wouldn't have 'em at a gift."

" Better than East, though; for they ain't quite so sharp," said Green, getting up and leaning his back against the mantelpiece. He wasn't a bad fellow, and couldn't help not being able to put down the unruly fifth-form. His eye twinkled as he went on, " Did I ever tell you how the young vagabond sold me last half?"

" No; how?"

" Well, he never half cleaned my study out—only just stuck the candlesticks in the cupboard, and swept the crumbs on to the floor. So at last I was mortal angry, and had him up, and made him go through the whole performance under my eyes. The dust the young scamp made nearly choked me, and showed that he hadn't swept the carpet before. Well, when it was all finished, 'Now, young gentleman,' says I, 'mind, I expect this to be done every morning—floor swept, table-cloth taken off and shaken, and everything dusted.' 'Very well,' grunts he. Not a bit of it though. I was quite sure, in a day or two, that he never took the table-cloth off even. So I laid a trap for him. I tore up some paper, and put half a dozen bits on my table one night, and the cloth over them as usual. Next morning after breakfast up I came, pulled off the cloth, and, sure enough, there was the paper, which fluttered down on to the floor. I was in a towering rage. 'I've got you now,' thought I, and sent for him, while I got out my cane. Up he came as cool as you please, with his hands in his pockets. 'Didn't I tell you to shake my table-cloth every morning?' roared I. 'Yes,' says he. 'Did you do it this morning?' 'Yes.' 'You young liar! I put these pieces of paper on the table last night, and if you'd taken the table-cloth off you'd have seen them, so I'm going to give you a good licking.' Then my youngster takes one hand out of his pocket, and just stoops down and picks up two of the bits of paper, and holds them out to me. There was written on each, in great round text, 'Harry East, his mark.' The young rogue had found my trap out, taken away my paper, and put some of his there, every bit ear-marked. I'd a great mind to lick him for his impudence; but, after all, one has no right to be laying traps, so I didn't. Of course I was at his mercy till the end of the half, and in his weeks my study was so frowzy I couldn't sit in it."

"They spoil one's things so, too," chimed in a third boy. "Hall and Brown were night-fags last week. I called 'fag,' and gave them my candlesticks to clean. Away they went, and didn't appear again. When they'd had time enough to clean them three times over, I went out to look after them. They weren't in the passages, so down I went into the hall, where I heard music; and there I found them sitting on the table, listening to Johnson, who was playing the flute, and my candlesticks stuck between the bars well into the fire, red-hot, clean spoiled. They've never stood straight since, and I must get some more. However, I gave them a good licking; that's one comfort."

Such were the sort of scrapes they were always getting into; and so, partly by their own faults, partly from circumstances, partly from the faults of others, they found themselves outlaws, ticket-of-leave men, or what you will in that line—in short, dangerous parties—and lived the sort of hand-to-mouth, wild, reckless life which such parties generally have to put up with. Nevertheless they never quite lost favour with young Brooke, who was now the cock of the house, and just getting into the sixth; and Diggs stuck to them like a man, and gave them store of good advice, by which they never in the least profited.

And even after the house mended, and law and order had been restored, which soon happened after young Brooke and Diggs got into the sixth, they couldn't easily or at once return into the paths of steadiness, and many of the old, wild, out-of-bounds habits stuck to them as firmly as ever. While they had been quite little boys, the scrapes they got into in the School hadn't much mattered to any one; but now they were in the upper school, all wrong-doers from which were sent up straight to the Doctor at once. So they began to come under his notice; and as they were a sort of leaders in a small way amongst their own contemporaries, his eye, which was everywhere, was upon them.

It was a toss-up whether they turned out well or ill, and so they were just the boys who caused most anxiety to such a master. You have been told of the first occasion on which they were sent up to the Doctor, and the remembrance of it was so pleasant that they had much less fear of him than most boys of their standing had. "It's all his look," Tom used to say to East, "that frightens fellows. Don't you remember, he never said anything to us my first half-year for being an hour late for locking-up?"

The next time that Tom came before him, however, the interview was of a very different kind. It happened just about the time at which we have now arrived, and was the first of a series of scrapes into which our hero managed now to tumble.

The river Avon at Rugby is a slow and not very clear stream, in which chub, dace, roach, and other coarse fish are (or were) plentiful enough, together with a fair sprinkling of small jack, but no fish worth sixpence either for sport or food. It is, however, a capital river for bathing, as it has many nice small pools and several good reaches for swimming, all within about a mile of one another, and at an easy twenty minutes' walk from the school. This mile of water is rented, or used to be rented, for bathing purposes by the trustees of the School, for the boys. The footpath to Brownsover crosses the river by "the Planks," a curious old single-plank bridge running for fifty or sixty yards into the flat meadows on each side of the river—for in the winter there are frequent floods. Above the Planks were the bathing-

places for the smaller boys—Sleath's, the first bathing-
place, where all new boys had to begin, until they had
proved to the bathing men (three steady individuals,
who were paid to attend daily through the summer to
prevent accidents) that they could swim pretty decently,
when they were allowed to go on to Anstey's, about one
hundred and fifty yards below. Here there was a hole
about six feet deep and twelve feet across, over which
the puffing urchins struggled to the opposite side, and
thought no small beer of themselves for having been
out of their depths. Below the Planks came larger and
deeper holes, the first of which was Wratislaw's, and the
last Swift's, a famous hole, ten or twelve feet deep in
parts, and thirty yards across, from which there was a
fine swimming reach right down to the mill. Swift's
was reserved for the sixth and fifth forms, and had a
spring board and two sets of steps : the others had
one set of steps each, and were used indifferently by
all the lower boys, though each house addicted itself
more to one hole than to another. The School-house at
this time affected Wratislaw's hole, and Tom and East,
who had learnt to swim like fishes, were to be found
there as regular as the clock through the summer, always
twice, and often three times a day.

Now the boys either had, or fancied they had, a right
also to fish at their pleasure over the whole of this part
of the river, and would not understand that the right
(if any) only extended to the Rugby side. As ill-luck
would have it, the gentleman who owned the opposite
bank, after allowing it for some time without inter-
ference, had ordered his keepers not to let the boys fish
on his side—the consequence of which had been that
there had been first wranglings and then fights between
the keepers and boys ; and so keen had the quarrel

become that the landlord and his keepers, after a duck-
ing had been inflicted on one of the latter, and a fierce
fight ensued thereon, had been up to the great school at
calling-over to identify the delinquents, and it was all
the Doctor himself and five or six masters could do to
keep the peace.   Not even his authority could prevent
the hissing ; and so strong was the feeling that the four
prepostors of the week walked up the school with their
canes, shouting "S-s-s-s-i-lenc-c-c-c-e" at the top of their
voices.   However, the chief offenders for the time were
flogged and kept in bounds; but the victorious party
had brought a nice hornet's nest about their ears.
The landlord was hissed at the School-gates as he rode
past, and when he charged his horse at the mob of boys,
and tried to thrash them with his whip, was driven back
by cricket-bats and wickets, and pursued with pebbles
and fives balls ; while the wretched keepers' lives were
a burden to them, from having to watch the waters so
closely.

The School-house boys of Tom's standing, one and all,
as a protest against this tyranny and cutting short of
their lawful amusements, took to fishing in all ways, and
especially by means of night-lines.   The little tackle-
maker at the bottom of the town would soon have made
his fortune had the rage lasted, and several of the barbers
began to lay in fishing-tackle.   The boys had this great
advantage over their enemies, that they spent a large
portion of the day in nature's garb by the river-side, and
so, when tired of swimming, would get out on the other
side and fish, or set night-lines, till the keepers hove in
sight, and then plunge in and swim back and mix with
the other bathers, and the keepers were too wise to follow
across the stream.

While things were in this state, one day Tom and three

or four others were bathing at Wratislaw's, and had, as a matter of course, been taking up and re-setting night-lines. They had all left the water, and were sitting or standing about at their toilets, in all costumes, from a shirt upwards, when they were aware of a man in a velveteen shooting-coat approaching from the other side. He was a new keeper, so they didn't recognize or notice him, till he pulled up right opposite, and began :—

"I see'd some of you young gentlemen over this side a-fishing just now."

"Hullo! who are you? What business is that of yours, old Velveteens?"

"I'm the new under-keeper, and master's told me to keep a sharp lookout on all o' you young chaps. And I tells 'ee I means business, and you'd better keep on your own side, or we shall fall out."

"Well, that's right, Velveteens; speak out, and let's know your mind at once."

"Look here, old boy," cried East, holding up a miserable, coarse fish or two and a small jack; "would you like to smell 'em and see which bank they lived under?"

"I'll give you a bit of advice, keeper," shouted Tom, who was sitting in his shirt paddling with his feet in the river: "you'd better go down there to Swift's, where the big boys are; they're beggars at setting lines, and'll put you up to a wrinkle or two for catching the five-pounders." Tom was nearest to the keeper, and that officer, who was getting angry at the chaff, fixed his eyes on our hero, as if to take a note of him for future use. Tom returned his gaze with a steady stare, and then broke into a laugh, and struck into the middle of a favourite School-house song,—

"As I and my companions
Were setting of a snare,

> The gamekeeper was watching us ;
>   For him we did not care :
> For we can wrestle and fight, my boys,
>   And jump out anywhere.
> For it's my delight of a likely night,
>   In the season of the year."

The chorus was taken up by the other boys with shouts of laughter, and the keeper turned away with a grunt, but evidently bent on mischief. The boys thought no more of the matter.

But now came on the May-fly season ; the soft, hazy summer weather lay sleepily along the rich meadows by Avon side, and the green and gray flies flickered with their graceful, lazy up-and-down flight over the reeds and the water and the meadows, in myriads upon myriads. The May-flies must surely be the lotus-eaters of the ephemeræ — the happiest, laziest, carelessest fly that dances and dreams out his few hours of sunshiny life by English rivers.

Every little pitiful, coarse fish in the Avon was on the alert for the flies, and gorging his wretched carcass with hundreds daily, the gluttonous rogues ! and every lover of the gentle craft was out to avenge the poor May-flies.

So one fine Thursday afternoon, Tom, having borrowed East's new rod, started by himself to the river. He fished for some time with small success—not a fish would rise at him ; but as he prowled along the bank, he was presently aware of mighty ones feeding in a pool on the opposite side, under the shade of a huge willow-tree. The stream was deep here, but some fifty yards below was a shallow, for which he made off hot-foot ; and forgetting landlords, keepers, solemn prohibitions of the Doctor, and everything else, pulled up his trousers, plunged across, and in three minutes was creeping along on all fours towards the clump of willows.

It isn't often that great chub, or any other coarse fish, are in earnest about anything; but just then they were thoroughly bent on feeding, and in half an hour Master Tom had deposited three thumping fellows at the foot of the giant willow. As he was baiting for a fourth pounder, and just going to throw in again, he became aware of a man coming up the bank not one hundred yards off. Another look told him that it was the under-keeper. Could he reach the shallow before him ? No, not carrying his rod. Nothing for it but the tree. So Tom laid his bones to it, shinning up as fast as he could, and dragging up his rod after him. He had just time to reach and crouch along upon a huge branch some ten feet up, which stretched out over the river, when the keeper arrived at the clump. Tom's heart beat fast as he came under the tree ; two steps more and he would have passed, when, as ill-luck would have it, the gleam on the scales of the dead fish caught his eye, and he made a dead point at the foot of the tree. He picked up the fish one by one ; his eye and touch told him that they had been alive and feeding within the hour. Tom crouched lower along the branch, and heard the keeper beating the clump. " If I could only get the rod hidden," thought he, and began gently shifting it to get it alongside of him ; " willow-trees don't throw out straight hickory shoots twelve feet long, with no leaves, worse luck." Alas ! the keeper catches the rustle, and then a sight of the rod, and then of Tom's hand and arm.

"Oh, be up ther', be 'ee ? " says he, running under the tree. " Now you come down this minute."

"Tree'd at last," thinks Tom, making no answer, and keeping as close as possible, but working away at the rod, which he takes to pieces. " I'm in for it, unless I can starve him out." And then he begins to meditate getting along the branch for a plunge, and scramble to the other side ; but the small branches are so thick, and the opposite bank so difficult, that the keeper will have lots of time to get round by the ford before he can get out, so he gives that up. And now he hears the keeper beginning to scramble up the trunk. That will never do ; so he scrambles himself back to where his branch joins the trunk, and stands with lifted rod.

"Hullo, Velveteens; mind your fingers if you come any higher."

The keeper stops and looks up, and then with a grin says, "Oh ! be you, be it, young measter ? Well, here's luck. Now I tells 'ee to come down at once, and 't'll be best for 'ee."

"Thank 'ee, Velveteens; I'm very comfortable," said Tom, shortening the rod in his hand, and preparing for battle.

"Werry well; please yourself," says the keeper, descending, however, to the ground again, and taking his seat on the bank. "I bean't in no hurry, so you may take your time. I'll l'arn 'ee to gee honest folk names afore I've done with 'ee."

"My luck as usual," thinks Tom ; "what a fool I was to give him a black! If I'd called him ' keeper,' now, I might get off. The return match is all his way."

The keeper quietly proceeded to take out his pipe, fill, and light it, keeping an eye on Tom, who now sat disconsolately across the branch, looking at keeper—a pitiful sight for men and fishes. The more he thought of it the less he liked it. "It must be getting near second calling-over," thinks he. Keeper smokes on stolidly. "If he takes me up, I shall be flogged safe enough. I can't sit here all night. Wonder if he'll rise at silver."

"I say, keeper," said he meekly, "let me go for two bob?"

"Not for twenty neither," grunts his persecutor.

And so they sat on till long past second calling-over, and the sun came slanting in through the willow-branches, and telling of locking-up near at hand.

"I'm coming down, keeper," said Tom at last, with a sigh, fairly tired out. "Now what are you going to do?"

"Walk 'ee up to School, and give 'ee over to the Doctor; them's my orders," says Velveteens, knocking the ashes out of his fourth pipe, and standing up and shaking himself.

"Very good," said Tom; "but hands off, you know. I'll go with you quietly, so no collaring or that sort of thing."

Keeper looked at him a minute. "Werry good," said he at last. And so Tom descended, and wended his way drearily by the side of the keeper, up to the School-house, where they arrived just at locking-up. As they passed the School-gates, the Tadpole and several others who were standing there caught the state of things, and rushed out, crying, "Rescue!" But Tom shook his head; so they only followed to the Doctor's gate, and went back sorely puzzled.

How changed and stern the Doctor seemed from the last time that Tom was up there, as the keeper told the story, not omitting to state how Tom had called him blackguard names. "Indeed, sir," broke in the culprit, "it was only Velveteens." The Doctor only asked one question.

"You know the rule about the banks, Brown?"

"Yes, sir."

"Then wait for me to-morrow, after first lesson."

"I thought so," muttered Tom.

"And about the rod, sir?" went on the keeper. "Master's told we as we might have all the rods——"

"Oh, please, sir," broke in Tom, "the rod isn't mine."

The Doctor looked puzzled; but the keeper, who was a good-hearted fellow, and melted at Tom's evident distress, gave up his claim. Tom was flogged next morning, and a few days afterwards met Velveteens, and presented him with half a crown for giving up the rod claim, and they became sworn friends; and I regret to say that Tom had many more fish from under the willow that May-fly season, and was never caught again by Velveteens.

It wasn't three weeks before Tom, and now East by his side, were again in the awful presence. This time, however, the Doctor was not so terrible. A few days before, they had been fagged at fives to fetch the balls that went off the court. While standing watching the game, they saw five or six nearly new balls hit on the top of the School. "I say, Tom," said East, when they were dismissed, "couldn't we get those balls somehow?"

"Let's try, anyhow."

So they reconnoitred the walls carefully, borrowed a coal-hammer from old Stumps, bought some big nails, and after one or two attempts, scaled the Schools, and possessed themselves of huge quantities of fives balls. The place pleased them so much that they spent all their spare time there, scratching and cutting their names on the top of every tower; and at last, having exhausted all other places, finished up with inscribing H. EAST, T. BROWN, on the minute-hand of the great clock; in the doing of which they held the minute-hand, and disturbed the clock's economy. So next morning, when masters and boys came trooping down to prayers, and entered the quadrangle, the injured minute-hand was indicating three minutes to the hour. They all pulled up, and took their time. When the hour struck, doors were closed, and half the school late. Thomas being set to make inquiry, discovers their names on the minute-hand, and reports accordingly; and they are sent for, a knot of their friends making derisive and pantomimic allusions to what their fate will be as they walk off.

But the Doctor, after hearing their story, doesn't make much of it, and only gives them thirty lines of Homer to learn by heart, and a lecture on the likelihood of such exploits ending in broken bones.

Alas! almost the next day was one of the great fairs in the town; and as several rows and other disagreeable accidents had of late taken place on these occasions, the Doctor gives out, after prayers in the morning, that no boy is to go down into the town. Wherefore East and Tom, for no earthly pleasure except that of doing what they are told not to do, start away, after second lesson, and making a short circuit through the fields, strike a back lane which leads into the town, go down it, and run plump upon one of the masters as they emerge into the High Street. The master in question, though a very clever, is not a righteous man. He has already caught several of his own pupils, and gives them lines to learn, while he sends East and Tom, who are not his pupils, up to the Doctor, who, on learning that they had been at prayers in the morning, flogs them soundly.

The flogging did them no good at the time, for the injustice of their captor was rankling in their minds; but it was just the end of the half, and on the next evening but one Thomas knocks at their door, and says the Doctor wants to see them. They look at one another in silent dismay. What can it be now? Which of their countless wrong-doings can he have heard of officially?

However, it's no use delaying, so up they go to the study. There they find the Doctor, not angry, but very grave. " He has sent for them to speak to very seriously before they go home. They have each been flogged several times in the half-year for direct and wilful breaches of rules. This cannot go on. They are doing no good to themselves or others, and now they are getting up in the School, and have influence. They seem to think that rules are made capriciously, and for the pleasure of the masters; but this is not so. They are made for the good of the whole School, and must and shall be obeyed. Those who thoughtlessly or wilfully break them will not be allowed to stay at the School. He should be sorry if they had to leave, as the School might do them both much good, and wishes them to think very seriously in the holidays over what he has said. Good-night."

And so the two hurry off horribly scared; the idea of having to leave has never crossed their minds, and is quite unbearable.

As they go out, they meet at the door old Holmes, a sturdy, cheery prepostor of another house, who goes in to the Doctor; and they hear his genial, hearty greeting of the newcomer, so different to their own reception, as the door closes, and return to their study with heavy hearts, and tremendous resolves to break no more rules.

Five minutes afterwards the master of their form—a late arrival and a model young master—knocks at the Doctor's study-door. " Come in!" And as he enters, the Doctor goes on, to Holmes—" You see, I do not know anything of the case officially, and if I take any notice of it at all, I must publicly expel the boy. I don't wish to do that, for I think there is some good in him. There's nothing for it but a good sound thrashing." He paused to shake hands with the master, which Holmes does also, and then prepares to leave.

" I understand. Good-night, sir."

" Good-night, Holmes. And remember," added the Doctor, emphasizing the words, " a good sound thrashing before the whole house."

The door closed on Holmes ; and the Doctor, in answer to the puzzled look of his lieutenant, explained shortly. " A gross case of bullying. Wharton, the head of the house, is a very good fellow, but slight and weak, and severe physical pain is the only way to deal with such a case ; so I have asked Holmes to take it up. He is very careful and trustworthy, and has plenty of strength. I wish all the sixth had as much. We must have it here, if we are to keep order at all."

Now I don't want any wiseacres to read this book ; but if they should, of course they will prick up their long ears, and howl, or rather bray, at the above story. Very good—I don't object ; but what I have to add for you boys is this, that Holmes called a levy of his house after breakfast next morning, made them a speech on the case of bullying in question, and then gave the bully a "good sound thrashing ; " and that years afterwards, that boy sought out Holmes, and thanked him, saying it had been the kindest act which had ever been done upon him, and the turning-point in his character ; and a very good fellow he became, and a credit to his School.

After some other talk between them, the Doctor said, " I want to speak to you about two boys in your form, East and Brown. I have just been speaking to them. What do you think of them ? "

" Well, they are not hard workers, and very thoughtless and full of spirits ; but I can't help liking them. I think they are sound, good fellows at the bottom."

"I'm glad of it. I think so too. But they make me very uneasy. They are taking the lead a good deal amongst the fags in my house, for they are very active, bold fellows. I should be sorry to lose them, but I shan't let them stay if I don't see them gaining character and manliness. In another year they may do great harm to all the younger boys."

"Oh, I hope you won't send them away," pleaded their master.

"Not if I can help it. But now I never feel sure, after any half-holiday, that I shan't have to flog one of them next morning, for some foolish, thoughtless scrape. I quite dread seeing either of them."

They were both silent for a minute. Presently the Doctor began again :—

"They don't feel that they have any duty or work to do in the school, and how is one to make them feel it ?"

"I think if either of them had some little boy to take care of, it would steady them. Brown is the most reckless of the two, I should say. East wouldn't get into so many scrapes without him."

"Well," said the Doctor, with something like a sigh, "I'll think of it." And they went on to talk of other subjects.

PART II.

" I [hold] it truth, with him who sings
    To one clear harp in divers tones,
    That men may rise on stepping-stones
Of their dead selves to higher things."
                                    TENNYSON.

CHAPTER I.

HOW THE TIDE TURNED.

" Once to every man and nation comes the moment to decide,
    In the strife of Truth with Falsehood, for the good or evil side.
        *   *   *   *
    Then it is the brave man chooses, while the coward stands aside,
    Doubting in his abject spirit, till his Lord is crucified."—LOWELL.

THE turning-point in our hero's school career had now
come, and the manner of it was as follows. On the evening of the first day of the next half-year, Tom, East, and
another School-house boy, who had just been dropped at
the Spread Eagle by the old Regulator, rushed into the
matron's room in high spirits, such as all real boys are
in when they first get back, however fond they may be
of home.

" Well, Mrs. Wixie," shouted one, seizing on the me-
thodical, active, little dark-eyed woman, who was busy
stowing away the linen of the boys who had already
arrived into their several pigeon-holes, " here we are
again, you see, as jolly as ever. Let us help you put
the things away."

" And, Mary," cried another (she was called indifferently by either name), " who's come back ? Has the
Doctor made old Jones leave ? How many new boys
are there ? "

" Am I and East to have Gray's study ? You know
you promised to get it for us if you could," shouted Tom.

" And am I to sleep in Number 4 ? " roared East.

" How's old Sam, and Bogle, and Sally ? "

"Bless the boys!" cries Mary, at last getting in a word; "why, you'll shake me to death. There, now, do go away up to the housekeeper's room and get your suppers; you know I haven't time to talk. You'll find plenty more in the house.—Now, Master East, do let those things alone. You're mixing up three new boys' things." And she rushed at East, who escaped round the open trunks holding up a prize.

"Hullo! look here, Tommy," shouted he; "here's fun!" and he brandished above his head some pretty little night-caps, beautifully made and marked, the work of loving fingers in some distant country home. The kind mother and sisters who sewed that delicate stitching with aching hearts little thought of the trouble they might be bringing on the young head for which they were meant. The little matron was wiser, and snatched the caps from East before he could look at the name on them.

"Now, Master East, I shall be very angry if you don't go," said she; "there's some capital cold beef and pickles upstairs, and I won't have you old boys in my room first night."

"Hurrah for the pickles! Come along, Tommy—come along, Smith. We shall find out who the young count is, I'll be bound. I hope he'll sleep in my room. Mary's always vicious first week."

As the boys turned to leave the room, the matron touched Tom's arm, and said, "Master Brown, please stop a minute; I want to speak to you."

"Very well, Mary.—I'll come in a minute, East. Don't finish the pickles."

"O Master Brown," went on the little matron, when the rest had gone, "you're to have Gray's study, Mrs. Arnold says. And she wants you to take in this young gentleman. He's a new boy, and thirteen years old, though he don't look it. He's very delicate, and has never been from home before. And I told Mrs. Arnold I thought you'd be kind to him, and see that they don't bully him at first. He's put into your form, and I've given him the bed next to yours in Number 4; so East can't sleep there this half."

Tom was rather put about by this speech. He had got the double study which he coveted, but here were conditions attached which greatly moderated his joy. He looked across the room, and in the far corner of the sofa was aware of a slight, pale boy, with large blue eyes and light fair hair, who seemed ready to shrink through the floor. He saw at a glance that the little stranger was just the boy whose first half-year at a public school would be misery to himself if he were left alone, or constant anxiety to any one who meant to see him through his troubles. Tom was too honest to take in the youngster, and then let him shift for himself; and if he took him as his chum instead of East, where were all his pet plans of having a bottled-beer cellar under his window, and making night-lines and slings, and plotting expeditions to Brownsover Mills and Caldecott's Spinney? East and he had made up their minds to get this study, and then every night from locking-up till ten they would be together to talk about fishing, drink bottled-beer, read Marryat's novels, and sort birds' eggs. And this new boy would most likely never go out of the close, and would be afraid of wet feet, and always getting laughed at, and called Molly, or Jenny, or some derogatory feminine nickname.

The matron watched him for a moment, and saw what was passing in his mind, and so, like a wise negotiator, threw in an appeal to his warm heart. " Poor little fellow," said she, in almost a whisper; "his father's dead, and he's got no brothers. And his mamma—such a kind, sweet lady—almost broke her heart at leaving him this morning; and she said one of his sisters was like to die of decline, and so——"

"Well, well," burst in Tom, with something like a sigh at the effort, "I suppose I must give up East. —Come along, young un. What's your name? We'll go and have some supper, and then I'll show you our study."

"His name's George Arthur," said the matron, walking up to him with Tom, who grasped his little delicate hand as the proper preliminary to making a chum of him, and felt as if he could have blown him away. "I've had his books and things put into the study, which his mamma has had new papered, and the sofa covered, and new green-baize curtains over the door" (the diplomatic matron threw this in, to show that the new boy was contributing largely to the partnership comforts). "And Mrs. Arnold told me to say," she added, "that she should like you both to come up to tea with her. You know the way, Master Brown, and the things are just gone up, I know."

Here was an announcement for Master Tom! He was to go up to tea the first night, just as if he were a sixth or fifth form boy, and of importance in the School world, instead of the most reckless young scapegrace amongst the fags. He felt himself lifted on to a higher social and moral platform at once. Nevertheless he couldn't give up without a sigh the idea of the jolly supper in the housekeeper's room with East and the rest, and a rush round to all the studies of his friends afterwards, to pour out the deeds and wonders of the holidays, to plot fifty plans for the coming half-year, and to gather news of who had left and what new boys had come, who had got who's study, and where the new prepostors slept. However, Tom consoled himself with thinking that he couldn't have done all this with the new boy at his heels, and so marched off along the passages to the Doctor's private house with his young charge in tow, in monstrous good-humour with himself and all the world.

It is needless, and would be impertinent, to tell how the two young boys were received in that drawing-room. The lady who presided there is still living, and has carried with her to her peaceful home in the north the respect and love of all those who ever felt and shared that gentle and high-bred hospitality. Ay, many is the brave heart, now doing its work and bearing its load in country curacies, London chambers, under the Indian sun, and in Australian towns and clearings, which looks back with fond and grateful memory to that School-house drawing-room, and dates much of its highest and best training to the lessons learnt there.

Besides Mrs. Arnold and one or two of the elder children, there were one of the younger masters, young Brooke (who was now in the sixth, and had succeeded to his brother's position and influence), and another sixth-form boy, talking together before the fire. The master and young Brooke, now a great strapping fellow six feet high, eighteen years old, and powerful as a coal-heaver, nodded kindly to Tom, to his intense glory, and then went on talking. The other did not notice them. The hostess, after a few kind words, which led the boys at once and insensibly to feel at their ease and to begin talking to one another, left them with her own children while she finished a letter. The young ones got on fast and well, Tom holding forth about a prodigious pony he had been riding out hunting, and hearing stories of

the winter glories of the lakes, when tea came in, and
immediately after the Doctor himself.

How frank, and kind, and manly was his greeting to
the party by the fire !   It did Tom's heart good to see him
and young Brooke shake hands, and look one another in
the face ; and he didn't fail to remark that Brooke was
nearly as tall and quite as broad as the Doctor.   And
his cup was full when in another moment his master
turned to him with another warm shake of the hand,
and, seemingly oblivious of all the late scrapes which he
had been getting into, said, " Ah, Brown, you here !
I hope you left your father and all well at home ? "

" Yes, sir, quite well."

" And this is the little fellow who is to share your
study.   Well, he doesn't look as we should like to see
him.   He wants some Rugby air, and cricket.   And you
must take him some good long walks, to Bilton Grange,
and Caldecott's Spinney, and show him what a little
pretty country we have about here."

Tom wondered if the Doctor knew that his visits to
Bilton Grange were for the purpose of taking rooks'
nests (a proceeding strongly discountenanced by the
owner thereof), and those to Caldecott's Spinney were
prompted chiefly by the conveniences for setting night-
lines.   What didn't the Doctor know ?   And what a
noble use he always made of it !   He almost resolved
to abjure rook-pies and night-lines for ever.   The tea
went merrily off, the Doctor now talking of holiday
doings, and then of the prospects of the half-year—what
chance there was for the Balliol scholarship, whether
the eleven would be a good one.   Everybody was at his
ease, and everybody felt that he, young as he might
be, was of some use in the little School world, and had
a work to do there.

Soon after tea the Doctor went off to his study, and the young boys a few minutes afterwards took their leave and went out of the private door which led from the Doctor's house into the middle passage.

At the fire, at the farther end of the passage, was a crowd of boys in loud talk and laughter. There was a sudden pause when the door opened, and then a great shout of greeting, as Tom was recognized marching down the passage.

" Hullo, Brown! where do you come from ? "

" Oh, I've been to tea with the Doctor," says Tom, with great dignity.

" My eye ! " cried East. " Oh ! so that's why Mary called you back, and you didn't come to supper. You lost something. That beef and pickles was no end good."

" I say, young fellow," cried Hall, detecting Arthur, and catching him by the collar, " what's your name ? Where do you come from ?   How old are you ? "

Tom saw Arthur shrink back and look scared as all the group turned to him, but thought it best to let him answer, just standing by his side to support in case of need.

" Arthur, sir.   I come from Devonshire."

" Don't call me ' sir,' you young muff.   How old are you ? "

" Thirteen."

" Can you sing ? "

The poor boy was trembling and hesitating. Tom struck in—" You be hanged, Tadpole. He'll have to sing, whether he can or not, Saturday twelve weeks, and that's long enough off yet."

" Do you know him at home, Brown ? "

" No ; but he's my chum in Gray's old study, and it's

near prayer-time, and I haven't had a look at it yet.—
Come along, Arthur."

Away went the two, Tom longing to get his charge
safe under cover, where he might advise him on his
deportment.

"What a queer chum for Tom Brown," was the comment at the fire; and it must be confessed so thought
Tom himself, as he lighted his candle, and surveyed the
new green-baize curtains and the carpet and sofa with
much satisfaction.

"I say, Arthur, what a brick your mother is to make
us so cozy! But look here now; you must answer straight
up when the fellows speak to you, and don't be afraid.
If you're afraid, you'll get bullied. And don't you say
you can sing; and don't you ever talk about home, or
your mother and sisters."

Poor little Arthur looked ready to cry.

"But, please," said he, "mayn't I talk about—about
home to you?"

"Oh yes; I like it. But don't talk to boys you don't
know, or they'll call you home-sick, or mamma's darling,
or some such stuff. What a jolly desk! Is that yours?
And what stunning binding! Why, your school-books
look like novels."

And Tom was soon deep in Arthur's goods and chattels,
all new, and good enough for a fifth-form boy, and hardly
thought of his friends outside till the prayer-bell rang.

I have already described the School-house prayers.
They were the same on the first night as on the other
nights, save for the gaps caused by the absence of those
boys who came late, and the line of new boys who stood
all together at the farther table—of all sorts and sizes,
like young bears with all their troubles to come, as Tom's
father had said to him when he was in the same position.

He thought of it as he looked at the line, and poor little slight Arthur standing with them, and as he was leading him upstairs to Number 4, directly after prayers, and showing him his bed. It was a huge, high, airy room, with two large windows looking on to the School close. There were twelve beds in the room. The one in the farthest corner by the fireplace, occupied by the sixth-form boy, who was responsible for the discipline of the room, and the rest by boys in the lower-fifth and other junior forms, all fags (for the fifth-form boys, as has been said, slept in rooms by themselves). Being fags, the eldest of them was not more than about sixteen years old, and were all bound to be up and in bed by ten. The sixth-form boys came to bed from ten to a quarter-past (at which time the old verger came round to put the candles out), except when they sat up to read.

Within a few minutes therefore of their entry, all the other boys who slept in Number 4 had come up. The little fellows went quietly to their own beds, and began undressing, and talking to each other in whispers; while the elder, amongst whom was Tom, sat chatting about on one another's beds, with their jackets and waistcoats off. Poor little Arthur was overwhelmed with the novelty of his position. The idea of sleeping in the room with strange boys had clearly never crossed his mind before, and was as painful as it was strange to him. He could hardly bear to take his jacket off; however, presently, with an effort, off it came, and then he paused and looked at Tom, who was sitting at the bottom of his bed talking and laughing.

"Please, Brown," he whispered, "may I wash my face and hands?"

"Of course, if you like," said Tom, staring; "that's your washhand-stand, under the window, second from your bed. You'll have to go down for more water in the morning if you use it all." And on he went with his talk, while Arthur stole timidly from between the beds out to his washhand-stand, and began his ablutions, thereby drawing for a moment on himself the attention of the room.

On went the talk and laughter. Arthur finished his washing and undressing, and put on his night-gown. He then looked round more nervously than ever. Two or three of the little boys were already in bed, sitting up with their chins on their knees. The light burned clear, the noise went on. It was a trying moment for the poor little lonely boy ; however, this time he didn't ask Tom what he might or might not do, but dropped on his knees by his bedside, as he had done every day from his child-hood, to open his heart to Him who heareth the cry and beareth the sorrows of the tender child, and the strong man in agony.

Tom was sitting at the bottom of his bed unlacing his boots, so that his back was towards Arthur, and he didn't see what had happened, and looked up in wonder at the sudden silence. Then two or three boys laughed and sneered, and a big, brutal fellow who was standing in the middle of the room picked up a slipper, and shied it at the kneeling boy, calling him a snivelling young shaver. Then Tom saw the whole, and the next moment the boot he had just pulled off flew straight at the head of the bully, who had just time to throw up his arm and catch it on his elbow.

"Confound you, Brown! what's that for ?" roared he, stamping with pain.

"Never mind what I mean," said Tom, stepping on to the floor, every drop of blood in his body tingling; "if any fellow wants the other boot, he knows how to get it."

What would have been the result is doubtful, for at this moment the sixth-form boy came in, and not another word could be said. Tom and the rest rushed into bed and finished their unrobing there, and the old verger, as punctual as the clock, had put out the candle in another minute, and toddled on to the next room, shutting their door with his usual " Good-night, gen'lm'n."

There were many boys in the room by whom that little scene was taken to heart before they slept. But sleep seemed to have deserted the pillow of poor Tom. For some time his excitement, and the flood of memories which chased one another through his brain, kept him from thinking or resolving. His head throbbed, his heart leapt, and he could hardly keep himself from springing out of bed and rushing about the room. Then the thought of his own mother came across him, and the promise he had made at her knee, years ago, never to forget to kneel by his bedside, and give himself up to his Father, before he laid his head on the pillow, from which it might never rise; and he lay down gently, and cried as if his heart would break. He was only fourteen years old.

It was no light act of courage in those days, my dear boys, for a little fellow to say his prayers publicly, even at Rugby. A few years later, when Arnold's manly piety had begun to leaven the School, the tables turned; before he died, in the School-house at least, and I believe in the other house, the rule was the other way. But poor Tom had come to school in other times. The first few nights after he came he did not kneel down because of the noise, but sat up in bed till the candle was out, and then stole out and said his prayers, in fear lest some one should find him out. So did many another poor little fellow. Then he began to think that he might just as

well say his prayers in bed, and then that it didn't
matter whether he was kneeling, or sitting, or lying down.
And so it had come to pass with Tom, as with all who
will not confess their Lord before men ; and for the last
year he had probably not said his prayers in earnest a
dozen times.

Poor Tom ! the first and bitterest feeling which was
like to break his heart was the sense of his own
cowardice. The vice of all others which he loathed was
brought in and burnt in on his own soul. He had lied
to his mother, to his conscience, to his God. How could
he bear it ? And then the poor little weak boy, whom
he had pitied and almost scorned for his weakness, had
done that which he, braggart as he was, dared not do.
The first dawn of comfort came to him in swearing to
himself that he would stand by that boy through thick
and thin, and cheer him, and help him, and bear his
burdens for the good deed done that night. Then he
resolved to write home next day and tell his mother all,
and what a coward her son had been. And then peace
came to him as he resolved, lastly, to bear his testimony
next morning. The morning would be harder than the
night to begin with, but he felt that he could not afford
to let one chance slip. Several times he faltered, for
the devil showed him first all his old friends calling
him " Saint " and " Square-toes," and a dozen hard
names, and whispered to him that his motives would be
misunderstood, and he would only be left alone with the
new boy ; whereas it was his duty to keep all means of
influence, that he might do good to the largest number.
And then came the more subtle temptation, " Shall I
not be showing myself braver than others by doing this ?
Have I any right to begin it now ? Ought I not rather
to pray in my own study, letting other boys know that I

do so, and trying to lead them to it, while in public at least I should go on as I have done?" However, his good angel was too strong that night, and he turned on his side and slept, tired of trying to reason, but resolved to follow the impulse which had been so strong, and in which he had found peace.

Next morning he was up and washed and dressed, all but his jacket and waistcoat, just as the ten minutes' bell began to ring, and then in the face of the whole room knelt down to pray. Not five words could he say—the bell mocked him; he was listening for every whisper in the room—what were they all thinking of him? He was ashamed to go on kneeling, ashamed to rise from his knees. At last, as it were from his inmost heart, a still, small voice seemed to breathe forth the words of the publican, "God be merciful to me a sinner!" He repeated them over and over, clinging to them as for his life, and rose from his knees comforted and humbled, and ready to face the whole world. It was not needed: two other boys besides Arthur had already followed his example, and he went down to the great School with a glimmering of another lesson in his heart—the lesson that he who has conquered his own coward spirit has conquered the whole outward world; and that other one which the old prophet learnt in the cave in Mount Horeb, when he hid his face, and the still, small voice asked, "What doest thou here, Elijah?" that however we may fancy ourselves alone on the side of good, the King and Lord of men is nowhere without His witnesses; for in every society, however seemingly corrupt and godless, there are those who have not bowed the knee to Baal.

He found, too, how greatly he had exaggerated the effect to be produced by his act. For a few nights there was a sneer or a laugh when he knelt down, but this passed off soon, and one by one all the other boys but three or four followed the lead. I fear that this was in some measure owing to the fact that Tom could probably have thrashed any boy in the room except the prepostor; at any rate, every boy knew that he would try upon very slight provocation, and didn't choose to run the risk of a hard fight because Tom Brown had taken a fancy to say his prayers. Some of the small boys of Number 4 communicated the new state of things to their chums, and in several other rooms the poor little fellows tried it on—in one instance or so, where the prepostor heard of it and interfered very decidedly, with partial success; but in the rest, after a short struggle, the confessors were bullied or laughed down, and the old state of things went on for some time longer. Before either Tom Brown or Arthur left the School-house, there was no room in which it had not become the regular custom. I trust it is so still, and that the old heathen state of things has gone out for ever.

CHAPTER II.

THE NEW BOY.

> " And Heaven's rich instincts in him grew,
>   As effortless as woodland nooks
>   Send violets up and paint them blue."—LOWELL.

I DO not mean to recount all the little troubles and annoyances which thronged upon Tom at the beginning of this half-year, in his new character of bear-leader to a gentle little boy straight from home. He seemed to himself to have become a new boy again, without any of the long-suffering and meekness indispensable for supporting that character with moderate success. From morning till night he had the feeling of responsibility on his mind, and even if he left Arthur in their study or in the close for an hour, was never at ease till he had him in sight again. He waited for him at the doors of the school after every lesson and every calling-over; watched that no tricks were played him, and none but the regulation questions asked; kept his eye on his plate at dinner and breakfast, to see that no unfair depredations were made upon his viands; in short, as East remarked, cackled after him like a hen with one chick.

Arthur took a long time thawing, too, which made it all the harder work; was sadly timid; scarcely ever spoke unless Tom spoke to him first; and, worst of all, would agree with him in everything—the hardest thing in the world for a Brown to bear. He got quite angry sometimes, as they sat together of a night in their study, at this provoking habit of agreement, and was on the point of breaking out a dozen times with a lecture upon the propriety of a fellow having a will of his own and speaking out, but managed to restrain himself by the thought that he might only frighten Arthur, and the remembrance of the lesson he had learnt from him on his first night at Number 4. Then he would resolve to sit still and not say a word till Arthur began; but he was always beat at that game, and had presently to begin talking in despair, fearing lest Arthur might think he was vexed at something if he didn't, and dog-tired of sitting tongue-tied.

It was hard work. But Tom had taken it up, and meant to stick to it, and go through with it so as to satisfy himself; in which resolution he was much assisted by the chaffing of East and his other old friends, who began to call him " dry-nurse," and otherwise to break their small wit on him. But when they took other ground, as they did every now and then, Tom was sorely puzzled.

"Tell you what, Tommy," East would say; "you'll spoil young Hopeful with too much coddling. Why can't you let him go about by himself and find his own level? He'll never be worth a button if you go on keeping him under your skirts."

"Well, but he ain't fit to fight his own way yet; I'm trying to get him to it every day, but he's very odd. Poor little beggar! I can't make him out a bit. He ain't a bit like anything I've ever seen or heard of—he seems all over nerves; anything you say seems to hurt him like a cut or a blow."

"That sort of boy's no use here," said East; "he'll only spoil. Now I'll tell you what to do, Tommy. Go and get a nice large band-box made, and put him in with plenty of cotton-wool and a pap-bottle, labelled 'With care—this side up,' and send him back to mamma."

"I think I shall make a hand of him though," said Tom, smiling, "say what you will. There's something about him, every now and then, which shows me he's got pluck somewhere in him. That's the only thing after all that'll wash, ain't it, old Scud? But how to get at it and bring it out?"

Tom took one hand out of his breeches-pocket and stuck it in his back hair for a scratch, giving his hat a tilt over his nose, his one method of invoking wisdom. He stared at the ground with a ludicrously puzzled look, and presently looked up and met East's eyes. That young gentleman slapped him on the back, and then put his arm round his shoulder, as they strolled through the quadrangle together. "Tom," said he, "blest if you ain't the best old fellow ever was. I do like to see you go into a thing. Hang it, I wish I could take things as you do; but I never can get higher than a joke. Everything's a joke. If I was going to be flogged next minute, I should be in a blue funk, but I couldn't help laughing at it for the life of me."

"Brown and East, you go and fag for Jones on the great fives court."

"Hullo, though, that's past a joke," broke out East, springing at the young gentleman who addressed them, and catching him by the collar.—"Here, Tommy, catch hold of him t'other side before he can holla."

The youth was seized, and dragged, struggling, out of the quadrangle into the School-house hall. He was one of the miserable little pretty white-handed, curly-headed boys, petted and pampered by some of the big fellows, who wrote their verses for them, taught them to drink and use bad language, and did all they could to spoil them for everything * in this world and the next. One of the avocations in which these young gentlemen took particular delight was in going about and getting fags for their protectors, when those heroes were playing any game. They carried about pencil and paper with them, putting down the names of all the boys they sent, always sending five times as many as were wanted, and getting all those thrashed who didn't go. The present youth belonged to a house which was very jealous of the School-house, and always picked out School-house fags when he could find them. However, this time he'd got the wrong sow by the ear. His captors slammed the great door of the hall, and East put his back against it, while Tom gave the prisoner a shake up, took away his list, and stood him up on the floor, while he proceeded leisurely to examine that document.

* A kind and wise critic, an old Rugbœan, notes here in the margin: "The small friend system was not so utterly bad from 1841-1847." Before that, too, there were many noble friendships between big and little boys; but I can't strike out the passage. Many boys will know why it is left in.

"Let me out, let me go!" screamed the boy, in a furious passion. "I'll go and tell Jones this minute, and he'll give you both the —— thrashing you ever had."

"Pretty little dear," said East, patting the top of his hat.—"Hark how he swears, Tom. Nicely brought up young man, ain't he, I don't think."

"Let me alone, —— you," roared the boy, foaming with rage, and kicking at East, who quietly tripped him up, and deposited him on the floor in a place of safety.

"Gently, young fellow," said he; "'tain't improving for little whippersnappers like you to be indulging in blasphemy; so you stop that, or you'll get something you won't like."

"I'll have you both licked when I get out, that I will," rejoined the boy, beginning to snivel.

"Two can play at that game, mind you," said Tom, who had finished his examination of the list. "Now you just listen here. We've just come across the fives court, and Jones has four fags there already—two more than he wants. If he'd wanted us to change, he'd have stopped us himself. And here, you little blackguard, you've got seven names down on your list besides ours, and five of them School-house." Tom walked up to him, and jerked him on to his legs; he was by this time whining like a whipped puppy. "Now just listen to me. We ain't going to fag for Jones. If you tell him you've sent us, we'll each of us give you such a thrashing as you'll remember." And Tom tore up the list and threw the pieces into the fire.

"And mind you, too," said East, "don't let me catch you again sneaking about the School-house, and picking up our fags. You haven't got the sort of hide to take a sound licking kindly." And he opened the door and sent the young gentleman flying into the quadrangle with a parting kick.

"Nice boy, Tommy," said East, shoving his hands in his pockets, and strolling to the fire.

"Worst sort we breed," responded Tom, following his example. "Thank goodness, no big fellow ever took to petting me."

"You'd never have been like that," said East. "I should like to have put him in a museum : Christian young gentleman, nineteenth century, highly educated. Stir him up with a long pole, Jack, and hear him swear like a drunken sailor. He'd make a respectable public open its eyes, I think."

"Think he'll tell Jones ? " said Tom.

"No," said East. "Don't care if he does."

"Nor I," said Tom. And they went back to talk about Arthur.

The young gentleman had brains enough not to tell Jones, reasoning that East and Brown, who were noted as some of the toughest fags in the School, wouldn't care three straws for any licking Jones might give them, and would be likely to keep their words as to passing it on with interest.

After the above conversation, East came a good deal to their study, and took notice of Arthur, and soon allowed to Tom that he was a thorough little gentleman, and would get over his shyness all in good time ; which much comforted our hero. He felt every day, too, the value of having an object in his life—something that drew him out of himself ; and it being the dull time of the year, and no games going about for which he much cared, was happier than he had ever yet been at school, which was saying a great deal.

The time which Tom allowed himself away from his charge was from locking-up till supper-time. During this hour or hour and a half he used to take his fling, going round to the studies of all his acquaintance, sparring or gossiping in the hall, now jumping the old iron-bound tables, or carving a bit of his name on them, then joining in some chorus of merry voices—in fact, blowing off his steam, as we should now call it.

This process was so congenial to his temper, and Arthur showed himself so pleased at the arrangement, that it was several weeks before Tom was ever in their study before supper. One evening, however, he rushed in to look for an old chisel, or some corks, or other article essential to his pursuit for the time being, and while rummaging about in the cupboards, looked up for a moment, and was caught at once by the figure of poor little Arthur. The boy was sitting with his elbows on the table, and his head leaning on his hands, and before him an open book, on which his tears were falling fast. Tom shut the door at once, and sat down on the sofa by Arthur, putting his arm round his neck.

"Why, young un, what's the matter?" said he kindly; "you ain't unhappy, are you?"

"Oh no, Brown," said the little boy, looking up with the great tears in his eyes; "you are so kind to me, I'm very happy."

"Why don't you call me Tom? Lots of boys do that I don't like half so much as you. What are you reading, then? Hang it! you must come about with me, and not mope yourself." And Tom cast down his eyes on the book, and saw it was the Bible. He was silent for a minute, and thought to himself, "Lesson Number 2, Tom Brown;" and then said gently, "I'm very glad to see this, Arthur, and ashamed that I don't read the Bible more myself. Do you read it every night before supper while I'm out?"

"Yes."

"Well, I wish you'd wait till afterwards, and then we'd read together. But, Arthur, why does it make you cry?"

"Oh, it isn't that I'm unhappy. But at home, while my father was alive, we always read the lessons after tea; and I love to read them over now, and try to remember what he said about them. I can't remember all, and I think I scarcely understand a great deal of what I do remember. But it all comes back to me so fresh that I can't help crying sometimes to think I shall never read them again with him."

Arthur had never spoken of his home before, and Tom hadn't encouraged him to do so, as his blundering school-boy reasoning made him think that Arthur would be softened and less manly for thinking of home. But now he was fairly interested, and forgot all about chisels and bottled beer; while with very little encouragement Arthur launched into his home history, and the prayer-bell put them both out sadly when it rang to call them to the hall.

From this time Arthur constantly spoke of his home, and above all, of his father, who had been dead about a year, and whose memory Tom soon got to love and reverence almost as much as his own son did.

Arthur's father had been the clergyman of a parish in the Midland counties, which had risen into a large town during the war, and upon which the hard years which followed had fallen with fearful weight. The trade had been half ruined; and then came the old, sad story, of masters reducing their establishments, men turned off and wandering about, hungry and wan in body, and fierce in soul, from the thought of wives and children

starving at home, and the last sticks of furniture going
to the pawnshop; children taken from school, and
lounging about the dirty streets and courts, too listless
almost to play, and squalid in rags and misery; and
then the fearful struggle between the employers and men
—lowerings of wages, strikes, and the long course of oft-
repeated crime, ending every now and then with a riot,
a fire, and the county yeomanry. There is no need here
to dwell upon such tales : the Englishman into whose
soul they have not sunk deep is not worthy the name.
You English boys, for whom this book is meant (God
bless your bright faces and kind hearts !), will learn it
all soon enough.

Into such a parish and state of society Arthur's father
had been thrown at the age of twenty-five—a young
married parson, full of faith, hope, and love. He had
battled with it like a man, and had lots of fine Utopian
ideas about the perfectibility of mankind, glorious
humanity, and such-like, knocked out of his head, and
a real, wholesome Christian love for the poor, struggling,
sinning men, of whom he felt himself one, and with and
for whom he spent fortune, and strength, and life, driven
into his heart. He had battled like a man, and gotten
a man's reward—no silver tea-pots or salvers, with
flowery inscriptions setting forth his virtues and the
appreciation of a genteel parish ; no fat living or stall,
for which he never looked, and didn't care ; no sighs and
praises of comfortable dowagers and well-got-up young
women, who worked him slippers, sugared his tea, and
adored him as " a devoted man ; " but a manly respect,
wrung from the unwilling souls of men who fancied his
order their natural enemies ; the fear and hatred of
every one who was false or unjust in the district, were
he master or man ; and the blessed sight of women and

children daily becoming more human and more homely, a comfort to themselves and to their husbands and fathers.

These things, of course, took time, and had to be fought for with toil and sweat of brain and heart, and with the life-blood poured out. All that, Arthur had laid his account to give, and took as a matter of course, neither pitying himself, nor looking on himself as a martyr, when he felt the wear and tear making him feel old before his time, and the stifling air of fever-dens telling on his health. His wife seconded him in everything. She had been rather fond of society, and much admired and run after before her marriage; and the London world to which she had belonged pitied poor Fanny Evelyn when she married the young clergyman, and went to settle in that smoky hole Turley, a very nest of Chartism and Atheism, in a part of the country which all the decent families had had to leave for years. However, somehow or other she didn't seem to care. If her husband's living had been amongst green fields and near pleasant neighbours she would have liked it better—that she never pretended to deny. But there they were. The air wasn't bad, after all; the people were very good sort of people —civil to you if you were civil to them, after the first brush; and they didn't expect to work miracles, and convert them all off-hand into model Christians. So he and she went quietly among the folk, talking to and treating them just as they would have done people of their own rank. They didn't feel that they were doing anything out of the common way, and so were perfectly natural, and had none of that condescension or consciousness of manner which so outrages the independent poor. And thus they gradually won respect and confidence; and after sixteen years he was looked up to by the whole neighbourhood as *the* just man, *the* man to whom masters and men could go in their strikes, and in all their quarrels and difficulties, and by whom the right and true word would be said without fear or favour. And the women had come round to take her advice, and go to her as a friend in all their troubles; while the children all worshipped the very ground she trod on.

They had three children, two daughters and a son, little Arthur, who came between his sisters. He had been a very delicate boy from his childhood; they thought he had a tendency to consumption, and so he had been kept at home and taught by his father, who had made a companion of him, and from whom he had gained good scholarship, and a knowledge of and interest in many subjects which boys in general never come across till they are many years older.

Just as he reached his thirteenth year, and his father had settled that he was strong enough to go to school, and, after much debating with himself, had resolved to send him there, a desperate typhus fever broke out in the town. Most of the other clergy, and almost all the doctors, ran away; the work fell with tenfold weight on those who stood to their work. Arthur and his wife both caught the fever, of which he died in a few days; and she recovered, having been able to nurse him to the end, and store up his last words. He was sensible to the last, and calm and happy, leaving his wife and children with fearless trust for a few years in the hands of the Lord and Friend who had lived and died for him, and for whom he, to the best of his power, had lived and died. His widow's mourning was deep and gentle. She was more affected by the request of the committee of a freethinking club, established in the town by some of the factory hands (which he had striven against with might and main, and nearly suppressed), that some of their number might

be allowed to help bear the coffin, than by anything else.
Two of them were chosen, who, with six other labouring
men, his own fellow-workmen and friends, bore him to
his grave—a man who had fought the Lord's fight even
unto the death. The shops were closed and the factories
shut that day in the parish, yet no master stopped the
day's wages ; but for many a year afterwards the towns-
folk felt the want of that brave, hopeful, loving parson
and his wife, who had lived to teach them mutual forbear-
ance and helpfulness, and had *almost* at last given them
a glimpse of what this old world would be if people would
live for God and each other instead of for themselves.

What has all this to do with our story ? Well, my
dear boys, let a fellow go on his own way, or you won't
get anything out of him worth having. I must show
you what sort of a man it was who had begotten and
trained little Arthur, or else you won't believe in him,
which I am resolved you shall do ; and you won't see
how he, the timid, weak boy, had points in him from
which the bravest and strongest recoiled, and made his
presence and example felt from the first on all sides, un-
consciously to himself, and without the least attempt at
proselytizing. The spirit of his father was in him, and
the Friend to whom his father had left him did not neg-
lect the trust.

After supper that night, and almost nightly for years
afterwards, Tom and Arthur, and by degrees East occasionally, and sometimes one, sometimes another, of their
friends, read a chapter of the Bible together, and talked
it over afterwards. Tom was at first utterly astonished,
and almost shocked, at the sort of way in which Arthur
read the book and talked about the men and women
whose lives were there told. The first night they happened to fall on the chapters about the famine in Egypt,

and Arthur began talking about Joseph as if he were a living statesman—just as he might have talked about Lord Grey and the Reform Bill, only that they were much more living realities to him. The book was to him, Tom saw, the most vivid and delightful history of real people, who might do right or wrong, just like any one who was walking about in Rugby—the Doctor, or the masters, or the sixth-form boys. But the astonishment soon passed off, the scales seemed to drop from his eyes, and the book became at once and for ever to him the great human and divine book, and the men and women, whom he had looked upon as something quite different from himself, became his friends and counsellors.

For our purposes, however, the history of one night's reading will be sufficient, which must be told here, now we are on the subject, though it didn't happen till a year afterwards, and long after the events recorded in the next chapter of our story.

Arthur, Tom, and East were together one night, and read the story of Naaman coming to Elisha to be cured of his leprosy. When the chapter was finished, Tom shut his Bible with a slap.

" I can't stand that fellow Naaman," said he, " after what he'd seen and felt, going back and bowing himself down in the house of Rimmon, because his effeminate scoundrel of a master did it. I wonder Elisha took the trouble to heal him. How he must have despised him ! "

" Yes ; there you go off as usual, with a shell on your head," struck in East, who always took the opposite side to Tom, half from love of argument, half from conviction. " How do you know he didn't think better of it ? How do you know his master was a scoundrel ? His letter don't look like it, and the book don't say so."

" I don't care," rejoined Tom ; " why did Naaman talk

about bowing down, then, if he didn't mean to do it ? He wasn't likely to get more in earnest when he got back to court, and away from the prophet."

" Well, but, Tom," said Arthur, " look what Elisha says to him—' Go in peace.' He wouldn't have said that if Naaman had been in the wrong."

" I don't see that that means more than saying, ' You're not the man I took you for.' "

" No, no ; that won't do at all," said East. " Read the words fairly, and take men as you find them. I like Naaman, and think he was a very fine fellow."

" I don't," said Tom positively.

" Well, I think East is right," said Arthur ; " I can't see but what it's right to do the best you can, though it mayn't be the best absolutely. Every man isn't born to be a martyr."

" Of course, of course," said East ; " but he's on one of his pet hobbies.—How often have I told you, Tom, that you must drive a nail where it'll go."

" And how often have I told you," rejoined Tom, " that it'll always go where you want, if you only stick to it and hit hard enough. I hate half-measures and compromises."

" Yes, he's a whole-hog man, is Tom. Must have the whole animal—hair and teeth, claws and tail," laughed East. "Sooner have no bread any day than half the loaf."

" I don't know," said Arthur—" it's rather puzzling ; " but ain't most right things got by proper compromises —I mean where the principle isn't given up ? "

" That's just the point," said Tom ; " I don't object to a compromise, where you don't give up your principle."

" Not you," said East laughingly.—" I know him of old, Arthur, and you'll find him out some day. There isn't such a reasonable fellow in the world, to hear him talk. He never wants anything but what's right and fair ; only when you come to settle what's right and fair, it's everything that he wants, and nothing that you want. And that's his idea of a compromise. Give me the Brown compromise when I'm on his side."

"Now, Harry," said Tom, "no more chaff. I'm serious. Look here. This is what makes my blood tingle." And he turned over the pages of his Bible and read, "Shadrach, Meshach, and Abed-nego answered and said to the king, O Nebuchadnezzar, we are not careful to answer thee in this matter. If it *be* so, our God whom we serve is able to deliver us from the burning fiery furnace, and he will deliver us out of thine hand, O king. But *if not*, be it known unto thee, O king, that we will *not* serve thy gods, nor worship the golden image which thou hast set up." He read the last verse twice, emphasizing the nots, and dwelling on them as if they gave him actual pleasure, and were hard to part with.

They were silent a minute, and then Arthur said, "Yes, that's a glorious story, but it don't prove your point, Tom, I think. There are times when there is only one way, and that the highest, and then the men are found to stand in the breach."

"There's always a highest way, and it's always the right one," said Tom. "How many times has the Doctor told us that in his sermons in the last year, I should like to know?"

"Well, you ain't going to convince us—is he, Arthur? No Brown compromise to-night," said East, looking at his watch. "But it's past eight, and we must go to first lesson. What a bore!"

So they took down their books and fell to work ; but Arthur didn't forget, and thought long and often over the conversation.

CHAPTER III.

ARTHUR MAKES A FRIEND.

" Let Nature be your teacher :
        Sweet is the lore which Nature brings.
        Our meddling intellect
        Misshapes the beauteous forms of things.
        We murder to dissect.
        Enough of Science and of Art :
        Close up those barren leaves ;
        Come forth, and bring with you a heart
        That watches and receives."—WORDSWORTH.

ABOUT six weeks after the beginning of the half, as Tom and Arthur were sitting one night before supper beginning their verses, Arthur suddenly stopped, and looked up, and said, " Tom, do you know anything of Martin ? "

" Yes," said Tom, taking his hand out of his back hair, and delighted to throw his Gradus ad Parnassum on to the sofa ; " I know him pretty well. He's a very good fellow, but as mad as a hatter. He's called Madman, you know. And never was such a fellow for getting all sorts of rum things about him. He tamed two snakes last half, and used to carry them about in his pocket ; and I'll be bound he's got some hedgehogs and rats in his cupboard now, and no one knows what besides."

" I should like very much to know him," said Arthur ; " he was next to me in the form to-day, and he'd lost his book and looked over mine, and he seemed so kind and gentle that I liked him very much."

" Ah, poor old Madman, he's always losing his books," said Tom, " and getting called up and floored because he hasn't got them."

" I like him all the better," said Arthur.

" Well, he's great fun, I can tell you," said Tom, throwing himself back on the sofa, and chuckling at the remem-

brance. "We had such a game with him one day last
half. He had been kicking up horrid stinks for some
time in his study, till I suppose some fellow told Mary,
and she told the Doctor. Anyhow, one day a little
before dinner, when he came down from the library, the
Doctor, instead of going home, came striding into the
hall. East and I and five or six other fellows were at
the fire, and preciously we stared, for he don't come in
like that once a year, unless it is a wet day and there's
a fight in the hall. 'East,' says he, 'just come and show
me Martin's study.' 'Oh, here's a game,' whispered
the rest of us; and we all cut upstairs after the Doctor,
East leading. As we got into the New Row, which was
hardly wide enough to hold the Doctor and his gown,
click, click, click, we heard in the old Madman's den.
Then that stopped all of a sudden, and the bolts went
to like fun. The Madman knew East's step, and thought
there was going to be a siege.

"'It's the Doctor, Martin. He's here and wants to
see you,' sings out East.

"Then the bolts went back slowly, and the door
opened, and there was the old Madman standing, looking precious scared—his jacket off, his shirt-sleeves up
to his elbows, and his long skinny arms all covered with
anchors and arrows and letters, tattooed in with gun-
powder like a sailor-boy's, and a stink fit to knock you
down coming out. 'Twas all the Doctor could do to
stand his ground, and East and I, who were looking in
under his arms, held our noses tight. The old magpie
was standing on the window-sill, all his feathers droop-
ing, and looking disgusted and half-poisoned.

"'What can you be about, Martin?' says the Doctor.
'You really mustn't go on in this way; you're a nuisance
to the whole passage.'

" ' Please, sir, I was only mixing up this powder; there isn't any harm in it. And the Madman seized nervously on his pestle and mortar, to show the Doctor the harmlessness of his pursuits, and went on pounding—click, click, click. He hadn't given six clicks before, puff! up went the whole into a great blaze, away went the pestle and mortar across the study, and back we tumbled into the passage. The magpie fluttered down into the court, swearing, and the Madman danced out, howling, with his fingers in his mouth. The Doctor caught hold of him, and called to us to fetch some water. ' There, you silly fellow,' said he, quite pleased, though, to find he wasn't much hurt, ' you see you don't know the least what you're doing with all these things ; and now, mind, you must give up practising chemistry by yourself.' Then he took hold of his arm and looked at it, and I saw he had to bite his lip, and his eyes twinkled ; but he said, quite grave, ' Here, you see, you've been making all these foolish marks on yourself, which you can never get out, and you'll be very sorry for it in a year or two. Now come down to the housekeeper's room, and let us see if you are hurt.' And away went the two, and we all stayed and had a regular turn-out of the den, till Martin came back with his hand bandaged and turned us out. However, I'll go and see what he's after, and tell him to come in after prayers to supper." And away went Tom to find the boy in question, who dwelt in a little study by himself, in New Row.

The aforesaid Martin, whom Arthur had taken such a fancy for, was one of those unfortunates who were at that time of day (and are, I fear, still) quite out of their places at a public school. If we knew how to use our boys, Martin would have been seized upon and educated as a natural philosopher. He had a passion for birds, beasts, and insects, and knew more of them and their habits than any one in Rugby—except perhaps the Doctor, who knew everything. He was also an experimental chemist on a small scale, and had made unto himself an electric machine, from which it was his greatest pleasure and glory to administer small shocks to any small boys who were rash enough to venture into his study. And this was by no means an adventure free from excitement ; for besides the probability of a snake dropping on to your head or twining lovingly up your leg, or a rat getting into your breeches-pocket in search of food, there was the animal and chemical odour to be faced, which always hung about the den, and the chance of being blown up in some of the many experiments which Martin was always trying, with the most wondrous results in the shape of explosions and smells that mortal boy ever heard of. Of course, poor Martin, in consequence of his pursuits, had become an Ishmaelite in the house. In the first place, he half-poisoned all his neighbours, and they in turn were always on the lookout to pounce upon any of his numerous live-stock, and drive him frantic by enticing his pet old magpie out of his window into a neighbouring study, and making the disreputable old bird drunk on toast soaked in beer and sugar. Then Martin, for his sins, inhabited a study looking into a small court some ten feet across, the window of which was completely commanded by those of the studies opposite in the Sick-room Row, these latter being at a slightly higher elevation. East, and another boy of an equally tormenting and ingenious turn of mind, now lived exactly opposite, and had expended huge pains and time in the preparation of instruments of annoyance for the behoof of Martin and his live colony. One morning an old basket made its appearance, suspended by a short cord outside Martin's window, in which were deposited an amateur nest containing four young hungry jackdaws, the pride and glory of Martin's life for the time being, and which he was currently asserted to have hatched upon his own person. Early in the morning and late at night he was to be seen half out of window, administering to the varied wants of his callow brood. After deep cogitation, East and his chum had spliced a knife on to the end of a fishing-rod; and having watched Martin out, had, after half an hour's severe sawing, cut the string by which the basket was suspended, and tumbled it on to the pavement below, with hideous remonstrance from the occupants. Poor Martin, returning from his short absence, collected the fragments and replaced his brood (except one whose neck had been broken in the descent) in their old location, suspending them this time by string and wire twisted together, defiant of any sharp instrument which his persecutors could command. But, like the Russian engineers at Sebastopol, East and his chum had an answer for every move of the adversary, and the next day had mounted a gun in the shape of a pea-shooter upon the ledge of their window, trained so as to bear exactly upon the spot which Martin had to occupy while tending his nurslings. The moment he began to feed they began to shoot. In vain did the enemy himself invest in a pea-shooter, and endeavour to answer the fire while he fed the young birds with his other hand; his attention was divided, and his shots flew wild, while every one of theirs told on his face and hands, and drove him into howlings and imprecations. He had been driven to ensconce the nest in a corner of his already too-well-filled den.

His door was barricaded by a set of ingenious bolts of his own invention, for the sieges were frequent by the neighbours when any unusually ambrosial odour spread itself from the den to the neighbouring studies. The door panels were in a normal state of smash, but the frame of the door resisted all besiegers, and behind it the owner carried on his varied pursuits—much in the same state of mind, I should fancy, as a border-farmer lived in, in the days of the moss-troopers, when his hold might be summoned or his cattle carried off at any minute of night or day.

"Open, Martin, old boy; it's only I, Tom Brown."

"Oh, very well; stop a moment." One bolt went back. "You're sure East isn't there?"

"No, no; hang it, open." Tom gave a kick, the other bolt creaked, and he entered the den.

Den indeed it was—about five feet six inches long by five wide, and seven feet high. About six tattered school-books, and a few chemical books, Taxidermy, Stanley on Birds, and an odd volume of Bewick, the latter in much better preservation, occupied the top shelves. The other shelves, where they had not been cut away and used by the owner for other purposes, were fitted up for the abiding-places of birds, beasts, and reptiles. There was no attempt at carpet or curtain. The table was entirely occupied by the great work of Martin, the electric machine, which was covered carefully with the remains of his table-cloth. The jackdaw cage occupied one wall; and the other was adorned by a small hatchet, a pair of climbing irons, and his tin candle-box, in which he was for the time being endeavouring to raise a hopeful young family of field-mice. As nothing should be let to lie useless, it was well that the candle-box was thus occupied, for candles Martin never had. A pound was issued to him weekly, as to the other boys; but as candles were available capital, and easily exchangeable for birds' eggs or young birds, Martin's pound invariably found its way in a few hours to Howlett's the bird-fancier's, in the Bilton road, who would give a hawk's or nightingale's egg or young linnet in exchange. Martin's ingenuity was therefore for ever on the rack to supply himself with a light. Just now he had hit upon a grand invention, and the den was lighted by a flaring cotton wick issuing from a ginger-beer bottle full of some doleful composition. When light altogether failed him, Martin would loaf about by the fires in the passages or hall, after the manner of Diggs, and try to do his verses or learn his lines by the firelight.

" Well, old boy, you haven't got any sweeter in the den this half. How that stuff in the bottle stinks ! Never mind; I ain't going to stop; but you come up after prayers to our study. You know young Arthur. We've got Gray's study. We'll have a good supper and talk about bird-nesting."

Martin was evidently highly pleased at the invitation, and promised to be up without fail.

As soon as prayers were over, and the sixth and fifth form boys had withdrawn to the aristocratic seclusion of their own room, and the rest, or democracy, had sat down to their supper in the hall, Tom and Arthur, having secured their allowances of bread and cheese, started on their feet to catch the eye of the prepostor of the week, who remained in charge during supper, walking up and down the hall. He happened to be an easy-going fellow, so they got a pleasant nod to their " Please may I go out ? " and away they scrambled to prepare for Martin a sumptuous banquet. This Tom had insisted on, for he was in great delight on the occasion, the reason of which delight must be expounded. The fact was that this was the first attempt at a friendship of his own which Arthur

had made, and Tom hailed it as a grand step. The ease
with which he himself became hail-fellow-well-met with
anybody, and blundered into and out of twenty friendships a half-year, made him sometimes sorry and sometimes angry at Arthur's reserve and loneliness. True,
Arthur was always pleasant, and even jolly, with any
boys who came with Tom to their study; but Tom felt
that it was only through him, as it were, that his chum
associated with others, and that but for him Arthur
would have been dwelling in a wilderness. This increased his consciousness of responsibility; and though
he hadn't reasoned it out and made it clear to himself,
yet somehow he knew that this responsibility, this trust
which he had taken on him without thinking about it,
head over heels in fact, was the centre and turning-point
of his school-life, that which was to make him or mar
him, his appointed work and trial for the time being.
And Tom was becoming a new boy, though with frequent
tumbles in the dirt and perpetual hard battle with himself, and was daily growing in manfulness and thoughtfulness, as every high-couraged and well-principled boy
must, when he finds himself for the first time consciously
at grips with self and the devil. Already he could turn
almost without a sigh from the School-gates, from which
had just scampered off East and three or four others of
his own particular set, bound for some jolly lark not quite
according to law, and involving probably a row with
louts, keepers, or farm-labourers, the skipping dinner or
calling-over, some of Phœbe Jennings's beer, and a very
possible flogging at the end of all as a relish. He had
quite got over the stage in which he would grumble to
himself—" Well, hang it, it's very hard of the Doctor
to have saddled me with Arthur. Why couldn't he have
chummed him with Fogey, or Thomkin, or any of the

fellows who never do anything but walk round the close, and finish their copies the first day they're set?" But although all this was past, he longed, and felt that he was right in longing, for more time for the legitimate pastimes of cricket, fives, bathing, and fishing, within bounds, in which Arthur could not yet be his companion; and he felt that when the "young un" (as he now generally called him) had found a pursuit and some other friend for himself, he should be able to give more time to the education of his own body with a clear conscience.

And now what he so wished for had come to pass; he almost hailed it as a special providence (as indeed it was, but not for the reasons he gave for it—what providences are?) that Arthur should have singled out Martin of all fellows for a friend. "The old Madman is the very fellow," thought he; "he will take him scrambling over half the country after birds' eggs and flowers, make him run and swim and climb like an Indian, and not teach him a word of anything bad, or keep him from his lessons. What luck!" And so, with more than his usual heartiness, he dived into his cupboard, and hauled out an old knuckle-bone of ham, and two or three bottles of beer, together with the solemn pewter only used on state occasions; while Arthur, equally elated at the easy accomplishment of his first act of volition in the joint establishment, produced from his side a bottle of pickles and a pot of jam, and cleared the table. In a minute or two the noise of the boys coming up from supper was heard, and Martin knocked and was admitted, bearing his bread and cheese; and the three fell to with hearty good-will upon the viands, talking faster than they ate, for all shyness disappeared in a moment before Tom's bottled-beer and hospitable ways. "Here's Arthur, a regular young town-mouse, with a natural taste for the woods, Martin, longing to break his neck climbing trees, and with a passion for young snakes."

"Well, I say," sputtered out Martin eagerly, "will you come to-morrow, both of you, to Caldecott's Spinney, then? for I know of a kestrel's nest, up a fir-tree. I can't get at it without help; and, Brown, you can climb against any one."

"Oh yes, do let us go," said Arthur; "I never saw a hawk's nest nor a hawk's egg."

"You just come down to my study, then, and I'll show you five sorts," said Martin.

"Ay, the old Madman has got the best collection in the house, out and out," said Tom; and then Martin, warming with unaccustomed good cheer and the chance of a convert, launched out into a proposed bird-nesting campaign, betraying all manner of important secrets— a golden-crested wren's nest near Butlin's Mound, a moor-hen who was sitting on nine eggs in a pond down the Barby road, and a kingfisher's nest in a corner of the old canal above Brownsover Mill. He had heard, he said, that no one had ever got a kingfisher's nest out perfect, and that the British Museum, or the Government, or somebody, had offered £100 to any one who could bring them a nest and eggs not damaged. In the middle of which astounding announcement, to which the others were listening with open ears, and already considering the application of the £100, a knock came to the door, and East's voice was heard craving admittance.

"There's Harry," said Tom; "we'll let him in. I'll keep him steady, Martin. I thought the old boy would smell out the supper."

The fact was, that Tom's heart had already smitten him for not asking his *fidus Achates* to the feast, although only an extempore affair; and though prudence and the desire to get Martin and Arthur together alone at first had overcome his scruples, he was now heartily glad to open the door, broach another bottle of beer, and hand over the old ham-knuckle to the searching of his old friend's pocket-knife.

"Ah, you greedy vagabonds," said East, with his mouth full, "I knew there was something going on when I saw you cut off out of hall so quick with your suppers. What a stunning tap, Tom! You are a wunner for bottling the swipes."

"I've had practice enough for the sixth in my time, and it's hard if I haven't picked up a wrinkle or two for my own benefit."

"Well, old Madman, and how goes the bird-nesting campaign? How's Howlett? I expect the young rooks'll be out in another fortnight, and then my turn comes."

"There'll be no young rooks fit for pies for a month yet; shows how much you know about it," rejoined Martin, who, though very good friends with East, regarded him with considerable suspicion for his propensity to practical jokes.

"Scud knows nothing and cares for nothing but grub and mischief," said Tom; "but young rook pie, specially when you've had to climb for them, is very pretty eating. —However, I say, Scud, we're all going after a hawk's nest to-morrow, in Caldecott's Spinney; and if you'll come and behave yourself, we'll have a stunning climb."

"And a bathe in Aganippe. Hooray! I'm your man."

"No, no; no bathing in Aganippe; that's where our betters go."

"Well, well, never mind. I'm for the hawk's nest, and anything that turns up."

And the bottled-beer being finished, and his hunger

appeased, East departed to his study, "that sneak Jones," as he informed them, who had just got into the sixth, and occupied the next study, having instituted a nightly visitation upon East and his chum, to their no small discomfort.

When he was gone Martin rose to follow, but Tom stopped him. " No one goes near New Row," said he, " so you may just as well stop here and do your verses, and then we'll have some more talk. We'll be no end quiet. Besides, no prepostor comes here now. We haven't been visited once this half."

So the table was cleared, the cloth restored, and the three fell to work with Gradus and dictionary upon the morning's vulgus.

They were three very fair examples of the way in which such tasks were done at Rugby, in the consulship of Plancus. And doubtless the method is little changed, for there is nothing new under the sun, especially at schools.

Now be it known unto all you boys who are at schools which do not rejoice in the time-honoured institution of the vulgus (commonly supposed to have been established by William of Wykeham at Winchester, and imported to Rugby by Arnold more for the sake of the lines which were learnt by heart with it than for its own intrinsic value, as I've always understood), that it is a short exercise in Greek or Latin verse, on a given subject, the minimum number of lines being fixed for each form.

The master of the form gave out at fourth lesson on the previous day the subject for next morning's vulgus, and at first lesson each boy had to bring his vulgus ready to be looked over ; and with the vulgus, a certain number of lines from one of the Latin or Greek poets then being construed in the form had to be got by heart. The master at first lesson called up each

boy in the form in order, and put him on in the lines.
If he couldn't say them, or seem to say them, by reading
them off the master's or some other boy's book who
stood near, he was sent back, and went below all the
boys who did so say or seem to say them ; but in either
case his vulgus was looked over by the master, who gave
and entered in his book, to the credit or discredit of the
boy, so many marks as the composition merited.   At
Rugby vulgus and lines were the first lesson every other
day in the week, on Tuesdays, Thursdays, and Saturdays ;
and as there were thirty-eight weeks in the school year,
it is obvious to the meanest capacity that the master of
each form had to set one hundred and fourteen subjects every year, two hundred and twenty-eight every
two years, and so on.   Now, to persons of moderate invention this was a considerable task, and human nature
being prone to repeat itself, it will not be wondered that
the masters gave the same subjects sometimes over again
after a certain lapse of time.   To meet and rebuke this
bad habit of the masters, the schoolboy mind, with its
accustomed ingenuity, had invented an elaborate system
of tradition.   Almost every boy kept his own vulgus
written out in a book, and these books were duly handed
down from boy to boy, till (if the tradition has gone on
till now) I suppose the popular boys, in whose hands
bequeathed vulgus-books have accumulated, are prepared with three or four vulguses on any subject in
heaven or earth, or in " more worlds than one," which an
unfortunate master can pitch upon.   At any rate, such
lucky fellows had generally one for themselves and one
for a friend in my time.   The only objection to the traditionary method of doing your vulguses was the risk
that the successions might have become confused, and
so that you and another follower of traditions should

show up the same identical vulgus some fine morning; in which case, when it happened, considerable grief was the result. But when did such risk hinder boys or men from short cuts and pleasant paths?

Now in the study that night Tom was the upholder of the traditionary method of vulgus doing. He carefully produced two large vulgus-books, and began diving into them, and picking out a line here, and an ending there (tags, as they were vulgarly called), till he had gotten all that he thought he could make fit. He then proceeded to patch his tags together with the help of his Gradus, producing an incongruous and feeble result of eight elegiac lines, the minimum quantity for his form, and finishing up with two highly moral lines extra, making ten in all, which he cribbed entire from one of his books, beginning " O genus humanum," and which he himself must have used a dozen times before, whenever an unfortunate or wicked hero, of whatever nation or language under the sun, was the subject. Indeed he began to have great doubts whether the master wouldn't remember them, and so only throw them in as extra lines, because in any case they would call off attention from the other tags, and if detected, being extra lines, he wouldn't be sent back to do more in their place, while if they passed muster again he would get marks for them.

The second method, pursued by Martin, may be called the dogged or prosaic method. He, no more than Tom, took any pleasure in the task, but having no old vulgus-books of his own, or any one's else, could not follow the traditionary method, for which too, as Tom remarked, he hadn't the genius. Martin then proceeded to write down eight lines in English, of the most matter-of-fact kind, the first that came into his head; and to convert these, line by line, by main force of Gradus and dictionary, into Latin that would scan. This was all he cared for—to produce eight lines with no false quantities or concords : whether the words were apt, or what the sense was, mattered nothing ; and as the article was all new, not a line beyond the minimum did the followers of the dogged method ever produce.

The third, or artistic method, was Arthur's. He considered first what point in the character or event which was the subject could most neatly be brought out within the limits of a vulgus, trying always to get his idea into the eight lines, but not binding himself to ten or even twelve lines if he couldn't do this. He then set to work, as much as possible without Gradus or other help, to clothe his idea in appropriate Latin or Greek, and would not be satisfied till he had polished it well up with the aptest and most poetic words and phrases he could get at.

A fourth method, indeed, was used in the school, but of too simple a kind to require a comment. It may be called the vicarious method, obtained amongst big boys of lazy or bullying habits, and consisted simply in making clever boys whom they could thrash do their whole vulgus for them, and construe it to them afterwards ; which latter is a method not to be encouraged, and which I strongly advise you all not to practise. Of the others, you will find the traditionary most troublesome, unless you can steal your vulguses whole (*experto crede*), and that the artistic method pays the best both in marks and other ways.

The vulguses being finished by nine o'clock, and Martin having rejoiced above measure in the abundance of light, and of Gradus and dictionary, and other conveniences almost unknown to him for getting through the work, and having been pressed by Arthur to come and do his verses there whenever he liked, the three boys went down to Martin's den, and Arthur was initiated into the lore of birds' eggs, to his great delight. The exquisite colouring and forms astonished and charmed him, who had scarcely ever seen any but a hen's egg or an ostrich's; and by the time he was lugged away to bed he had learned the names of at least twenty sorts, and dreamed of the glorious perils of tree-climbing, and that he had found a roc's egg in the island as big as Sinbad's, and clouded like a tit-lark's, in blowing which Martin and he had nearly been drowned in the yolk.

CHAPTER IV.

THE BIRD-FANCIERS.

" I have found out a gift for my fair—
   I have found where the wood-pigeons breed;
But let me the plunder forbear,
   She would say 'twas a barbarous deed."—ROWE.

" And now, my lad, take them five shilling,
   And on my advice in future think;
So Billy pouched them all so willing,
   And got that night disguised in drink."—*MS. Ballad.*

THE next morning, at first lesson, Tom was turned back in his lines, and so had to wait till the second round; while Martin and Arthur said theirs all right, and got out of school at once. When Tom got out and ran down to breakfast at Harrowell's they were missing, and Stumps informed him that they had swallowed down their breakfasts and gone off together—where, he couldn't say. Tom hurried over his own breakfast, and went first to Martin's study and then to his own; but no signs of the missing boys were to be found. He felt half angry and jealous of Martin. Where could they be gone?

He learnt second lesson with East and the rest in no

very good temper, and then went out into the quadrangle. About ten minutes before school Martin and
Arthur arrived in the quadrangle breathless; and catching sight of him, Arthur rushed up, all excitement, and
with a bright glow on his face.

"O Tom, look here!" cried he, holding out three
moor-hen's eggs; "we've been down the Barby road
to the pool Martin told us of last night, and just see
what we've got."

Tom wouldn't be pleased, and only looked out for
something to find fault with.

"Why, young un," said he, "what have you been
after? You don't mean to say you've been wading?"

The tone of reproach made poor little Arthur shrink up
in a moment and look piteous; and Tom with a shrug of
his shoulders turned his anger on Martin.

"Well, I didn't think, Madman, that you'd have been
such a muff as to let him be getting wet through at this
time of day. You might have done the wading yourself."

"So I did, of course; only he would come in too, to
see the nest. We left six eggs in. They'll be hatched
in a day or two."

"Hang the eggs!" said Tom; "a fellow can't turn his
back for a moment but all his work's undone. He'll be
laid up for a week for this precious lark, I'll be bound."

"Indeed, Tom, now," pleaded Arthur, "my feet ain't
wet, for Martin made me take off my shoes and stockings
and trousers."

"But they are wet, and dirty too; can't I see?" answered Tom; "and you'll be called up and floored when
the master sees what a state you're in. You haven't
looked at second lesson, you know."

O Tom, you old humbug! you to be upbraiding any

one with not learning their lessons! If you hadn't been floored yourself now at first lesson, do you mean to say you wouldn't have been with them? And you've taken away all poor little Arthur's joy and pride in his first birds' eggs, and he goes and puts them down in the study, and takes down his books with a sigh, thinking he has done something horribly wrong, whereas he has learnt on in advance much more than will be done at second lesson.

But the old Madman hasn't, and gets called up, and makes some frightful shots, losing about ten places, and all but getting floored. This somewhat appeases Tom's wrath, and by the end of the lesson he has regained his temper. And afterwards in their study he begins to get right again, as he watches Arthur's intense joy at seeing Martin blowing the eggs and gluing them carefully on to bits of cardboard, and notes the anxious, loving looks which the little fellow casts sidelong at him. And then he thinks, "What an ill-tempered beast I am! Here's just what I was wishing for last night come about, and I'm spoiling it all," and in another five minutes has swallowed the last mouthful of his bile, and is repaid by seeing his little sensitive plant expand again and sun itself in his smiles.

After dinner the Madman is busy with the preparations for their expedition, fitting new straps on to his climbing-irons, filling large pill-boxes with cotton-wool, and sharpening East's small axe. They carry all their munitions into calling-over, and directly afterwards, having dodged such prepostors as are on the lookout for fags at cricket, the four set off at a smart trot down the Lawford footpath, straight for Caldecott's Spinney and the hawk's nest.

Martin leads the way in high feather; it is quite a new sensation to him, getting companions, and he finds it very pleasant, and means to show them all manner of proofs of his science and skill. Brown and East may be better at cricket and football and games, thinks he, but out in the fields and woods see if I can't teach them something. He has taken the leadership already, and strides away in front with his climbing-irons strapped under one arm, his pecking-bag under the other, and his pockets and hat full of pill-boxes, cotton-wool, and other etceteras. Each of the others carries a pecking-bag, and East his hatchet.

When they had crossed three or four fields without a check, Arthur began to lag; and Tom seeing this shouted to Martin to pull up a bit. "We ain't out hare-and-hounds. What's the good of grinding on at this rate?"

"There's the Spinney," said Martin, pulling up on the brow of a slope at the bottom of which lay Lawford brook, and pointing to the top of the opposite slope; "the nest is in one of those high fir-trees at this end. And down by the brook there I know of a sedge-bird's nest. We'll go and look at it coming back."

"Oh, come on; don't let us stop," said Arthur, who was getting excited at the sight of the wood. So they broke into a trot again, and were soon across the brook, up the slope, and into the Spinney. Here they advanced as noiselessly as possible, lest keepers or other enemies should be about, and stopped at the foot of a tall fir, at the top of which Martin pointed out with pride the kestrel's nest, the object of their quest.

"Oh, where? which is it?" asks Arthur, gaping up in the air, and having the most vague idea of what it would be like.

"There, don't you see?" said East, pointing to a lump of mistletoe in the next tree, which was a beech. He saw that Martin and Tom were busy with the climbing-irons, and couldn't resist the temptation of hoaxing. Arthur stared and wondered more than ever.

"Well, how curious! It doesn't look a bit like what I expected," said he.

"Very odd birds, kestrels," said East, looking waggishly at his victim, who was still star-gazing.

"But I thought it was in a fir-tree?" objected Arthur.

"Ah, don't you know? That's a new sort of fir which old Caldecott brought from the Himalayas."

"Really!" said Arthur; "I'm glad I know that. How unlike our firs they are! They do very well too here, don't they? The Spinney's full of them."

"What's that humbug he's telling you?" cried Tom, looking up, having caught the word Himalayas, and suspecting what East was after.

"Only about this fir," said Arthur, putting his hand on the stem of the beech.

"Fir!" shouted Tom; "why, you don't mean to say, young un, you don't know a beech when you see one?"

Poor little Arthur looked terribly ashamed, and East exploded in laughter which made the wood ring.

"I've hardly ever seen any trees," faltered Arthur.

"What a shame to hoax him, Scud!" cried Martin. —"Never mind, Arthur; you shall know more about trees than he does in a week or two."

"And isn't that the kestrel's nest, then?" asked Arthur.

"That! Why, that's a piece of mistletoe. There's the nest, that lump of sticks up this fir."

"Don't believe him, Arthur," struck in the incorrigible East; "I just saw an old magpie go out of it."

Martin did not deign to reply to this sally, except by a grunt, as he buckled the last buckle of his climbing-irons, and Arthur looked reproachfully at East without speaking.

But now came the tug of war. It was a very difficult tree to climb until the branches were reached, the first of which was some fourteen feet up, for the trunk was too large at the bottom to be swarmed; in fact, neither of the boys could reach more than half round it with their arms. Martin and Tom, both of whom had irons on, tried it without success at first; the fir bark broke away where they stuck the irons in as soon as they leant any weight on their feet, and the grip of their arms wasn't enough to keep them up; so, after getting up three or four feet, down they came slithering to the ground, barking their arms and faces. They were furious, and East sat by laughing and shouting at each failure, " Two to one on the old magpie ! "

" We must try a pyramid," said Tom at last. " Now, Scud, you lazy rascal, stick yourself against the tree ! "

" I dare say ! and have you standing on my shoulders with the irons on. What do you think my skin's made of ? " However, up he got, and leant against the tree, putting his head down and clasping it with his arms as far as he could.

" Now then, Madman," said Tom, " you next."

" No, I'm lighter than you ; you go next." So Tom got on East's shoulders, and grasped the tree above, and then Martin scrambled up on to Tom's shoulders, amidst the totterings and groanings of the pyramid, and, with a spring which sent his supporters howling to the ground, clasped the stem some ten feet up, and remained clinging. For a moment or two they thought he couldn't get up; but then, holding on with arms and teeth, he worked first one iron then the other firmly into the bark, got another grip with his arms, and in another minute had hold of the lowest branch.

" All up with the old magpie now," said East ; and

after a minute's rest, up went Martin, hand over hand, watched by Arthur with fearful eagerness.

" Isn't it very dangerous ? " said he.

" Not a bit," answered Tom ; " you can't hurt if you only get good hand-hold. Try every branch with a good pull before you trust it, and then up you go."

Martin was now amongst the small branches close to the nest, and away dashed the old bird, and soared up above the trees, watching the intruder.

" All right—four eggs ! " shouted he.

" Take 'em all ! " shouted East ; " that'll be one a-piece."

" No, no ; leave one, and then she won't care," said Tom.

We boys had an idea that birds couldn't count, and were quite content as long as you left one egg. I hope it is so.

Martin carefully put one egg into each of his boxes and the third into his mouth, the only other place of safety, and came down like a lamplighter. All went well till he was within ten feet of the ground, when, as the trunk enlarged, his hold got less and less firm, and at last down he came with a run, tumbling on to his back on the turf, spluttering and spitting out the remains of the great egg, which had broken by the jar of his fall.

" Ugh, ugh ! something to drink—ugh ! it was addled," spluttered he, while the wood rang again with the merry laughter of East and Tom.

Then they examined the prizes, gathered up their things, and went off to the brook, where Martin swallowed huge draughts of water to get rid of the taste ; and they visited the sedge-bird's nest, and from thence struck across the country in high glee, beating the hedges and brakes as they went along ; and Arthur at last, to his intense delight, was allowed to climb a small hedgerow oak for a magpie's nest with Tom, who kept all round him like a mother, and showed him where to hold and how to throw his weight ; and though he was in a great fright, didn't show it, and was applauded by all for his lissomness.

They crossed a road soon afterwards, and there, close to them, lay a great heap of charming pebbles.

"Look here," shouted East ; "here's luck ! I've been longing for some good, honest pecking this half-hour. Let's fill the bags, and have no more of this foozling bird-nesting."

No one objected, so each boy filled the fustian bag he carried full of stones. They crossed into the next field, Tom and East taking one side of the hedges, and the other two the other side. Noise enough they made certainly, but it was too early in the season for the young birds, and the old birds were too strong on the wing for our young marksmen, and flew out of shot after the first discharge. But it was great fun, rushing along the hedgerows, and discharging stone after stone at blackbirds and chaffinches, though no result in the shape of slaughtered birds was obtained ; and Arthur soon entered into it, and rushed to head back the birds, and shouted, and threw, and tumbled into ditches, and over and through hedges, as wild as the Madman himself.

Presently the party, in full cry after an old blackbird (who was evidently used to the thing and enjoyed the fun, for he would wait till they came close to him, and then fly on for forty yards or so, and, with an impudent flicker of his tail, dart into the depths of the quickset), came beating down a high double hedge, two on each side.

"There he is again," "Head him," "Let drive," "I had him there," "Take care where you're throwing, Madman." The shouts might have been heard a quarter of a mile off. They were heard some two hundred yards off by a farmer and two of his shepherds, who were doctoring sheep in a fold in the next field.

Now, the farmer in question rented a house and yard situate at the end of the field in which the young bird-fanciers had arrived, which house and yard he didn't occupy or keep any one else in. Nevertheless, like a brainless and unreasoning Briton, he persisted in maintaining on the premises a large stock of cocks, hens, and other poultry. Of course, all sorts of depredators visited the place from time to time : foxes and gipsies wrought havoc in the night ; while in the daytime, I regret to have to confess that visits from the Rugby boys, and consequent disappearances of ancient and respectable fowls were not unfrequent. Tom and East had during the period of their outlawry visited the farm in question for felonious purposes, and on one occasion had conquered and slain a duck there, and borne away the carcass triumphantly, hidden in their handkerchiefs. However, they were sickened of the practice by the trouble and anxiety which the wretched duck's body caused them. They carried it to Sally Harrowell's. in hopes of a good supper ; but she, after examining it, made a long face, and refused to dress or have anything to do with it. Then they took it into their study, and began plucking it themselves ; but what to do with the feathers, where to hide them ?

"Good gracious, Tom, what a lot of feathers a duck has ! " groaned East, holding a bagful in his hand, and looking disconsolately at the carcass, not yet half plucked.

"And I do think he's getting high, too, already," said

Tom, smelling at him cautiously, " so we must finish him up soon."

" Yes, all very well; but how are we to cook him ? I'm sure I ain't going to try it on in the hall or passages ; we can't afford to be roasting ducks about—our character's too bad."

" I wish we were rid of the brute," said Tom, throwing him on the table in disgust. And after a day or two more it became clear that got rid of he must be ; so they packed him and sealed him up in brown paper, and put him in the cupboard of an unoccupied study, where he was found in the holidays by the matron, a gruesome body.

They had never been duck-hunting there since, but others had, and the bold yeoman was very sore on the subject, and bent on making an example of the first boys he could catch. So he and his shepherds crouched behind the hurdles, and watched the party, who were approaching all unconscious.

Why should that old guinea-fowl be lying out in the hedge just at this particular moment of all the year ? Who can say ? Guinea-fowls always are; so are all other things, animals, and persons, requisite for getting one into scrapes—always ready when any mischief can come of them. At any rate, just under East's nose popped out the old guinea-hen, scuttling along and shrieking, " Come back, come back," at the top of her voice. Either of the other three might perhaps have withstood the temptation, but East first lets drive the stone he has in his hand at her, and then rushes to turn her into the hedge again. He succeeds, and then they are all at it for dear life, up and down the hedge in full cry, the " Come back, come back," getting shriller and fainter every minute.

Meantime, the farmer and his men steal over the hurdles and creep down the hedge towards the scene of action. They are almost within a stone's throw of Martin, who is pressing the unlucky chase hard, when Tom catches sight of them, and sings out, " Louts, 'ware louts, your side !   Madman, look ahead ! " and then catching hold of Arthur, hurries him away across the field towards Rugby as hard as they can tear. Had he been by himself, he would have stayed to see it out with the others, but now his heart sinks and all his pluck goes. The idea of being led up to the Doctor with Arthur for bagging fowls quite unmans and takes half the run out of him.

However, no boys are more able to take care of themselves than East and Martin ; they dodge the pursuers, slip through a gap, and come pelting after Tom and Arthur, whom they catch up in no time. The farmer and his men are making good running about a field behind. Tom wishes to himself that they had made off in any other direction, but now they are all in for it together, and must see it out.

" You won't leave the young un, will you ? " says he, as they haul poor little Arthur, already losing wind from the fright, through the next hedge. " Not we," is the answer from both. The next hedge is a stiff one ; the pursuers gain horribly on them, and they only just pull Arthur through, with two great rents in his trousers, as the foremost shepherd comes up on the other side. As they start into the next field, they are aware of two figures walking down the footpath in the middle of it, and recognize Holmes and Diggs taking a constitutional. Those good-natured fellows immediately shout, " On." " Let's go to them and surrender," pants Tom.   Agreed. And in another minute the four boys, to the great astonishment of those worthies, rush breathless up to Holmes and Diggs, who pull up to see what is the matter; and then the whole is explained by the appearance of the farmer and his men, who unite their forces and bear down on the knot of boys.

There is no time to explain, and Tom's heart beats frightfully quick, as he ponders, " Will they stand by us?"

The farmer makes a rush at East and collars him; and that young gentleman, with unusual discretion, instead of kicking his shins, looks appealingly at Holmes, and stands still.

"Hullo there; not so fast," says Holmes, who is bound to stand up for them till they are proved in the wrong. " Now what's all this about?"

" I've got the young varmint at last, have I," pants the farmer; " why, they've been a-skulking about my yard and stealing my fowls—that's where 'tis; and if I doan't have they flogged for it, every one on 'em, my name ain't Thompson."

Holmes looks grave and Diggs's face falls. They are quite ready to fight—no boys in the school more so; but they are prepostors, and understand their office, and can't uphold unrighteous causes.

" I haven't been near his old barn this half," cries East. " Nor I," " Nor I," chime in Tom and Martin.

" Now, Willum, didn't you see 'em there last week?"

" Ees, I seen 'em sure enough," says Willum, grasping a prong he carried, and preparing for action.

The boys deny stoutly, and Willum is driven to admit that " if it worn't they 'twas chaps as like 'em as two peas'n;" and " leastways he'll swear he see'd them two in the yard last Martinmas," indicating East and Tom.

Holmes has had time to meditate. "Now, sir," says he to Willum, "you see you can't remember what you have seen, and I believe the boys."

"I doan't care," blusters the farmer; "they was arter my fowls to-day—that's enough for I.—Willum, you catch hold o' t'other chap. They've been a-sneaking about this two hours, I tells 'ee," shouted he, as Holmes stands between Martin and Willum, "and have druv a matter of a dozen young pullets pretty nigh to death."

"Oh, there's a whacker!" cried East; "we haven't been within a hundred yards of his barn; we haven't been up here above ten minutes, and we've seen nothing but a tough old guinea-hen, who ran like a greyhound."

"Indeed, that's all true, Holmes, upon my honour," added Tom; "we weren't after his fowls; guinea-hen ran out of the hedge under our feet, and we've seen nothing else."

"Drat their talk. Thee catch hold o' t'other, Willum, and come along wi' un."

"Farmer Thompson," said Holmes, warning off Willum and the prong with his stick, while Diggs faced the other shepherd, cracking his fingers like pistol-shots, "now listen to reason. The boys haven't been after your fowls, that's plain."

"Tells 'ee I see'd 'em. Who be you, I should like to know?"

"Never you mind, farmer," answered Holmes. "And now I'll just tell you what it is: you ought to be ashamed of yourself for leaving all that poultry about, with no one to watch it, so near the School. You deserve to have it all stolen. So if you choose to come up to the Doctor with them, I shall go with you, and tell him what I think of it."

The farmer began to take Holmes for a master; besides, he wanted to get back to his flock. Corporal punishment was out of the question, the odds were too great; so he began to hint at paying for the damage. Arthur jumped at this, offering to pay anything, and the farmer immediately valued the guinea-hen at half a sovereign.

"Half a sovereign!" cried East, now released from the farmer's grip; "well, that is a good one! The old hen ain't hurt a bit, and she's seven years old, I know, and as tough as whipcord; she couldn't lay another egg to save her life."

It was at last settled that they should pay the farmer two shillings, and his man one shilling; and so the matter ended, to the unspeakable relief of Tom, who hadn't been able to say a word, being sick at heart at the idea of what the Doctor would think of him; and now the whole party of boys marched off down the footpath towards Rugby. Holmes, who was one of the best boys in the School, began to improve the occasion. "Now, you youngsters," said he, as he marched along in the middle of them, "mind this; you're very well out of this scrape. Don't you go near Thompson's barn again; do you hear?"

Profuse promises from all, especially East.

"Mind, I don't ask questions," went on Mentor, "but I rather think some of you have been there before this after his chickens. Now, knocking over other people's chickens, and running off with them, is stealing. It's a nasty word, but that's the plain English of it. If the chickens were dead and lying in a shop, you wouldn't take them, I know that, any more than you would apples out of Griffith's basket; but there's no real difference between chickens running about and apples on a tree, and the same articles in a shop. I wish our morals were sounder in such matters. There's nothing so mischievous as these school distinctions, which jumble up right and wrong, and justify things in us for which poor boys would be sent to prison." And good old Holmes delivered his soul on the walk home of many wise sayings, and, as the song says,

"Gee'd 'em a sight of good advice;"

which same sermon sank into them all, more or less, and very penitent they were for several hours. But truth compels me to admit that East, at any rate, forgot it all in a week, but remembered the insult which had been put upon him by Farmer Thompson, and with the Tadpole and other hair-brained youngsters committed a raid on the barn soon afterwards, in which they were caught by the shepherds and severely handled, besides having to pay eight shillings—all the money they had in the world—to escape being taken up to the Doctor.

Martin became a constant inmate in the joint study from this time, and Arthur took to him so kindly that Tom couldn't resist slight fits of jealousy, which, however, he managed to keep to himself. The kestrel's eggs had not been broken, strange to say, and formed the nucleus of Arthur's collection, at which Martin worked heart and soul, and introduced Arthur to Howlett the bird-fancier, and instructed him in the rudiments of the art of stuffing. In token of his gratitude, Arthur allowed Martin to tattoo a small anchor on one of his wrists; which decoration, however, he carefully concealed from Tom. Before the end of the half-year he had trained into a bold climber and good runner, and, as Martin had foretold, knew twice as much about trees, birds, flowers, and many other things, as our good-hearted and facetious young friend Harry East.

CHAPTER V.

THE FIGHT.

" Surgebat Macnevisius
Et mox jactabat ultro,
Pugnabo tuâ gratiâ
Feroci hoc Mactwoltro."—*Etonian.*

THERE is a certain sort of fellow—we who are used to studying boys all know him well enough—of whom you can predicate with almost positive certainty, after he has been a month at school, that he is sure to have a fight, and with almost equal certainty that he will have but one. Tom Brown was one of these; and as it is our well-weighed intention to give a full, true, and correct account of Tom's only single combat with a school-fellow in the manner of our old friend *Bell's Life*, let those young persons whose stomachs are not strong, or who think a good set-to with the weapons which God has given us all an uncivilized, unchristian, or ungentlemanly affair, just skip this chapter at once, for it won't be to their taste.

It was not at all usual in those days for two School-house boys to have a fight. Of course there were exceptions, when some cross-grained, hard-headed fellow came up who would never be happy unless he was quarrelling with his nearest neighbours, or when there was some class-dispute, between the fifth form and the fags, for instance, which required blood-letting; and a champion was picked out on each side tacitly, who settled the matter by a good hearty mill. But, for the most part, the constant use of those surest keepers of the peace, the boxing-gloves, képt the School-house boys from fighting one another. Two or three nights in every week the gloves were brought out, either in the hall or fifth-form room; and every boy who was ever likely to fight at all knew all his neighbours' prowess perfectly well, and could tell to a nicety what chance he would have in a stand-up fight with any other boy in the house. But, of course, no such experience could be gotten as regarded boys in other houses; and as most of the other houses were more or less jealous of the School-house, collisions were frequent.

After all, what would life be without fighting, I should like to know? From the cradle to the grave, fighting, rightly understood, is the business, the real highest, honestest business of every son of man. Every one who is worth his salt has his enemies, who must be beaten, be they evil thoughts and habits in himself, or spiritual wickednesses in high places, or Russians, or Border-ruffians, or Bill, Tom, or Harry, who will not let him live his life in quiet till he has thrashed them.

It is no good for quakers, or any other body of men, to uplift their voices against fighting. Human nature is too strong for them, and they don't follow their own precepts. Every soul of them is doing his own piece of fighting, somehow and somewhere. The world might be a better world without fighting, for anything I know, but it wouldn't be our world; and therefore I am dead against crying peace when there is no peace, and isn't meant to be. I am as sorry as any man to see folk fighting the wrong people and the wrong things, but I'd a deal sooner see them doing that than that they should have no fight in them. So having recorded, and being about to record, my hero's fights of all sorts, with all sorts of enemies, I shall now proceed to give an account of his passage-at-arms with the only one of his school-fellows whom he ever had to encounter in this manner.

It was drawing towards the close of Arthur's first half-year, and the May evenings were lengthening out. Lock-

ing-up was not till eight o'clock, and everybody was
beginning to talk about what he would do in the holidays.
The shell, in which form all our *dramatis personæ* now
are, were reading, amongst other things, the last book of
Homer's "Iliad," and had worked through it as far as the
speeches of the women over Hector's body. It is a whole
school-day, and four or five of the School-house boys
(amongst whom are Arthur, Tom, and East) are preparing
third lesson together. They have finished the regulation
forty lines, and are for the most part getting very tired,
notwithstanding the exquisite pathos of Helen's lamentation. And now several long four-syllabled words come
together, and the boy with the dictionary strikes work.

"I am not going to look out any more words," says
he; "we've done the quantity. Ten to one we shan't
get so far. Let's go out into the close."

"Come along, boys," cries East, always ready to leave
"the grind," as he called it; "our old coach is laid up,
you know, and we shall have one of the new masters,
who's sure to go slow and let us down easy."

So an adjournment to the close was carried *nem. con.*,
little Arthur not daring to uplift his voice; but, being
deeply interested in what they were reading, stayed
quietly behind, and learnt on for his own pleasure.

As East had said, the regular master of the form was
unwell, and they were to be heard by one of the new
masters—quite a young man, who had only just left the
university. Certainly it would be hard lines if, by dawdling as much as possible in coming in and taking their
places, entering into long-winded explanations of what
was the usual course of the regular master of the form,
and others of the stock contrivances of boys for wasting
time in school, they could not spin out the lesson so that
he should not work them through more than the forty

lines. As to which quantity there was a perpetual fight going on between the master and his form—the latter insisting, and enforcing by passive resistance, that it was the prescribed quantity of Homer for a shell lesson; the former, that there was no fixed quantity, but that they must always be ready to go on to fifty or sixty lines if there were time within the hour. However, notwithstanding all their efforts, the new master got on horribly quick. He seemed to have the bad taste to be really interested in the lesson, and to be trying to work them up into something like appreciation of it, giving them good, spirited English words, instead of the wretched bald stuff into which they rendered poor old Homer, and construing over each piece himself to them, after each boy, to show them how it should be done.

Now the clock strikes the three-quarters; there is only a quarter of an hour more, but the forty lines are all but done. So the boys, one after another, who are called up, stick more and more, and make balder and ever more bald work of it. The poor young master is pretty near beat by this time, and feels ready to knock his head against the wall, or his fingers against somebody else's head. So he gives up altogether the lower and middle parts of the form, and looks round in despair at the boys on the top bench, to see if there is one out of whom he can strike a spark or two, and who will be too chivalrous to murder the most beautiful utterances of the most beautiful woman of the old world. His eye rests on Arthur, and he calls him up to finish construing Helen's speech. Whereupon all the other boys draw long breaths, and begin to stare about and take it easy. They are all safe : Arthur is the head of the form, and sure to be able to construe, and that will tide on safely till the hour strikes.

Arthur proceeds to read out the passage in Greek before construing it, as the custom is. Tom, who isn't paying much attention, is suddenly caught by the falter in his voice as he reads the two lines—

ἀλλὰ σὺ τόν γ' ἐπέεσσι παραιφάμενος κατέρυκες,
Σῇ τ' ἀγανοφροσύνῃ καὶ σοῖς ἀγανοῖς ἐπέεσσιν.

He looks up at Arthur. "Why, bless us," thinks he, "what can be the matter with the young un? He's never going to get floored. He's sure to have learnt to the end." Next moment he is reassured by the spirited tone in which Arthur begins construing, and betakes himself to drawing dogs' heads in his notebook, while the master, evidently enjoying the change, turns his back on the middle bench and stands before Arthur, beating a sort of time with his hand and foot, and saying, "Yes, yes," "Very well," as Arthur goes on.

But as he nears the fatal two lines, Tom catches that falter, and again looks up. He sees that there is something the matter; Arthur can hardly get on at all. What can it be?

Suddenly at this point Arthur breaks down altogether, and fairly bursts out crying, and dashes the cuff of his jacket across his eyes, blushing up to the roots of his hair, and feeling as if he should like to go down suddenly through the floor. The whole form are taken aback; most of them stare stupidly at him, while those who are gifted with presence of mind find their places and look steadily at their books, in hopes of not catching the master's eye and getting called up in Arthur's place.

The master looks puzzled for a moment, and then seeing, as the fact is, that the boy is really affected to tears by the most touching thing in Homer, perhaps in all profane poetry put together, steps up to him and lays his hand kindly on his shoulder, saying, "Never mind, my little man; you've construed very well. Stop a minute; there's no hurry."

Now, as luck would have it, there sat next above Tom on that day, in the middle bench of the form, a big boy, by name Williams, generally supposed to be the cock of the shell, therefore of all the school below the fifths. The small boys, who are great speculators on the prowess of their elders, used to hold forth to one another about Williams's great strength, and to discuss whether East or Brown would take a licking from him. He was called Slogger Williams, from the force with which it was supposed he could hit. In the main, he was a rough, good-natured fellow enough, but very much alive to his own dignity. He reckoned himself the king of the form, and kept up his position with the strong hand, especially in the matter of forcing boys not to construe more than the legitimate forty lines. He had already grunted and grumbled to himself when Arthur went on reading beyond the forty lines; but now that he had broken down just in the middle of all the long words, the Slogger's wrath was fairly roused.

"Sneaking little brute," muttered he, regardless of prudence—"clapping on the water-works just in the hardest place; see if I don't punch his head after fourth lesson."

"Whose?" said Tom, to whom the remark seemed to be addressed.

"Why, that little sneak, Arthur's," replied Williams.

"No, you shan't," said Tom.

"Hullo!" exclaimed Williams, looking at Tom with great surprise for a moment, and then giving him a sudden dig in the ribs with his elbow, which sent Tom's books flying on to the floor, and called the attention of the master, who turned suddenly round, and seeing the state of things, said,—

"Williams, go down three places, and then go on."

The Slogger found his legs very slowly, and proceeded to go below Tom and two other boys with great disgust; and then, turning round and facing the master, said, "I haven't learnt any more, sir; our lesson is only forty lines."

"Is that so?" said the master, appealing generally to the top bench. No answer.

"Who is the head boy of the form?" said he, waxing wroth.

"Arthur, sir," answered three or four boys, indicating our friend.

"Oh, your name's Arthur. Well, now, what is the length of your regular lesson?"

Arthur hesitated a moment, and then said, "We call it only forty lines, sir."

"How do you mean—you call it?"

"Well, sir, Mr. Graham says we ain't to stop there when there's time to construe more."

"I understand," said the master.—"Williams, go down three more places, and write me out the lesson in Greek and English.—And now, Arthur, finish construing."

"Oh! would I be in Arthur's shoes after fourth lesson?" said the little boys to one another; but Arthur finished Helen's speech without any further catastrophe, and the clock struck four, which ended third lesson.

Another hour was occupied in preparing and saying fourth lesson, during which Williams was bottling up his wrath; and when five struck, and the lessons for the day were over, he prepared to take summary vengeance on the innocent cause of his misfortune.

Tom was detained in school a few minutes after the rest, and on coming out into the quadrangle, the first thing he saw was a small ring of boys, applauding Williams, who was holding Arthur by the collar.

"There, you young sneak," said he, giving Arthur a cuff on the head with his other hand; "what made you say that——"

"Hullo!" said Tom, shouldering into the crowd; "you drop that, Williams; you shan't touch him."

"Who'll stop me?" said the Slogger, raising his hand again.

"I," said Tom; and suiting the action to the word, he struck the arm which held Arthur's arm so sharply that the Slogger dropped it with a start, and turned the full current of his wrath on Tom.

"Will you fight?"

"Yes, of course."

"Huzza! There's going to be a fight between Slogger Williams and Tom Brown!"

The news ran like wildfire about, and many boys who were on their way to tea at their several houses turned back, and sought the back of the chapel, where the fights come off.

"Just run and tell East to come and back me," said Tom to a small School-house boy, who was off like a rocket to Harrowell's, just stopping for a moment to poke his head into the School-house hall, where the lower boys were already at tea, and sing out, "Fight! Tom Brown and Slogger Williams."

Up start half the boys at once, leaving bread, eggs, butter, sprats, and all the rest to take care of themselves. The greater part of the remainder follow in a minute, after swallowing their tea, carrying their food in their hands to consume as they go. Three or four only remain, who steal the butter of the more impetuous, and make to themselves an unctuous feast.

In another minute East and Martin tear through the quadrangle, carrying a sponge, and arrive at the scene of action just as the combatants are beginning to strip.

Tom felt he had got his work cut out for him, as he stripped off his jacket, waistcoat, and braces. East tied his handkerchief round his waist, and rolled up his shirt-sleeves for him. "Now, old boy, don't you open your mouth to say a word, or try to help yourself a bit—we'll do all that; you keep all your breath and strength for the Slogger." Martin meanwhile folded the clothes, and put them under the chapel rails; and now Tom, with East to handle him, and Martin to give him a knee, steps out on the turf, and is ready for all that may come; and here is the Slogger too, all stripped, and thirsting for the fray.

It doesn't look a fair match at first glance: Williams is nearly two inches taller, and probably a long year older than his opponent, and he is very strongly made about the arms and shoulders—" peels well," as the little knot of big fifth-form boys, the amateurs, say, who stand outside the ring of little boys, looking complacently on, but taking no active part in the proceedings. But down below he is not so good by any means—no spring from the loins, and feeblish, not to say shipwrecky, about the knees. Tom, on the contrary, though not half so strong in the arms, is good all over, straight, hard, and springy, from neck to ankle, better perhaps in his legs than any-where. Besides, you can see by the clear white of his eye, and fresh, bright look of his skin, that he is in tip-top training, able to do all he knows; while the Slogger looks rather sodden, as if he didn't take much exercise and ate too much tuck. The time-keeper is chosen, a large ring made, and the two stand up opposite one another for a moment, giving us time just to make our little observations.

"If Tom'll only condescend to fight with his head and heels," as East mutters to Martin, "we shall do."

But seemingly he won't, for there he goes in, making play with both hands. Hard all is the word; the two stand to one another like men; rally follows rally in quick succession, each fighting as if he thought to finish the whole thing out of hand. "Can't last at this rate," say the knowing ones, while the partisans of each make the air ring with their shouts and counter-shouts of encouragement, approval, and defiance.

"Take it easy, take it easy; keep away; let him come after you," implores East, as he wipes Tom's face after the first round with a wet sponge, while he sits back on Martin's knee, supported by the Madman's long arms, which tremble a little from excitement.

"Time's up," calls the time-keeper.

"There he goes again, hang it all!" growls East, as his man is at it again, as hard as ever. A very severe round follows, in which Tom gets out and out the worst of it, and is at last hit clean off his legs, and deposited on the grass by a right-hander from the Slogger.

Loud shouts rise from the boys of Slogger's house, and the School-house are silent and vicious, ready to pick quarrels anywhere.

"Two to one in half-crowns on the big un," says Rattle, one of the amateurs, a tall fellow, in thunder-and-lightning waistcoat, and puffy, good-natured face.

"Done!" says Groove, another amateur of quieter look, taking out his notebook to enter it, for our friend Rattle sometimes forgets these little things.

Meantime East is freshening up Tom with the sponges for next round, and has set two other boys to rub his hands.

"Tom, old boy," whispers he, "this may be fun for
you, but it's death to me. He'll hit all the fight out of
you in another five minutes, and then I shall go and
drown myself in the island ditch. Feint him; use your
legs; draw him about. He'll lose his wind then in no
time, and you can go into him. Hit at his body too;
we'll take care of his frontispiece by-and-by."

Tom felt the wisdom of the counsel, and saw already
that he couldn't go in and finish the Slogger off at mere
hammer and tongs, so changed his tactics completely in
the third round. He now fights cautiously, getting away
from and parrying the Slogger's lunging hits, instead of
trying to counter, and leading his enemy a dance all
round the ring after him. "He's funking; go in,
Williams," "Catch him up," "Finish him off," scream
the small boys of the Slogger party.

"Just what we want," thinks East, chuckling to himself, as he sees Williams, excited by these shouts, and
thinking the game in his own hands, blowing himself
in his exertions to get to close quarters again, while Tom
is keeping away with perfect ease.

They quarter over the ground again and again, Tom
always on the defensive.

The Slogger pulls up at last for a moment, fairly blown.

"Now, then, Tom," sings out East, dancing with delight. Tom goes in in a twinkling, and hits two heavy
body blows, and gets away again before the Slogger can
catch his wind, which when he does he rushes with blind
fury at Tom, and being skilfully parried and avoided,
overreaches himself and falls on his face, amidst terrific
cheers from the School-house boys.

"Double your two to one?" says Groove to Rattle,
notebook in hand.

"Stop a bit," says that hero, looking uncomfortably at

Williams, who is puffing away on his second's knee, winded enough, but little the worse in any other way.

After another round the Slogger too seems to see that he can't go in and win right off, and has met his match or thereabouts. So he too begins to use his head, and tries to make Tom lose his patience, and come in before his time. And so the fight sways on, now one and now the other getting a trifling pull.

Tom's face begins to look very one-sided—there are little queer bumps on his forehead, and his mouth is bleeding ; but East keeps the wet sponge going so scientifically that he comes up looking as fresh and bright as ever. Williams is only slightly marked in the face, but by the nervous movement of his elbows you can see that Tom's body blows are telling. In fact, half the vice of the Slogger's hitting is neutralized, for he daren't lunge out freely for fear of exposing his sides. It is too interesting by this time for much shouting, and the whole ring is very quiet.

"All right, Tommy," whispers East ; " hold on's the horse that's to win. We've got the last. Keep your head, old boy."

But where is Arthur all this time ? Words cannot paint the poor little fellow's distress. He couldn't muster courage to come up to the ring, but wandered up and down from the great fives court to the corner of the chapel rails, now trying to make up his mind to throw himself between them, and try to stop them ; then thinking of running in and telling his friend Mary, who he knew, would instantly report to the Doctor. The stories he had heard of men being killed in prize-fights rose up horribly before him.

Once only, when the shouts of " Well done, Brown ! " " Huzza for the School-house ! " rose higher than ever, he ventured up to the ring, thinking the victory was won. Catching sight of Tom's face in the state I have described, all fear of consequences vanishing out of his mind; he rushed straight off to the matron's room, beseeching her to get the fight stopped, or he should die.

But it's time for us to get back to the close. What is this fierce tumult and confusion? The ring is broken, and high and angry words are being bandied about. "It's all fair "—" It isn't "—" No hugging ! " The fight is stopped. The combatants, however, sit there quietly, tended by their seconds, while their adherents wrangle in the middle. East can't help shouting challenges to two or three of the other side, though he never leaves Tom for a moment, and plies the sponges as fast as ever.

The fact is, that at the end of the last round, Tom, seeing a good opening, had closed with his opponent, and after a moment's struggle, had thrown him heavily, by help of the fall he had learnt from his village rival in the Vale of White Horse. Williams hadn't the ghost of a chance with Tom at wrestling.; and the conviction broke at once on the Slogger faction that if this were allowed their man must be licked. There was a strong feeling in the School against catching hold and throwing, though it was generally ruled all fair within limits; so the ring was broken and the fight stopped.

The School-house are overruled—the fight is on again, but there is to be no throwing ; and East, in high wrath, threatens to take his man away after next round (which he don't mean to do, by the way), when suddenly young Brooke comes through the small gate at the end of the chapel. The School-house faction rush to him. " Oh, hurrah ! now we shall get fair play."

" Please, Brooke, come up. They won't let Tom Brown throw him."

"Throw whom?" says Brooke, coming up to the ring. "Oh! Williams, I see. Nonsense! Of course he may throw him, if he catches him fairly above the waist."

Now, young Brooke, you're in the sixth, you know, and you ought to stop all fights. He looks hard at both boys. "Anything wrong?" says he to East, nodding at Tom.

"Not a bit."

"Not beat at all?"

"Bless you, no! Heaps of fight in him.—Ain't there, Tom?"

Tom looks at Brooke and grins.

"How's he?" nodding at Williams.

"So so; rather done, I think, since his last fall. He won't stand above two more."

"Time's up!" The boys rise again and face one another. Brooke can't find it in his heart to stop them just yet, so the round goes on, the Slogger waiting for Tom, and reserving all his strength to hit him out should he come in for the wrestling dodge again, for he feels that that must be stopped, or his sponge will soon go up in the air.

And now another newcomer appears on the field, to wit, the under-porter, with his long brush and great wooden receptacle for dust under his arm. He has been sweeping out the schools.

"You'd better stop, gentlemen," he says; "the Doctor knows that Brown's fighting—he'll be out in a minute."

"You go to Bath, Bill," is all that that excellent servitor gets by his advice; and being a man of his hands, and a stanch upholder of the School-house, can't help stopping to look on for a bit, and see Tom Brown, their pet craftsman, fight a round.

It is grim earnest now, and no mistake. Both boys

feel this, and summon every power of head, hand, and eye to their aid. A piece of luck on either side, a foot slipping, a blow getting well home, or another fall, may decide it. Tom works slowly round for an opening; he has all the legs, and can choose his own time. The Slogger waits for the attack, and hopes to finish it by some heavy right-handed blow. As they quarter slowly over the ground, the evening sun comes out from behind a cloud and falls full on Williams's face. Tom darts in; the heavy right hand is delivered, but only grazes his head. A short rally at close quarters, and they close; in another moment the Slogger is thrown again heavily for the third time.

"I'll give you three or two on the little one in half-crowns," said Groove to Rattle.

"No, thank 'ee," answers the other, diving his hands farther into his coat-tails.

Just at this stage of the proceedings, the door of the turret which leads to the Doctor's library suddenly opens, and he steps into the close, and makes straight for the ring, in which Brown and the Slogger are both seated on their seconds' knees for the last time.

"The Doctor! the Doctor!" shouts some small boy who catches sight of him, and the ring melts away in a few seconds, the small boys tearing off, Tom collaring his jacket and waistcoat, and slipping through the little gate by the chapel, and round the corner to Harrowell's with his backers, as lively as need be; Williams and his backers making off not quite so fast across the close; Groove, Rattle, and the other bigger fellows trying to combine dignity and prudence in a comical manner, and walking off fast enough, they hope, not to be recognized, and not fast enough to look like running away.

Young Brooke alone remains on the ground by the

time the Doctor gets there, and touches his hat, not without a slight inward qualm.

"Hah! Brooke. I am surprised to see you here. Don't you know that I expect the sixth to stop fighting?"

Brooke felt much more uncomfortable than he had expected, but he was rather a favourite with the Doctor for his openness and plainness of speech, so blurted out, as he walked by the Doctor's side, who had already turned back,—

"Yes, sir, generally. But I thought you wished us to exercise a discretion in the matter too—not to inter-fere too soon."

"But they have been fighting this half-hour and more," said the Doctor.

"Yes, sir; but neither was hurt. And they're the sort of boys who'll be all the better friends now, which they wouldn't have been if they had been stopped any earlier—before it was so equal."

"Who was fighting with Brown?" said the Doctor.

"Williams, sir, of Thompson's. He is bigger than Brown, and had the best of it at first, but not when you came up, sir. There's a good deal of jealousy between our house and Thompson's, and there would have been more fights if this hadn't been let go on, or if either of them had had much the worst of it."

"Well but, Brooke," said the Doctor, "doesn't this look a little as if you exercised your discretion by only stopping a fight when the School-house boy is getting the worst of it?"

Brooke, it must be confessed, felt rather gravelled.

"Now remember," added the Doctor, as he stopped at the turret-door, "this fight is not to go on; you'll see to that. And I expect you to stop all fights in future at once."

"Very well, sir," said young Brooke, touching his hat, and not sorry to see the turret-door close behind the Doctor's back.

Meantime Tom and the stanchest of his adherents had reached Harrowell's, and Sally was bustling about to get them a late tea, while Stumps had been sent off to Tew, the butcher, to get a piece of raw beef for Tom's eye, which was to be healed off-hand, so that he might show well in the morning. He was not a bit the worse, except a slight difficulty in his vision, a singing in his ears, and a sprained thumb, which he kept in a cold-water bandage, while he drank lots of tea, and listened to the babel of voices talking and speculating of nothing but the fight, and how Williams would have given in after another fall (which he didn't in the least believe), and how on earth the Doctor could have got to know of it—such bad luck! He couldn't help thinking to himself that he was glad he hadn't won; he liked it better as it was, and felt very friendly to the Slogger. And then poor little Arthur crept in and sat down quietly near him, and kept looking at him and the raw beef with such plaintive looks that Tom at last burst out laughing.

"Don't make such eyes, young un," said he; "there's nothing the matter."

"Oh, but, Tom, are you much hurt? I can't bear thinking it was all for me."

"Not a bit of it; don't flatter yourself. We were sure to have had it out sooner or later."

"Well, but you won't go on, will you? You'll promise me you won't go on?"

"Can't tell about that—all depends on the houses. We're in the hands of our countrymen, you know. Must fight for the School-house flag, if so be."

However, the lovers of the science were doomed to disappointment this time. Directly after locking-up, one of the night-fags knocked at Tom's door.

"Brown, young Brooke wants you in the sixth-form room."

Up went Tom to the summons, and found the magnates sitting at their supper.

"Well, Brown," said young Brooke, nodding to him, "how do you feel?"

"Oh, very well, thank you, only I've sprained my thumb, I think."

"Sure to do that in a fight. Well, you hadn't the worst of it, I could see. Where did you learn that throw?"

"Down in the country when I was a boy."

"Hullo! why, what are you now? Well, never mind; you're a plucky fellow. Sit down and have some supper."

Tom obeyed, by no means loath. And the fifth-form boy next filled him a tumbler of bottled beer, and he ate and drank, listening to the pleasant talk, and wondering how soon he should be in the fifth, and one of that much-envied society.

As he got up to leave, Brooke said, "You must shake hands to-morrow morning; I shall come and see that done after first lesson."

And so he did. And Tom and the Slogger shook hands with great satisfaction and mutual respect. And for the next year or two, whenever fights were being talked of, the small boys who had been present shook their heads wisely, saying, "Ah! but you should just have seen the fight between Slogger Williams and Tom Brown!"

And now, boys all, three words before we quit the

subject. I have put in this chapter on fighting of malice prepense, partly because I want to give you a true picture of what everyday school life was in my time, and not a kid-glove and go-to-meeting-coat picture, and partly because of the cant and twaddle that's talked of boxing and fighting with fists nowadays. Even Thackeray has given in to it; and only a few weeks ago there was some rampant stuff in the *Times* on the subject, in an article on field sports.

Boys will quarrel, and when they quarrel will sometimes fight. Fighting with fists is the natural and English way for English boys to settle their quarrels. What substitute for it is there, or ever was there, amongst any nation under the sun? What would you like to see take its place?

Learn to box, then, as you learn to play cricket and football. Not one of you will be the worse, but very much the better, for learning to box well. Should you never have to use it in earnest, there's no exercise in the world so good for the temper and for the muscles of the back and legs.

As to fighting, keep out of it if you can, by all means. When the time comes, if it ever should, that you have to say "Yes" or "No" to a challenge to fight, say "No" if you can—only take care you make it clear to yourselves why you say "No." It's a proof of the highest courage, if done from true Christian motives. It's quite right and justifiable, if done from a simple aversion to physical pain and danger. But don't say "No" because you fear a licking, and say or think it's because you fear God, for that's neither Christian nor honest. And if you do fight, fight it out; and don't give in while you can stand and see.

CHAPTER VI.

FEVER IN THE SCHOOL.

" This our hope for all that's mortal,
    And we too shall burst the bond ;
Death keeps watch beside the portal,
    But 'tis life that dwells beyond."

                                    JOHN STERLING.

Two years have passed since the events recorded in the
last chapter, and the end of the summer half-year is
again drawing on.   Martin has left and gone on a cruise
in the South Pacific, in one of his uncle's ships ; the old
magpie, as disreputable as ever, his last bequest to
Arthur, lives in the joint study.   Arthur is nearly sixteen, and at the head of the twenty, having gone up
the school at the rate of a form a half-year. East and
Tom have been much more deliberate in their progress,
and are only a little way up the fifth form. Great
strapping boys they are, but still thorough boys, filling
about the same place in the house that young Brooke
filled when they were new boys, and much the same
sort of fellows. Constant intercourse with Arthur has
done much for both of them, especially for Tom ; but
much remains yet to be done, if they are to get all the
good out of Rugby which is to be got there in these
times.   Arthur is still frail and delicate, with more spirit
than body ; but, thanks to his intimacy with them and
Martin, has learned to swim, and run, and play cricket,
and has never hurt himself by too much reading.

One evening, as they were all sitting down to supper
in the fifth-form room, some one started a report that
a fever had broken out at one of the boarding-houses.
" They say," he added, " that Thompson is very ill, and
that Dr. Robertson has been sent for from Northampton."

"Then we shall all be sent home," cried another. "Hurrah! five weeks' extra holidays, and no fifth-form examination!"

"I hope not," said Tom; "there'll be no Marylebone match then at the end of the half."

Some thought one thing, some another, many didn't believe the report; but the next day, Tuesday, Dr. Robertson arrived, and stayed all day, and had long conferences with the Doctor.

On Wednesday morning, after prayers, the Doctor addressed the whole school. There were several cases of fever in different houses, he said; but Dr. Robertson, after the most careful examination, had assured him that it was not infectious, and that if proper care were taken, there could be no reason for stopping the school-work at present. The examinations were just coming on, and it would be very unadvisable to break up now. However, any boys who chose to do so were at liberty to write home, and, if their parents wished it, to leave at once. He should send the whole school home if the fever spread.

The next day Arthur sickened, but there was no other case. Before the end of the week thirty or forty boys had gone, but the rest stayed on. There was a general wish to please the Doctor, and a feeling that it was cowardly to run away.

On the Saturday Thompson died, in the bright afternoon, while the cricket-match was going on as usual on the big-side ground. The Doctor, coming from his death-bed, passed along the gravel-walk at the side of the close, but no one knew what had happened till the next day. At morning lecture it began to be rumoured, and by afternoon chapel was known generally; and a feeling of seriousness and awe at the actual presence of death among them came over the whole school. In all the long years of his ministry the Doctor perhaps never spoke words which sank deeper than some of those in that day's sermon.

"When I came yesterday from visiting all but the very death-bed of him who has been taken from us, and looked around upon all the familiar objects and scenes within our own ground, where your common amusements were going on with your common cheerfulness and activity, I felt there was nothing painful in witnessing that; it did not seem in any way shocking or out of tune with those feelings which the sight of a dying Christian must be supposed to awaken. The unsuitableness in point of natural feeling between scenes of mourning and scenes of liveliness did not at all present itself. But I did feel that if at that moment any of those faults had been brought before me which sometimes occur amongst us; had I heard that any of you had been guilty of falsehood, or of drunkenness, or of any other such sin; had I heard from any quarter the language of profaneness, or of unkindness, or of indecency; had I heard or seen any signs of that wretched folly which courts the laugh of fools by affecting not to dread evil and not to care for good, then the unsuitableness of any of these things with the scene I had just quitted would indeed have been most intensely painful. And why? Not because such things would really have been worse than at any other time, but because at such a moment the eyes are opened really to know good and evil, because we then feel what it is so to live as that death becomes an infinite blessing, and what it is so to live also that it were good for us if we had never been born."

Tom had gone into chapel in sickening anxiety about

Arthur, but he came out cheered and strengthened by those grand words, and walked up alone to their study. And when he sat down and looked round, and saw Arthur's straw hat and cricket-jacket hanging on their pegs, and marked all his little neat arrangements, not one of which had been disturbed, the tears indeed rolled down his cheeks ; but they were calm and blessed tears, and he repeated to himself, " Yes, Geordie's eyes are opened; he knows what it is so to live as that death becomes an infinite blessing. But do I ? O God, can I bear to lose him ? "

The week passed mournfully away. No more boys sickened, but Arthur was reported worse each day, and his mother arrived early in the week. Tom made many appeals to be allowed to see him, and several times tried to get up to the sick-room ; but the housekeeper was always in the way, and at last spoke to the Doctor, who kindly but peremptorily forbade him.

Thompson was buried on the Tuesday, and the burial service, so soothing and grand always, but beyond all words solemn when read over a boy's grave to his companions, brought him much comfort, and many strange new thoughts and longings. He went back to his regular life, and played cricket and bathed as usual. It seemed to him that this was the right thing to do, and the new thoughts and longings became more brave and healthy for the effort. The crisis came on Saturday, the day week that Thompson had died ; and during that long afternoon Tom sat in his study reading his Bible, and going every half-hour to the housekeeper's room, expecting each time to hear that the gentle and brave little spirit had gone home. But God had work for Arthur to do. The crisis passed : on Sunday evening he was declared out of danger : on Monday he sent a message to

Tom that he was almost well, had changed his room, and was to be allowed to see him the next day.

It was evening when the housekeeper summoned him to the sick-room. Arthur was lying on the sofa by the open window, through which the rays of the western sun stole gently, lighting up his white face and golden hair. Tom remembered a German picture of an angel which he knew; often had he thought how transparent and golden and spirit-like it was; and he shuddered to think how like it Arthur looked, and felt a shock as if his blood had all stopped short, as he realized how near the other world his friend must have been to look like that. Never till that moment had he felt how his little chum had twined himself round his heart-strings; and as he stole gently across the room and knelt down, and put his arm round Arthur's head on the pillow, felt ashamed and half-angry at his own red and brown face, and the bounding sense of health and power which filled every fibre of his body, and made every movement of mere living a joy to him. He needn't have troubled himself: it was this very strength and power so different from his own which drew Arthur so to him.

Arthur laid his thin, white hand, on which the blue veins stood out so plainly, on Tom's great brown fist, and smiled at him; and then looked out of the window again, as if he couldn't bear to lose a moment of the sunset, into the tops of the great feathery elms, round which the rooks were circling and clanging, returning in flocks from their evening's foraging parties. The elms rustled; the sparrows in the ivy just outside the window chirped and fluttered about, quarrelling, and making it up again; the rooks, young and old, talked in chorus, and the merry shouts of the boys and the sweet click of the cricket-bats came up cheerily from below.

"Dear George," said Tom, "I am so glad to be let up to see you at last. I've tried hard to come so often, but they wouldn't let me before."

"Oh, I know, Tom; Mary has told me every day about you, and how she was obliged to make the Doctor speak to you to keep you away. I'm very glad you didn't get up, for you might have caught it; and you couldn't stand being ill, with all the matches going on. And you're in the eleven, too, I hear. I'm so glad."

"Yes; ain't it jolly?" said Tom proudly. "I'm ninth too. I made forty at the last pie-match, and caught three fellows out. So I was put in above Jones and Tucker. Tucker's so savage, for he was head of the twenty-two."

"Well, I think you ought to be higher yet," said Arthur, who was as jealous for the renown of Tom in games as Tom was for his as a scholar.

"Never mind. I don't care about cricket or anything now you're getting well, Geordie; and I shouldn't have hurt, I know, if they'd have let me come up. Nothing hurts me. But you'll get about now directly, won't you? You won't believe how clean I've kept the study. All your things are just as you left them; and I feed the old magpie just when you used, though I have to come in from big-side for him, the old rip. He won't look pleased all I can do, and sticks his head first on one side and then on the other, and blinks at me before he'll begin to eat, till I'm half inclined to box his ears. And whenever East comes in, you should see him hop off to the window, dot and go one, though Harry wouldn't touch a feather of him now."

Arthur laughed. "Old Gravey has a good memory; he can't forget the sieges of poor Martin's den in old times." He paused a moment, and then went on:

"You can't think how often I've been thinking of old Martin since I've been ill. I suppose one's mind gets restless, and likes to wander off to strange, unknown places. I wonder what queer new pets the old boy has got. How he must be revelling in the thousand new birds, beasts, and fishes!"

Tom felt a pang of jealousy, but kicked it out in a moment. "Fancy him on a South Sea island, with the Cherokees, or Patagonians, or some such wild niggers!" (Tom's ethnology and geography were faulty, but sufficient for his needs.) "They'll make the old Madman cock medicine-man, and tattoo him all over. Perhaps he's cutting about now all blue, and has a squaw and a wigwam. He'll improve their boomerangs, and be able to throw them too, without having old Thomas sent after him by the Doctor to take them away."

Arthur laughed at the remembrance of the boomerang story, but then looked grave again, and said, "He'll convert all the island, I know."

"Yes, if he don't blow it up first."

"Do you remember, Tom, how you and East used to laugh at him and chaff him, because he said he was sure the rooks all had calling-over or prayers, or something of the sort, when the locking-up bell rang? Well, I declare," said Arthur, looking up seriously into Tom's laughing eyes, "I do think he was right. Since I've been lying here, I've watched them every night; and, do you know, they really do come and perch, all of them, just about locking-up time; and then first there's a regular chorus of caws; and then they stop a bit, and one old fellow, or perhaps two or three in different trees, caw solos; and then off they all go again, fluttering about and cawing anyhow till they roost."

"I wonder if the old blackies do talk," said Tom,

looking up at them. "How they must abuse me and East, and pray for the Doctor for stopping the slinging!"

"There! look, look!" cried Arthur; "don't you see the old fellow without a tail coming up? Martin used to call him the 'clerk.' He can't steer himself. You never saw such fun as he is in a high wind, when he can't steer himself home, and gets carried right past the trees, and has to bear up again and again before he can perch."

The locking-up bell began to toll, and the two boys were silent, and listened to it. The sound soon carried Tom off to the river and the woods, and he began to go over in his mind the many occasions on which he had heard that toll coming faintly down the breeze, and had to pack his rod in a hurry and make a run for it, to get in before the gates were shut. He was roused with a start from his memories by Arthur's voice, gentle and weak from his late illness.

"Tom, will you be angry if I talk to you very seriously?"

"No, dear old boy, not I. But ain't you faint, Arthur, or ill? What can I get you? Don't say anything to hurt yourself now—you are very weak; let me come up again."

"No, no; I shan't hurt myself. I'd sooner speak to you now, if you don't mind. I've asked Mary to tell the Doctor that you are with me, so you needn't go down to calling-over; and I mayn't have another chance, for I shall most likely have to go home for change of air to get well, and mayn't come back this half."

"Oh, do you think you must go away before the end of the half? I'm so sorry. It's more than five weeks yet to the holidays, and all the fifth-form examination and half the cricket-matches to come yet. And what shall I do all that time alone in our study? Why, Arthur, it will be more than twelve weeks before I see you again. Oh, hang it, I can't stand that! Besides, who's to keep me up to working at the examination books? I shall come out bottom of the form, as sure as eggs is eggs."

Tom was rattling on, half in joke, half in earnest, for he wanted to get Arthur out of his serious vein, thinking it would do him harm; but Arthur broke in,—

"Oh, please, Tom, stop, or you'll drive all I had to say out of my head. And I'm already horribly afraid I'm going to make you angry."

"Don't gammon, young un," rejoined Tom (the use of the old name, dear to him from old recollections, made Arthur start and smile and feel quite happy); "you know you ain't afraid, and you've never made me angry since the first month we chummed together. Now I'm going to be quite sober for a quarter of an hour, which is more than I am once in a year; so make the most of it; heave ahead, and pitch into me right and left."

"Dear Tom, I ain't going to pitch into you," said Arthur piteously; "and it seems so cocky in me to be advising you, who've been my backbone ever since I've been at Rugby, and have made the school a paradise to me. Ah, I see I shall never do it, unless I go head over heels at once, as you said when you taught me to swim. Tom, I want you to give up using vulgus-books and cribs."

Arthur sank back on to his pillow with a sigh, as if the effort had been great; but the worst was now over, and he looked straight at Tom, who was evidently taken aback. He leant his elbows on his knees, and stuck his hands into his hair, whistled a verse of "Billy Taylor," and then was quite silent for another minute. Not a shade crossed his face, but he was clearly puzzled. At last he looked up, and caught Arthur's anxious look, took his hand, and said simply,—

"Why, young un?"

"Because you're the honestest boy in Rugby, and that ain't honest."

"I don't see that."

"What were you sent to Rugby for?"

"Well, I don't know exactly—nobody ever told me: I suppose because all boys are sent to a public school in England."

"But what do you think yourself? What do you want to do here, and to carry away?"

Tom thought a minute. "I want to be A1 at cricket and football, and all the other games, and to make my hands keep my head against any fellow, lout or gentleman. I want to get into the sixth before I leave, and to please the Doctor; and I want to carry away just as much Latin and Greek as will take me through Oxford respectably. There, now, young un; I never thought of it before, but that's pretty much about my figure. Ain't it all on the square? What have you got to say to that?"

"Why, that you are pretty sure to do all that you want, then."

"Well, I hope so. But you've forgot one thing—what I want to leave behind me. I want to leave behind me," said Tom, speaking slow, and looking much moved, "the name of a fellow who never bullied a little boy, or turned his back on a big one."

Arthur pressed his hand, and after a moment's silence went on, "You say, Tom, you want to please the Doctor. Now, do you want to please him by what he thinks you do, or by what you really do?"

"By what I really do, of course."

"Does he think you use cribs and vulgus-books?"

Tom felt at once that his flank was turned, but he couldn't give in. "He was at Winchester himself," said he; "he knows all about it."

"Yes; but does he think *you* use them? Do you think he approves of it?"

"You young villain!" said Tom, shaking his fist at Arthur, half vexed and half pleased, "I never think about it. Hang it! there, perhaps he don't. Well, I suppose he don't."

Arthur saw that he had got his point; he knew his friend well, and was wise in silence as in speech. He only said, "I would sooner have the doctor's good opinion of me as I really am than any man's in the world."

After another minute, Tom began again, "Look here, young un. How on earth am I to get time to play the matches this half if I give up cribs? We're in the middle of that long crabbed chorus in the Agamemnon. I can only just make head or tail of it with the crib. Then there's Pericles's speech coming on in Thucydides, and 'The Birds' to get up for the examination, besides the Tacitus." Tom groaned at the thought of his accumulated labours. "I say, young un, there's only five weeks or so left to holidays. Mayn't I go on as usual for this half? I'll tell the Doctor about it some day, or you may."

Arthur looked out of the window. The twilight had come on, and all was silent. He repeated in a low voice: "In this thing the Lord pardon thy servant, that when my master goeth into the house of Rimmon to worship there, and he leaneth on my hand, and I bow down myself in the house of Rimmon, when I bow down myself in the house of Rimmon, the Lord pardon thy servant in this thing."

Not a word more was said on the subject, and the boys were again silent—one of those blessed, short silences in which the resolves which colour a life are so often taken.

Tom was the first to break it. " You've been very ill indeed, haven't you, Geordie ? " said he, with a mixture of awe and curiosity, feeling as if his friend had been in some strange place or scene, of which he could form no idea, and full of the memory of his own thoughts during the last week.

" Yes, very. I'm sure the Doctor thought I was going to die. He gave me the Sacrament last Sunday, and you can't think what he is when one is ill. He said such brave, and tender, and gentle things to me, I felt quite light and strong after it, and never had any more fear. My mother brought our old medical man, who attended me when I was a poor sickly child. He said my constitution was quite changed, and that I'm fit for anything now. If it hadn't, I couldn't have stood three days of this illness. That's all thanks to you, and the games you've made me fond of."

" More thanks to old Martin," said Tom ; " he's been your real friend."

" Nonsense, Tom ; he never could have done for me what you have."

" Well, I don't know ; I did little enough. Did they tell you—you won't mind hearing it now, I know—that poor Thompson died last week ? The other three boys are getting quite round, like you."

" Oh yes, I heard of it."

Then Tom, who was quite full of it, told Arthur of the burial-service in the chapel, and how it had impressed him, and, he believed, all the other boys. " And though the Doctor never said a word about it," said he, " and it was a half-holiday and match-day, there wasn't a game played in the close all the afternoon, and the boys all went about as if it were Sunday."

"I'm very glad of it," said Arthur. "But, Tom, I've had such strange thoughts about death lately. I've never told a soul of them, not even my mother. Sometimes I think they're wrong, but, do you know, I don't think in my heart I could be sorry at the death of any of my friends."

Tom was taken quite aback. "What in the world is the young un after now?" thought he; "I've swallowed a good many of his crotchets, but this altogether beats me. He can't be quite right in his head." He didn't want to say a word, and shifted about uneasily in the dark; however, Arthur seemed to be waiting for an answer, so at last he said, "I don't think I quite see what you mean, Geordie. One's told so often to think about death that I've tried it on sometimes, especially this last week. But we won't talk of it now. I'd better go. You're getting tired, and I shall do you harm."

"No, no; indeed I ain't, Tom. You must stop till nine; there's only twenty minutes. I've settled you shall stop till nine. And oh! do let me talk to you—I must talk to you. I see it's just as I feared. You think I'm half mad. Don't you, now?"

"Well, I did think it odd what you said, Geordie, as you ask me."

Arthur paused a moment, and then said quickly, "I'll tell you how it all happened. At first, when I was sent to the sick-room, and found I had really got the fever, I was terribly frightened. I thought I should die, and I could not face it for a moment. I don't think it was sheer cowardice at first, but I thought how hard it was to be taken away from my mother and sisters and you all, just as I was beginning to see my way to many things, and to feel that I might be a man and do a man's work. To die without having fought, and worked, and given one's life away, was too hard to bear. I got terribly impatient, and accused God of injustice, and strove to justify myself. And the harder I strove the deeper I sank. Then the image of my dear father often came across me, but I turned from it. Whenever it came, a heavy, numbing throb seemed to take hold of my heart, and say, 'Dead—dead—dead.' And I cried out, 'The living, the living shall praise Thee, O God; the dead cannot praise thee. There is no work in the grave; in the night no man can work. But I can work. I can do great things. I *will* do great things. Why wilt thou slay me?' And so I struggled and plunged, deeper and deeper, and went down into a living black tomb. I was alone there, with no power to stir or think; alone with myself; beyond the reach of all human fellowship; beyond Christ's reach, I thought, in my nightmare. You, who are brave and bright and strong, can have no idea of that agony. Pray to God you never may. Pray as for your life."

Arthur stopped—from exhaustion, Tom thought; but what between his fear lest Arthur should hurt himself, his awe, and his longing for him to go on, he couldn't ask, or stir to help him.

Presently he went on, but quite calm and slow. "I don't know how long I was in that state—for more than a day, I know; for I was quite conscious, and lived my outer life all the time, and took my medicines, and spoke to my mother, and heard what they said. But I didn't take much note of time. I thought time was over for me, and that that tomb was what was beyond. Well, on last Sunday morning, as I seemed to lie in that tomb, alone, as I thought, for ever and ever, the black, dead wall was cleft in two, and I was caught up and borne through into the light by some great power, some living, mighty spirit. Tom, do you remember the living creatures and the wheels in Ezekiel? It was just like that. 'When they went, I heard the noise of their wings, like the noise of great waters, as the voice of the Almighty, the voice of speech, as the noise of an host; when they stood, they let down their wings.' 'And they went every one straight forward: whither the spirit was to go, they went; and they turned not when they went.' And we rushed through the bright air, which was full of myriads of living creatures, and paused on the brink of a great river. And the power held me up, and I knew that that great river was the grave, and death dwelt there, but not the death I had met in the black tomb. That, I felt, was gone for ever. For on the other bank of the great river I saw men and women and children rising up pure and bright, and the tears were wiped from their eyes, and they put on glory and strength, and all weariness and pain fell away. And beyond were a multitude which no man could number, and they worked at some great work; and they who rose from the river went on and joined in the work. They all worked, and each worked in a different way, but all at the same work. And I saw there my father, and the men in the old town whom I knew when I was a child—many a hard, stern man, who never came to church, and whom they called atheist and infidel. There they were, side by side with my father, whom I had seen toil and die for them, and women and little children, and the seal was on the foreheads of all. And I longed to see what the work was, and could not; so I tried to plunge in the river, for I thought I would join them, but I could not. Then I looked about to see how they got into the river. And this I could not see, but I saw myriads on this side, and they too worked, and I knew that it was the same work, and the same seal was on their foreheads. And though I saw that there was toil and anguish in the work of these, and that most that were working were blind and feeble, yet I longed no more to plunge into the river, but more and more to know what the work was. And as I looked I saw my mother and my sisters, and I saw the Doctor, and you, Tom, and hundreds more whom I knew; and at last I saw myself too, and I was toiling and doing ever so little a piece of the great work. Then it all melted away, and the power left me, and as it left me I thought I heard a voice say, ' The vision is for an appointed time; though it tarry, wait for it, for in the end it shall speak and not lie, it shall surely come, it shall not tarry.' It was early morning I know, then—it was so quiet and cool, and my mother was fast asleep in the chair by my bedside; but it wasn't only a dream of mine. I know it wasn't a dream. Then I fell into a deep sleep, and only woke after afternoon chapel; and the Doctor came and gave me the Sacrament, as I told you. I told him and my mother I should get well—I knew I should; but I couldn't tell them why. Tom," said Arthur gently, after another minute, " do you see why I could not grieve now to see my dearest friend die ? It can't be—it isn't—all fever or illness. God would never have let me see it so clear if it wasn't true. I don't understand it all yet; it will take me my life and longer to do that—to find out what the work is."

When Arthur stopped there was a long pause. Tom could not speak; he was almost afraid to breathe, lest he should break the train of Arthur's thoughts. He longed to hear more, and to ask questions. In another minute nine o'clock struck, and a gentle tap at the door called them both back into the world again. They did not answer, however, for a moment; and so the door opened, and a lady came in carrying a candle.

She went straight to the sofa, and took hold of Arthur's hand, and then stooped down and kissed him.

"My dearest boy, you feel a little feverish again. Why didn't you have lights? You've talked too much, and excited yourself in the dark."

"Oh no, mother; you can't think how well I feel. I shall start with you to-morrow for Devonshire. But, mother, here's my friend—here's Tom Brown. You know him?"

"Yes, indeed; I've known him for years," she said, and held out her hand to Tom, who was now standing up behind the sofa. This was Arthur's mother : tall and slight and fair, with masses of golden hair drawn back from the broad, white forehead, and the calm blue eye meeting his so deep and open—the eye that he knew so well, for it was his friend's over again, and the lovely, tender mouth that trembled while he looked—she stood there, a woman of thirty-eight, old enough to be his mother, and one whose face showed the lines which must be written on the faces of good men's wives and widows, but he thought he had never seen anything so beautiful. He couldn't help wondering if Arthur's sisters were like her.

Tom held her hand, and looked on straight in her face ; he could neither let it go nor speak.

"Now, Tom," said Arthur, laughing, "where are your manners? You'll stare my mother out of countenance." Tom dropped the little hand with a sigh. "There, sit down, both of you.—Here, dearest mother; there's room here." And he made a place on the sofa for her.—"Tom, you needn't go ; I'm sure you won't be called up at first lesson." Tom felt that he would risk being floored at every lesson for the rest of his natural school-life sooner than go, so sat down. "And now," said Arthur, "I have realized one of the dearest wishes of my life—to see you two together."

And then he led away the talk to their home in Devonshire, and the red, bright earth, and the deep green combes, and the peat streams like cairngorm pebbles, and the wild moor with its high, cloudy tors for a giant background to the picture, till Tom got jealous, and stood up for the clear chalk streams, and the emerald water meadows and great elms and willows of the dear old royal county, as he gloried to call it. And the mother sat on quiet and loving, rejoicing in their life. The quarter to ten struck, and the bell rang for bed, before they had well begun their talk, as it seemed.

Then Tom rose with a sigh to go.

"Shall I see you in the morning, Geordie?" said he, as he shook his friend's hand. "Never mind, though; you'll be back next half. And I shan't forget the house of Rimmon."

Arthur's mother got up and walked with him to the door, and there gave him her hand again; and again his eyes met that deep, loving look, which was like a spell upon him. Her voice trembled slightly as she said, "Good-night. You are one who knows what our Father has promised to the friend of the widow and the fatherless. May He deal with you as you have dealt with me and mine!"

Tom was quite upset; he mumbled something about owing everything good in him to Geordie, looked in her face again, pressed her hand to his lips, and rushed downstairs to his study, where he sat till old Thomas came kicking at the door, to tell him his allowance would be stopped if he didn't go off to bed. (It would have been stopped anyhow, but that he was a great favourite with the old gentleman, who loved to come out in the afternoons into the close to Tom's wicket, and bowl slow twisters to him, and talk of the glories of bygone Surrey heroes, with whom he had played former generations.) So Tom roused himself, and took up his candle to go to bed; and then for the first time was aware of a beautiful new fishing-rod, with old Eton's mark on it, and a splendidly-bound Bible, which lay on his table, on the title-page of which was written—"TOM BROWN, from his affectionate and grateful friends, Frances Jane Arthur; George Arthur."

I leave you all to guess how he slept, and what he dreamt of.

CHAPTER VII.

HARRY EAST'S DILEMMAS AND DELIVERANCES.

> " The Holy Supper is kept indeed,
> In whatso we share with another's need—
> Not that which we give, but what we share,
> For the gift without the giver is bare.
> Who bestows himself with his alms feeds three,—
> Himself, his hungering neighbour, and Me."
> LOWELL, *The Vision of Sir Launfal.*

THE next morning, after breakfast, Tom, East, and Gower met as usual to learn their second lesson together. Tom had been considering how to break his proposal of giving up the crib to the others, and having found no better way (as indeed none better can ever be found by man or boy), told them simply what had happened; how he had been to see Arthur, who had talked to him upon the subject, and what he had said, and for his part he had made up his mind, and wasn't going to use cribs any more; and not being quite sure of his ground, took the high and pathetic tone, and was proceeding to say "how that, having learnt his lessons with them for so many years, it would grieve him much to put an end to the arrangement, and he hoped, at any rate, that if they wouldn't go on with him, they should still be just as good friends, and respect one another's motives; but——"

Here the other boys, who had been listening with open eyes and ears, burst in,—

"Stuff and nonsense!" cried Gower. "Here, East, get down the crib and find the place."

"O Tommy, Tommy!" said East, proceeding to do as he was bidden, "that it should ever have come to this! I knew Arthur'd be the ruin of you some day, and you of me. And now the time's come." And he made a doleful face.

"I don't know about ruin," answered Tom; "I know that you and I would have had the sack long ago if it hadn't been for him. And you know it as well as I."

"Well, we were in a baddish way before he came, I own; but this new crotchet of his is past a joke."

"Let's give it a trial, Harry; come. You know how often he has been right and we wrong."

"Now, don't you two be jawing away about young Square-toes," struck in Gower. "He's no end of a sucking wiseacre, I dare say; but we've no time to lose, and I've got the fives court at half-past nine."

"I say, Gower," said Tom appealingly, "be a good fellow, and let's try if we can't get on without the crib."

"What! in this chorus? Why, we shan't get through ten lines."

"I say, Tom," cried East, having hit on a new idea, "don't you remember, when we were in the upper fourth, and old Momus caught me construing off the leaf of a crib which I'd torn out and put in my book, and which

10

would float out on to the floor, he sent me up to be flogged for it ? "

" Yes, I remember it very well."

" Well, the Doctor, after he'd flogged me, told me himself that he didn't flog me for using a translation, but for taking it in to lesson, and using it there when I hadn't learnt a word before I came in. He said there was no harm in using a translation to get a clue to hard passages, if you tried all you could first to make them out without."

" Did he, though ? " said Tom ; " then Arthur must be wrong."

" Of course he is," said Gower—" the little prig. We'll only use the crib when we can't construe without it.—Go ahead, East."

And on this agreement they started—Tom, satisfied with having made his confession, and not sorry to have a *locus pœnitentiæ*, and not to be deprived altogether of the use of his old and faithful friend.

The boys went on as usual, each taking a sentence in turn, and the crib being handed to the one whose turn it was to construe. Of course Tom couldn't object to this, as, was it not simply lying there to be appealed to in case the sentence should prove too hard altogether for the construer ? But it must be owned that Gower and East did not make very tremendous exertions to conquer their sentences before having recourse to its help. Tom, however, with the most heroic virtue and gallantry, rushed into his sentence, searching in a high-minded manner for nominative and verb, and turning over his dictionary frantically for the first hard word that stopped him. But in the meantime Gower, who was bent on getting to fives, would peep quietly into the crib, and then suggest, " Don't you think this is the meaning ? " " I think you must take it this way, Brown." And as

Tom didn't see his way to not profiting by these suggestions, the lesson went on about as quickly as usual, and
Gower was able to start for the fives court within five
minutes of the half-hour.

When Tom and East were left face to face, they looked
at one another for a minute, Tom puzzled, and East choke-
full of fun, and then burst into a roar of laughter.

"Well, Tom," said East, recovering himself, "I don't
see any objection to the new way. It's about as good as
the old one, I think, besides the advantage it gives one of
feeling virtuous, and looking down on one's neighbours."

Tom shoved his hand into his back hair. "I ain't so
sure," said he; "you two fellows carried me off my legs.
I don't think we really tried one sentence fairly. Are
you sure you remember what the Doctor said to you?"

"Yes. And I'll swear I couldn't make out one of my
sentences to-day—no, nor ever could. I really don't
remember," said East, speaking slowly and impressively,
"to have come across one Latin or Greek sentence this
half that I could go and construe by the light of nature.
Whereby I am sure Providence intended cribs to be
used."

"The thing to find out," said Tom meditatively, "is
how long one ought to grind at a sentence without looking at the crib. Now I think if one fairly looks out all
the words one don't know, and then can't hit it, that's
enough."

"To be sure, Tommy," said East demurely, but with
a merry twinkle in his eye. "Your new doctrine too,
old fellow," added he, "when one comes to think of it,
is a cutting at the root of all school morality. You'll
take away mutual help, brotherly love, or, in the vulgar
tongue, giving construes, which I hold to be one of our
highest virtues. For how can you distinguish between

getting a construe from another boy and using a crib ? Hang it, Tom, if you're going to deprive all our school-fellows of the chance of exercising Christian benevolence and being good Samaritans, I shall cut the concern."

"I wish you wouldn't joke about it, Harry; it's hard enough to see one's way—a precious sight harder than I thought last night. But I suppose there's a use and an abuse of both, and one'll get straight enough somehow. But you can't make out, anyhow, that one has a right to use old vulgus-books and copy-books."

"Hullo, more heresy! How fast a fellow goes down-hill when he once gets his head before his legs. Listen to me, Tom. Not use old vulgus-books! Why, you Goth, ain't we to take the benefit of the wisdom and admire and use the work of past generations ? Not use old copy-books ! Why, you might as well say we ought to pull down Westminster Abbey, and put up a go-to-meeting shop with churchwarden windows; or never read Shakespeare, but only Sheridan Knowles. Think of all the work and labour that our predecessors have be-stowed on these very books ; and are we to make their work of no value ? "

"I say, Harry, please don't chaff; I'm really serious."

"And then, is it not our duty to consult the pleasure of others rather than our own, and above all, that of our masters ? Fancy, then, the difference to them in looking over a vulgus which has been carefully touched and re-touched by themselves and others, and which must bring them a sort of dreamy pleasure, as if they'd met the thought or expression of it somewhere or another—before they were born perhaps—and that of cutting up, and making picture-frames round all your and my false quantities, and other monstrosities. Why, Tom, you wouldn't be so cruel as never to let old Momus hum over

the ' O genus humanum ' again, and then look up doubt-
ingly through his spectacles, and end by smiling and
giving three extra marks for it—just for old sake's sake,
I suppose."

" Well," said Tom, getting up in something as like a
huff as he was capable of, " it's deuced hard that when
a fellow's really trying to do what he ought, his best
friends'll do nothing but chaff him and try to put him
down." And he stuck his books under his arm and his
hat on his head, preparatory to rushing out into the
quadrangle, to testify with his own soul of the faithless-
ness of friendships.

" Now don't be an ass, Tom," said East, catching hold
of him; " you know me well enough by this time ; my
bark's worse than my bite. You can't expect to ride
your new crotchet without anybody's trying to stick a
nettle under his tail and make him kick you off—especially as we shall all have to go on foot still. But now
sit down, and let's go over it again. I'll be as serious
as a judge."

Then Tom sat himself down on the table, and waxed
eloquent about all the righteousnesses and advantages of
the new plan, as was his wont whenever he took up
anything, going into it as if his life depended upon it,
and sparing no abuse which he could think of, of the
opposite method, which he denounced as ungentlemanly,
cowardly, mean, lying, and no one knows what besides:
" Very cool of Tom," as East thought, but didn't say,
" seeing as how he only came out of Egypt himself last
night at bedtime."

" Well, Tom," said he at last, " you see, when you and
I came to school there were none of these sort of notions:
You may be right—I dare say you are. Only what one
has always felt about the masters is, that it's a fair trial

of skill and last between us and them—like a match at football or a battle. We're natural enemies in school— that's the fact. We've got to learn so much Latin and Greek, and do so many verses, and they've got to see that we do it. If we can slip the collar and do so much less without getting caught, that's one to us. If they can get more out of us, or catch us shirking, that's one to them. All's fair in war but lying. If I run my luck against theirs, and go into school without looking at my lessons, and don't get called up, why am I a snob or a sneak ? I don't tell the master I've learnt it. He's got to find out whether I have or not. What's he paid for ? If he calls me up and I get floored, he makes me write it out in Greek and English. Very good. He's caught me, and I don't grumble. I grant you, if I go and snivel to him, and tell him I've really tried to learn it, but found it so hard without a translation, or say I've had a tooth-ache, or any humbug of that kind, I'm a snob. That's my school morality ; it's served me, and you too, Tom, for the matter of that, these five years. And it's all clear and fair, no mistake about it. We understand it, and they understand it, and I don't know what we're to come to with any other."

Tom looked at him pleased and a little puzzled. He had never heard East speak his mind seriously before, and couldn't help feeling how completely he had hit his own theory and practice up to that time.

" Thank you, old fellow," said he. " You're a good old brick to be serious, and not put out with me. I said more than I meant, I dare say ; only you see I know I'm right. Whatever you and Gower and the rest do, I shall hold on. I must. And as it's all new and an uphill game, you see, one must hit hard and hold on tight at first."

"Very good," said East; "hold on and hit away, only don't hit under the line."

"But I must bring you over, Harry, or I shan't be comfortable. Now, I'll allow all you've said. We've always been honourable enemies with the masters. We found a state of war when we came, and went into it of course. Only don't you think things are altered a good deal? I don't feel as I used to the masters. They seem to me to treat one quite differently."

"Yes, perhaps they do," said East; "there's a new set you see, mostly, who don't feel sure of themselves yet. They don't want to fight till they know the ground."

"I don't think it's only that," said Tom. "And then the Doctor, he does treat one so openly, and like a gentleman, and as if one was working with him."

"Well, so he does," said East; "he's a splendid fellow, and when I get into the sixth I shall act accordingly. Only you know he has nothing to do with our lessons now, except examining us. I say, though," looking at his watch, "it's just the quarter. Come along."

As they walked out they got a message, to say that Arthur was just starting, and would like to say goodbye. So they went down to the private entrance of the School-house, and found an open carriage, with Arthur propped up with pillows in it, looking already better, Tom thought.

They jumped up on to the steps to shake hands with him, and Tom mumbled thanks for the presents he had found in his study, and looked round anxiously for Arthur's mother.

East, who had fallen back into his usual humour, looked quaintly at Arthur, and said,—

"So you've been at it again, through that hot-headed convert of yours there. He's been making our lives a

burden to us all the morning about using cribs. I shall
get floored to a certainty at second lesson, if I'm called
up."

Arthur blushed and looked down. Tom struck in,—

"Oh, it's all right. He's converted already; he
always comes through the mud after us, grumbling
and sputtering."

The clock struck, and they had to go off to school,
wishing Arthur a pleasant holiday, Tom, lingering behind a moment to send his thanks and love to Arthur's
mother.

Tom renewed the discussion after second lesson, and
succeeded so far as to get East to promise to give the
new plan a fair trial.

Encouraged by his success, in the evening, when they
were sitting alone in the large study, where East lived
now almost, " *vice* Arthur on leave," after examining the
new fishing-rod, which both pronounced to be the genuine
article (" play enough to throw a midge tied on a single
hair against the wind, and strength enough to hold a
grampus "), they naturally began talking about Arthur.
Tom, who was still bubbling over with last night's scene
and all the thoughts of the last week, and wanting to
clinch and fix the whole in his own mind, which he could
never do without first going through the process of belabouring somebody else with it all, suddenly rushed
into the subject of Arthur's illness, and what he had
said about death.

East had given him the desired opening. After a serio-
comic grumble, " that life wasn't worth having, now they
were tied to a young beggar who was always 'raising
his standard;' and that he, East, was like a prophet's
donkey, who was obliged to struggle on after the donkey-
man who went after the prophet; that he had none of

the pleasure of starting the new crotchets, and didn't half understand them, but had to take the kicks and carry the luggage as if he had all the fun," he threw his legs up on to the sofa, and put his hands behind his head, and said,—

" Well, after all, he's the most wonderful little fellow I ever came across. There ain't such a meek, humble boy in the school. Hanged if I don't think now, really, Tom, that he believes himself a much worse fellow than you or I, and that he don't think he has more influence in the house than Dot Bowles, who came last quarter, and isn't ten yet. But he turns you and me round his little finger, old boy—there's no mistake about that." And East nodded at Tom sagaciously.

" Now or never!" thought Tom; so, shutting his eyes and hardening his heart, he went straight at it, repeating all that Arthur had said, as near as he could remember it, in the very words, and all he had himself thought. The life seemed to ooze out of it as he went on, and several times he felt inclined to stop, give it all up, and change the subject. But somehow he was borne on; he had a necessity upon him to speak it all out, and did so. At the end he looked at East with some anxiety, and was delighted to see that that young gentleman was thoughtful and attentive. The fact is, that in the stage of his inner life at which Tom had lately arrived, his intimacy with and friendship for East could not have lasted if he had not made him aware of, and a sharer in, the thoughts that were beginning to exercise him. Nor indeed could the friendship have lasted if East had shown no sympathy with these thoughts ; so that it was a great relief to have unbosomed himself, and to have found that his friend could listen.

Tom had always had a sort of instinct that East's levity

was only skin-deep, and this instinct was a true one. East had no want of reverence for anything he felt to be real; but his was one of those natures that burst into what is generally called recklessness and impiety the moment they feel that anything is being poured upon them for their good which does not come home to their inborn sense of right, or which appeals to anything like self-interest in them. Daring and honest by nature, and outspoken to an extent which alarmed all respectabilities, with a constant fund of animal health and spirits which he did not feel bound to curb in any way, he had gained for himself with the steady part of the school (including as well those who wished to appear steady as those who really were so) the character of a boy with whom it would be dangerous to be intimate; while his own hatred of everything cruel, or underhand, or false, and his hearty respect for what he could see to be good and true, kept off the rest.

Tom, besides being very like East in many points of character, had largely developed in his composition the capacity for taking the weakest side. This is not putting it strongly enough: it was a necessity with him; he couldn't help it any more than he could eating or drinking. He could never play on the strongest side with any heart at football or cricket, and was sure to make friends with any boy who was unpopular, or down on his luck.

Now, though East was not what is generally called unpopular, Tom felt more and more every day, as their characters developed, that he stood alone, and did not make friends among their contemporaries, and therefore sought him out. Tom was himself much more popular, for his power of detecting humbug was much less acute, and his instincts were much more sociable. He was at this period of his life, too, largely given to taking people for what they gave themselves out to be ; but his single-ness of heart, fearlessness, and honesty were just what East appreciated, and thus the two had been drawn into great intimacy.

This intimacy had not been interrupted by Tom's guardianship of Arthur.

East had often, as has been said, joined them in read-ing the Bible ; but their discussions had almost always turned upon the characters of the men and women of whom they read, and not become personal to themselves. In fact, the two had shrunk from personal religious dis-cussion, not knowing how it might end, and fearful of risking a friendship very dear to both, and which they felt somehow, without quite knowing why, would never be the same, but either tenfold stronger or sapped at its foundation, after such a communing together.

What a bother all this explaining is !   I wish we could get on without it. But we can't. However, you'll all find, if you haven't found it out already, that a time comes in every human friendship when you must go down into the depths of yourself, and lay bare what is there to your friend, and wait in fear for his answer. A few moments may do it ; and it may be (most likely will be, as you are English boys) that you will never do it but once. But done it must be, if the friendship is to be worth the name. You must find what is there, at the very root and bottom of one another's hearts ; and if you are at one there, nothing on earth can or at least ought to sunder you.

East had remained lying down until Tom finished speaking, as if fearing to interrupt him ; he now sat up at the table, and leant his head on one hand, taking up a pencil with the other, and working little holes with it in the table-cover. After a bit he looked up, stopped the pencil, and said, " Thank you very much, old fellow. There's no other boy in the house would have done it for me but you or Arthur. I can see well enough," he went on, after a pause, " all the best big fellows look on me with suspicion; they think I'm a devil-may-care, reckless young scamp. So I am—eleven hours out of twelve, but not the twelfth. Then all of our contemporaries worth knowing follow suit, of course : we're very good friends at games and all that, but not a soul of them but you and Arthur ever tried to break through the crust, and see whether there was anything at the bottom of me; and then the bad ones I won't stand, and they know that."

" Don't you think that's half fancy, Harry ? "

" Not a bit of it," said East bitterly, pegging away with his pencil. " I see it all plain enough. Bless you, you think everybody's as straightforward and kind-hearted as you are."

" Well, but what's the reason of it ? There must be a reason. You can play all the games as well as any one, and sing the best song, and are the best company in the house. You fancy you're not liked, Harry. It's all fancy."

" I only wish it was, Tom. I know I could be popular enough with all the bad ones; but that I won't have, and the good ones won't have me."

" Why not ? " persisted Tom; " you don't drink or swear, or get out at night; you never bully, or cheat at lessons. If you only showed you liked it, you'd have all the best fellows in the house running after you."

" Not I," said East. Then with an effort he went on, " I'll tell you what it is. I never stop the Sacrament. I can see, from the Doctor downwards, how that tells against me."

" Yes, I've seen that," said Tom, " and I've been very sorry for it, and Arthur and I have talked about it. I've often thought of speaking to you, but it's so hard to begin on such subjects. I'm very glad you've opened it. Now, why don't you ? "

" I've never been confirmed," said East.

" Not been confirmed ! " said Tom, in astonishment. " I never thought of that. Why weren't you confirmed with the rest of us nearly three years ago ? I always thought you'd been confirmed at home."

" No," answered East sorrowfully ; " you see this was how it happened. Last Confirmation was soon after Arthur came, and you were so taken up with him I hardly saw either of you. Well, when the Doctor sent round for us about it, I was living mostly with Green's set. You know the sort. They all went in. I dare say it was all right, and they got good by it ; I don't want to judge them. Only all I could see of their reasons drove me just the other way. 'Twas ' because the Doctor liked it ; ' ' no boy got on who didn't stay the Sacrament ; ' it was the ' correct thing,' in fact, like having a good hat to wear on Sundays. I couldn't stand it. I didn't feel that I wanted to lead a different life. I was very well content as I was, and I wasn't going to sham religious to curry favour with the Doctor, or any one else."

East stopped speaking, and pegged away more diligently than ever with his pencil. Tom was ready to cry. He felt half sorry at first that he had been confirmed himself. He seemed to have deserted his earliest friend—to have left him by himself at his worst need for those long years. He got up and went and sat by East, and put his arm over his shoulder.

" Dear old boy," he said, " how careless and selfish

I've been.   But why didn't you come and talk to Arthur and me ? "

"I wish to Heaven I had," said East, "but I was a fool.   It's too late talking of it now."

"Why too late ?   You want to be confirmed now, don't you ? "

"I think so," said East. "I've thought about it a good deal; only, often I fancy I must be changing, because I see it's to do me good here—just what stopped me last time.   And then I go back again."

"I'll tell you now how 'twas with me," said Tom warmly.   "If it hadn't been for Arthur, I should have done just as you did.   I hope I should.   I honour you for it.   But then he made it out just as if it was taking the weak side before all the world—going in once for all against everything that's strong and rich, and proud and respectable, a little band of brothers against the whole world.   And the Doctor seemed to say so too, only he said a great deal more."

"Ah ! " groaned East, "but there again, that's just another of my difficulties whenever I think about the matter.   I don't want to be one of your saints, one of your elect, whatever the right phrase is.   My sympathies are all the other way—with the many, the poor devils who run about the streets and don't go to church.   Don't stare, Tom ; mind, I'm telling you all that's in my heart —as far as I know it—but it's all a muddle.   You must be gentle with me if you want to land me.   Now I've seen a deal of this sort of religion; I was bred up in it, and I can't stand it.   If nineteen-twentieths of the world are to be left to uncovenanted mercies, and that sort of thing, which means in plain English to go to hell, and the other twentieth are to rejoice at it all, why——"

"Oh ! but, Harry, they ain't, they don't," broke in

Tom, really shocked. "Oh, how I wish Arthur hadn't gone! I'm such a fool about these things. But it's all you want too, East; it is indeed. It cuts both ways somehow, being confirmed and taking the Sacrament. It makes you feel on the side of all the good and all the bad too, of everybody in the world. Only there's some great dark strong power, which is crushing you and everybody else. That's what Christ conquered, and we've got to fight. What a fool I am! I can't explain. If Arthur were only here!"

"I begin to get a glimmering of what you mean," said East.

"I say, now," said Tom eagerly, "do you remember how we both hated Flashman?"

"Of course I do," said East; "I hate him still. What then?"

"Well, when I came to take the Sacrament, I had a great struggle about that. I tried to put him out of my head; and when I couldn't do that, I tried to think of him as evil—as something that the Lord who was loving me hated, and which I might hate too. But it wouldn't do. I broke down; I believe Christ Himself broke me down. And when the Doctor gave me the bread and wine, and leant over me praying, I prayed for poor Flashman, as if it had been you or Arthur."

East buried his face in his hands on the table. Tom could feel the table tremble. At last he looked up. "Thank you again, Tom," said he; "you don't know what you may have done for me to-night. I think I see now how the right sort of sympathy with poor devils is got at."

"And you'll stop the Sacrament next time, won't you?" said Tom.

"Can I, before I'm confirmed?"

" Go and ask the Doctor."

" I will."

That very night, after prayers, East followed the Doctor, and the old verger bearing the candle, upstairs. Tom watched, and saw the Doctor turn round when he heard footsteps following him closer than usual, and say, " Hah, East ! Do you want to speak to me, my man ? "

" If you please, sir." And the private door closed, and Tom went to his study in a state of great trouble of mind.

It was almost an hour before East came back. Then he rushed in breathless.

" Well, it's all right," he shouted, seizing Tom by the hand. " I feel as if a ton weight were off my mind."

" Hurrah," said Tom. " I knew it would be; but tell us all about it."

" Well, I just told him all about it. You can't think how kind and gentle he was, the great grim man, whom I've feared more than anybody on earth. When I stuck, he lifted me just as if I'd been a little child. And he seemed to know all I'd felt, and to have gone through it all. And I burst out crying—more than I've done this five years; and he sat down by me, and stroked my head; and I went blundering on, and told him all— much worse things than I've told you. And he wasn't shocked a bit, and didn't snub me, or tell me I was a fool, and it was all nothing but pride or wickedness, though I dare say it was. And he didn't tell me not to follow out my thoughts, and he didn't give me any cut- and-dried explanation. But when I'd done he just talked a bit. I can hardly remember what he said yet ; but it seemed to spread round me like healing, and strength, and light, and to bear me up, and plant me on a rock, where I could hold my footing and fight for myself. I don't know what to do, I feel so happy. And it's all owing to you, dear old boy!" And he seized Tom's hand again.

"And you're to come to the Communion?" said Tom.

"Yes, and to be confirmed in the holidays."

Tom's delight was as great as his friend's. But he hadn't yet had out all his own talk, and was bent on improving the occasion : so he proceeded to propound Arthur's theory about not being sorry for his friends' deaths, which he had hitherto kept in the background, and by which he was much exercised ; for he didn't feel it honest to take what pleased him, and throw over the rest, and was trying vigorously to persuade himself that he should like all his best friends to die off-hand.

But East's powers of remaining serious were exhausted, and in five minutes he was saying the most ridiculous things he could think of, till Tom was almost getting angry again.

Despite of himself, however, he couldn't help laughing and giving it up, when East appealed to him with, "Well, Tom, you ain't going to punch my head, I hope, because I insist upon being sorry when you got to earth?"

And so their talk finished for that time, and they tried to learn first lesson, with very poor success, as appeared next morning, when they were called up and narrowly escaped being floored, which ill-luck, however, did not sit heavily on either of their souls.

CHAPTER VIII.

TOM BROWN'S LAST MATCH.

" Heaven grant the manlier heart, that timely, ere
Youth fly, with life's real tempest would be coping ;
          The fruit of dreamy hoping
          Is, waking, blank despair."—CLOUGH, *Ambarvalia.*

THE curtain now rises upon the last act of our little
drama, for hard-hearted publishers warn me that a single
volume must of necessity have an end. Well, well ! the
pleasantest things must come to an end. I little thought
last long vacation, when I began these pages to help
while away some spare time at a watering-place, how
vividly many an old scene which had lain hid away
for years in some dusty old corner of my brain, would
come back again, and stand before me as clear and
bright as if it had happened yesterday. The book has
been a most grateful task to me, and I only hope that
all you, my dear young friends, who read it (friends
assuredly you must be, if you get as far as this), will
be half as sorry to come to the last stage as I am.

Not but what there has been a solemn and a sad side
to it. As the old scenes became living, and the actors
in them became living too, many a grave in the Crimea
and distant India, as well as in the quiet churchyards
of our dear old country, seemed to open and send forth
their dead, and their voices and looks and ways were
again in one's ears and eyes, as in the old School-days.
But this was not sad. How should it be, if we believe
as our Lord has taught us ? How should it be, when
one more turn of the wheel, and we shall be by their
sides again, learning from them again, perhaps, as we
did when we were new boys.

Then there were others of the old faces so dear to us

once who had somehow or another just gone clean out of sight. Are they dead or living? We know not, but the thought of them brings no sadness with it. Wherever they are, we can well believe they are doing God's work and getting His wages.

But are there not some, whom we still see sometimes in the streets, whose haunts and homes we know, whom we could probably find almost any day in the week if we were set to do it, yet from whom we are really farther than we are from the dead, and from those who have gone out of our ken? Yes, there are and must be such; and therein lies the sadness of old School memories. Yet of these our old comrades, from whom more than time and space separate us, there are some by whose sides we can feel sure that we shall stand again when time shall be no more. We may think of one another now as dangerous fanatics or narrow bigots, with whom no truce is possible, from whom we shall only sever more and more to the end of our lives, whom it would be our respective duties to imprison or hang, if we had the power. We must go our way, and they theirs, as long as flesh and spirit hold together; but let our own Rugby poet speak words of healing for this trial:—

> " To veer how vain! on, onward strain,
>   Brave barks, in light, in darkness too;
> Through winds and tides one compass guides,—
>   To that, and your own selves, be true.
>
> " But, O blithe breeze, and O great seas,
>   Though ne'er that earliest parting past,
> On your wide plain they join again;
>   Together lead them home at last.
>
> " One port, methought, alike they sought,
>   One purpose hold where'er they fare.
> O bounding breeze, O rushing seas,
>   At last, at last, unite them there!" *

---

* Clough, *Ambarvalia.*

This is not mere longing; it is prophecy. So over these too, our old friends, who are friends no more, we sorrow not as men without hope. It is only for those who seem to us to have lost compass and purpose, and to be driven helplessly on rocks and quicksands, whose lives are spent in the service of the world, the flesh, and the devil, for self alone, and not for their fellow-men, their country, or their God, that we must mourn and pray without sure hope and without light, trusting only that He, in whose hands they as well as we are, who has died for them as well as for us, who sees all His creatures

> " With larger other eyes than ours,
> To make allowance for us all,"

will, in His own way and at His own time, lead them also home.

*   *   *   *   *

Another two years have passed, and it is again the end of the summer half-year at Rugby; in fact, the School has broken up. The fifth-form examinations were over last week, and upon them have followed the speeches, and the sixth-form examinations for exhibitions; and they too are over now. The boys have gone to all the winds of heaven, except the town boys and the eleven, and the few enthusiasts besides who have asked leave to stay in their houses to see the result of the cricket matches. For this year the Wellesburn return match and the Marylebone match are played at Rugby, to the great delight of the town and neighbourhood, and the sorrow of those aspiring young cricketers who have been reckoning for the last three months on showing off at Lord's ground.

The Doctor started for the Lakes yesterday morning, after an interview with the captain of the eleven, in the presence of Thomas, at which he arranged in what school the cricket dinners were to be, and all other

matters necessary for the satisfactory carrying out of
the festivities, and warned them as to keeping all
spirituous liquors out of the close, and having the gates
closed by nine o'clock.

The Wellesburn match was played out with great
success yesterday, the School winning by three wickets;
and to-day the great event of the cricketing year, the
Marylebone match, is being played. What a match it
has been! The London eleven came down by an afternoon train yesterday, in time to see the end of the
Wellesburn match; and as soon as it was over, their
leading men and umpire inspected the ground, criticising
it rather unmercifully. The captain of the School eleven,
and one or two others, who had played the Lord's match
before, and knew old Mr. Aislabie and several of the
Lord's men, accompanied them; while the rest of the
eleven looked on from under the Three Trees with admiring eyes, and asked one another the names of the
illustrious strangers, and recounted how many runs each
of them had made in the late matches in *Bell's Life*.
They looked such hard-bitten, wiry, whiskered fellows
that their young adversaries felt rather desponding as
to the result of the morrow's match. The ground was
at last chosen, and two men set to work upon it to water
and roll; and then, there being yet some half-hour of
daylight, some one had suggested a dance on the turf.
The close was half full of citizens and their families, and
the idea was hailed with enthusiasm. The cornopean
player was still on the ground. In five minutes the
eleven and half a dozen of the Wellesburn and Marylebone men got partners somehow or another, and a merry
country-dance was going on, to which every one flocked,
and new couples joined in every minute, till there were
a hundred of them going down the middle and up again;

and the long line of school buildings looked gravely down on them, every window glowing with the last rays of the western sun; and the rooks clanged about in the tops of the old elms, greatly excited, and resolved on having their country-dance too; and the great flag flapped lazily in the gentle western breeze. Altogether it was a sight which would have made glad the heart of our brave old founder, Lawrence Sheriff, if he were half as good a fellow as I take him to have been. It was a cheerful sight to see. But what made it so valuable in the sight of the captain of the School eleven was that he there saw his young hands shaking off their shyness and awe of the Lord's men, as they crossed hands and capered about on the grass together; for the strangers entered into it all, and threw away their cigars, and danced and shouted like boys; while old Mr. Aislabie stood by looking on in his white hat, leaning on a bat, in benevolent enjoyment. "This hop will be worth thirty runs to us to-morrow, and will be the making of Raggles and Johnson," thinks the young leader, as he revolves many things in his mind, standing by the side of Mr. Aislabie, whom he will not leave for a minute, for he feels that the character of the School for courtesy is resting on his shoulders.

But when a quarter to nine struck, and he saw old Thomas beginning to fidget about with the keys in his hand, he thought of the Doctor's parting monition, and stopped the cornopean at once, notwithstanding the loud-voiced remonstrances from all sides; and the crowd scattered away from the close, the eleven all going into the School-house, where supper and beds were provided for them by the Doctor's orders.

Deep had been the consultations at supper as to the order of going in, who should bowl the first over, whether it would be best to play steady or freely; and the youngest hands declared that they shouldn't be a bit nervous, and praised their opponents as the jolliest fellows in the world, except perhaps their old friends the Wellesburn men. How far a little good-nature from their elders will go with the right sort of boys!

The morning had dawned bright and warm, to the intense relief of many an anxious youngster, up betimes to mark the signs of the weather. The eleven went down in a body before breakfast, for a plunge in the cold bath in a corner of the close. The ground was in splendid order, and soon after ten o'clock, before spectators had arrived, all was ready, and two of the Lord's men took their places at the wickets—the School, with the usual liberality of young hands, having put their adversaries in first. Old Bailey stepped up to the wicket, and called play, and the match has begun.

*　　　*　　　*　　　*　　　*

"Oh, well bowled! well bowled, Johnson!" cries the captain, catching up the ball and sending it high above the rook trees, while the third Marylebone man walks away from the wicket, and old Bailey gravely sets up the middle stump again and puts the bails on.

"How many runs?" Away scamper three boys to the scoring-table, and are back again in a minute amongst the rest of the eleven, who are collected together in a knot between wicket. "Only eighteen runs, and three wickets down!" "Huzza for old Rugby!" sings out Jack Raggles, the long-stop, toughest and burliest of boys, commonly called "Swiper Jack," and forthwith stands on his head, and brandishes his legs in the air in triumph, till the next boy catches hold of his heels, and throws him over on to his back.

"Steady there; don't be such an ass, Jack," says the

captain; "we haven't got the best wicket yet. Ah, look out now at cover-point," adds he, as he sees a long-armed bare-headed, slashing-looking player coming to the wicket. "And, Jack, mind your hits. He steals more runs than any man in England."

And they all find that they have got their work to do now. The newcomer's off-hitting is tremendous, and his running like a flash of lightning. He is never in his ground except when his wicket is down. Nothing in the whole game so trying to boys. He has stolen three byes in the first ten minutes, and Jack Raggles is furious, and begins throwing over savagely to the farther wicket, until he is sternly stopped by the captain. It is all that young gentlemen can do to keep his team steady, but he knows that everything depends on it, and faces his work bravely. The score creeps up to fifty; the boys begin to look blank; and the spectators, who are now mustering strong, are very silent. The ball flies off his bat to all parts of the field, and he gives no rest and no catches to any one. But cricket is full of glorious chances, and the goddess who presides over it loves to bring down the most skilful players. Johnson, the young bowler, is getting wild, and bowls a ball almost wide to the off; the batter steps out and cuts it beautifully to where cover-point is standing very deep—in fact almost off the ground. The ball comes skimming and twisting along about three feet from the ground; he rushes at it, and it sticks somehow or other in the fingers of his left hand, to the utter astonishment of himself and the whole field. Such a catch hasn't been made in the close for years, and the cheering is maddening: 'Pretty cricket," says the captain, throwing himself on the ground by the deserted wicket with a long breath. He feels that a crisis has passed.

I wish I had space to describe the match—how the captain stumped the next man off a leg-shooter, and bowled small cobs to old Mr. Aislabie, who came in for the last wicket; how the Lord's men were out by half-past twelve o'clock for ninety-eight runs; how the captain of the School eleven went in first to give his men pluck, and scored twenty-five in beautiful style; how Rugby was only four behind in the first innings; what a glorious dinner they had in the fourth-form school; and how the cover-point hitter sang the most topping comic songs, and old Mr. Aislabie made the best speeches that ever were heard, afterwards. But I haven't space—that's the fact; and so you must fancy it all, and carry yourselves on to half-past seven o'clock, when the School are again in, with five wickets down, and only thirty-two runs to make to win. The Marylebone men played carelessly in their second innings, but they are working like horses now to save the match.

There is much healthy, hearty, happy life scattered up and down the close; but the group to which I beg to call your especial attention is there, on the slope of the island, which looks towards the cricket-ground. It consists of three figures; two are seated on a bench, and one on the ground at their feet. The first, a tall, slight and rather gaunt man, with a bushy eyebrow and a dry, humorous smile, is evidently a clergyman. He is carelessly dressed, and looks rather used up, which isn't much to be wondered at, seeing that he has just finished six weeks of examination work; but there he basks, and spreads himself out in the evening sun, bent on enjoying life, though he doesn't quite know what to do with his arms and legs. Surely it is our friend the young master, whom we have had glimpses of before, but his face has gained a great deal since we last came across him.

And by his side, in white flannel shirt and trousers, straw hat, the captain's belt, and the untanned yellow cricket shoes which all the eleven wear, sits a strapping figure, near six feet high, with ruddy, tanned face and whiskers, curly brown hair, and a laughing, dancing eye. He is leaning forward with his elbows resting on his knees, and dandling his favourite bat, with which he has made thirty or forty runs to-day, in his strong brown hands. It is Tom Brown, grown into a young man nineteen years old, a prepostor and captain of the eleven, spending his last day as a Rugby boy, and, let us hope, as much wiser as he is bigger, since we last had the pleasure of coming across him.

And at their feet on the warm, dry ground, similarly dressed, sits Arthur, Turkish fashion, with his bat across his knees. He too is no longer a boy—less of a boy, in fact, than Tom, if one may judge from the thoughtfulness of his face, which is somewhat paler, too, than one could wish ; but his figure, though slight, is well knit and active, and all his old timidity has disappeared, and is replaced by silent, quaint fun, with which his face twinkles all over, as he listens to the broken talk between the other two, in which he joins every now and then.

All three are watching the game eagerly, and joining in the cheering which follows every good hit. It is pleasing to see the easy, friendly footing which the pupils are on with their master, perfectly respectful, yet with no reserve and nothing forced in their intercourse. Tom has clearly abandoned the old theory of "natural enemies" in this case at any rate.

But it is time to listen to what they are saying, and see what we can gather out of it.

"I don't object to your theory," says the master, "and I allow you have made a fair case for yourself. But now, in such books as Aristophanes, for instance, you've been reading a play this half with the Doctor, haven't you?"

"Yes, the Knights," answered Tom.

"Well, I'm sure you would have enjoyed the wonderful humour of it twice as much if you had taken more pains with your scholarship."

"Well, sir, I don't believe any boy in the form enjoyed the sets-to between Cleon and the Sausage-seller more than I did—eh, Arthur?" said Tom, giving him a stir with his foot.

"Yes, I must say he did," said Arthur. "I think, sir, you've hit upon the wrong book there."

"Not a bit of it," said the master. "Why, in those very passages of arms, how can you thoroughly appreciate them unless you are master of the weapons? and the weapons are the language, which you, Brown, have never half worked at; and so, as I say, you must have lost all the delicate shades of meaning which make the best part of the fun."

"Oh, well played! bravo, Johnson!" shouted Arthur, dropping his bat and clapping furiously; and Tom joined in with a "Bravo, Johnson!" which might have been heard at the chapel.

"Eh! what was it? I didn't see," inquired the master. "They only got one run, I thought?"

"No, but such a ball, three-quarters length, and coming straight for his leg bail. Nothing but that turn of the wrist could have saved him, and he drew it away to leg for a safe one.—Bravo, Johnson!"

"How well they are bowling, though," said Arthur; "they don't mean to be beat, I can see."

"There now," struck in the master; "you see that's just what I have been preaching this half-hour. The delicate play is the true thing. I don't understand cricket, so I don't enjoy those fine draws which you tell me are the best play, though when you or Raggles hit a ball hard away for six I am as delighted as any one. Don't you see the analogy?"

"Yes, sir," answered Tom, looking up roguishly, "I see; only the question remains whether I should have got most good by understanding Greek particles or cricket thoroughly. I'm such a thick, I never should have had time for both."

"I see you are an incorrigible," said the master, with a chuckle; "but I refute you by an example. Arthur there has taken in Greek and cricket too."

"Yes, but no thanks to him; Greek came natural to him. Why, when he first came I remember he used to read Herodotus for pleasure as I did Don Quixote, and couldn't have made a false concord if he'd tried ever so hard; and then I looked after his cricket."

"Out! Bailey has given him out. Do you see, Tom?" cries Arthur. "How foolish of them to run so hard."

"Well, it can't be helped; he has played very well. Whose turn is it to go in?"

"I don't know; they've got your list in the tent."

"Let's go and see," said Tom, rising; but at this moment Jack Raggles and two or three more came running to the island moat.

"O Brown, mayn't I go in next?" shouts the Swiper.

"Whose name is next on the list?" says the captain.

"Winter's, and then Arthur's," answers the boy who carries it; "but there are only twenty-six runs to get, and no time to lose. I heard Mr. Aislabie say that the stumps must be drawn at a quarter past eight exactly."

" Oh, do let the Swiper go in," chorus the boys; so Tom yields against his better judgment.

" I dare say now I've lost the match by this nonsense," he says, as he sits down again; "they'll be sure to get Jack's wicket in three or four minutes; however, you'll have the chance, sir, of seeing a hard hit or two," adds he, smiling, and turning to the master.

"Come, none of your irony, Brown," answers the master. "I'm beginning to understand the game scientifically. What a noble game it is, too!"

"Isn't it? But it's more than a game. It's an institution," said Tom.

"Yes," said Arthur—"the birthright of British boys old and young, as *habeas corpus* and trial by jury are of British men."

"The discipline and reliance on one another which it teaches is so valuable, I think," went on the master, "it ought to be such an unselfish game. It merges the individual in the eleven; he doesn't play that he may win, but that his side may."

"That's very true," said Tom, "and that's why football and cricket, now one comes to think of it, are such much better games than fives or hare-and-hounds, or any others where the object is to come in first or to win for oneself, and not that one's side may win."

"And then the captain of the eleven!" said the master, "what a post is his in our School-world! almost as hard as the Doctor's—requiring skill and gentleness and firmness, and I know not what other rare qualities."

"Which don't he may wish he may get!" said Tom, laughing; "at any rate he hasn't got them yet, or he wouldn't have been such a flat to-night as to let Jack Raggles go in out of his turn."

"Ah, the Doctor never would have done that," said

Arthur demurely. "Tom, you've a great deal to learn yet in the art of ruling."

"Well, I wish you'd tell the Doctor so then, and get him to let me stop till I'm twenty. I don't want to leave, I'm sure."

"What a sight it is," broke in the master, "the Doctor as a ruler! Perhaps ours is the only little corner of the British Empire which is thoroughly, wisely, and strongly ruled just now. I'm more and more thankful every day of my life that I came here to be under him."

"So am I, I'm sure," said Tom, "and more and more sorry that I've got to leave."

"Every place and thing one sees here reminds one of some wise act of his," went on the master. "This island now—you remember the time, Brown, when it was laid out in small gardens, and cultivated by frost-bitten fags in February and March?"

"Of course I do," said Tom; "didn't I hate spending two hours in the afternoon grubbing in the tough dirt with the stump of a fives bat? But turf-cart was good fun enough."

"I dare say it was, but it was always leading to fights with the townspeople; and then the stealing flowers out of all the gardens in Rugby for the Easter show was abominable."

"Well, so it was," said Tom, looking down, "but we fags couldn't help ourselves. But what has that to do with the Doctor's ruling?"

"A great deal, I think," said the master; "what brought island-fagging to an end?"

"Why, the Easter speeches were put off till midsummer," said Tom, "and the sixth had the gymnastic poles put up here."

"Well, and who changed the time of the speeches,

and put the idea of gymnastic poles into the heads of their worships the sixth form ? " said the master.

" The Doctor, I suppose," said Tom. " I never thought of that."

" Of course you didn't," said the master, " or else, fag as you were, you would have shouted with the whole school against putting down old customs. And that's the way that all the Doctor's reforms have been carried out when he has been left to himself—quietly and naturally, putting a good thing in the place of a bad, and letting the bad die out ; no wavering, and no hurry— the best thing that could be done for the time being, and patience for the rest."

" Just Tom's own way," chimed in Arthur, nudging Tom with his elbow—" driving a nail where it will go ; " to which allusion Tom answered by a sly kick.

" Exactly so," said the master, innocent of the allusion and by-play.

Meantime Jack Raggles, with his sleeves tucked up above his great brown elbows, scorning pads and gloves, has presented himself at the wicket ; and having run one for a forward drive of Johnson's, is about to receive his first ball. There are only twenty-four runs to make, and four wickets to go down—a winning match if they play decently steady. The ball is a very swift one, and rises fast, catching Jack on the outside of the thigh, and bounding away as if from india-rubber, while they run two for a leg-bye amidst great applause and shouts from Jack's many admirers. The next ball is a beautifully-pitched ball for the outer stump, which the reckless and unfeeling Jack catches hold of, and hits right round to leg for five, while the applause becomes deafening. Only seventeen runs to get with four wickets ! The game is all but ours !

It is over now, and Jack walks swaggering about his wicket, with his bat over his shoulder, while Mr. Aislabie holds a short parley with his men. Then the cover-point hitter, that cunning man, goes on to bowl slow twisters: Jack waves his hand triumphantly towards the tent, as much as to say, " See if I don't finish it all off now in three hits.".

Alas, my son Jack, the enemy is too old for thee: The first ball of the over Jack steps out and meets, swiping with all his force. If he had only allowed for the twist ! But he hasn't, and so the ball goes spinning up straight in the air, as if it would never come down again. Away runs Jack, shouting and trusting to the chapter of accidents; but the bowler runs steadily under it, judging every spin, and calling out, " I have it," catches it, and playfully pitches it on to the back of the stalwart Jack, who is departing with a rueful countenance.

" I knew how it would be," says Tom, rising. " Come along; the game's getting very serious."

So they leave the island and go to the tent; and after deep consultation, Arthur is sent in, and goes off to the wicket with a last exhortation from Tom to play steady and keep his bat straight. To the suggestions that Winter is the best bat left, Tom only replies, " Arthur is the steadiest, and Johnson will make the runs if the wicket is only kept up."

" I am surprised to see Arthur in the eleven," said the master, as they stood together in front of the dense crowd, which was now closing in round the ground.

" Well, I'm not quite sure that he ought to be in for his play," said Tom, " but I couldn't help putting him in. It will do him so much good, and you can't think what I owe him."

The master smiled. The clock strikes eight, and the whole field becomes fevered with excitement. Arthur, after two narrow escapes, scores one, and Johnson gets the ball. The bowling and fielding are superb, and Johnson's batting worthy the occasion. He makes here a two, and there a one, managing to keep the ball to himself, and Arthur backs up and runs perfectly. Only eleven runs to make now, and the crowd scarcely breathe. At last Arthur gets the ball again, and actually drives it forward for two, and feels prouder than when he got the three best prizes, at hearing Tom's shout of joy, " Well played, well played, young un ! "

But the next ball is too much for the young hand, and his bails fly different ways. Nine runs to make, and two wickets to go down : it is too much for human nerves.

Before Winter can get in, the omnibus which is to take the Lord's men to the train pulls up at the side of the close, and Mr. Aislabie and Tom consult, and give out that the stumps will be drawn after the next over. And so ends the great match. Winter and Johnson carry out their bats, and, it being a one day's match, the Lord's men are declared the winners, they having scored the most in the first innings.

But such a defeat is a victory : so think Tom and all the School eleven, as they accompany their conquerors to the omnibus, and send them off with three ringing cheers, after Mr. Aislabie has shaken hands all round, saying to Tom, " I must compliment you, sir, on your eleven, and I hope we shall have you for a member if you come up to town."

As Tom and the rest of the eleven were turning back into the close, and everybody was beginning to cry out for another country-dance, encouraged by the success of the night before, the young master, who was just leaving the close, stopped him, and asked him to come up to tea at half-past eight, adding, " I won't keep you more than half an hour, and ask Arthur to come up too."

" I'll come up with you directly, if you'll let me," said Tom, " for I feel rather melancholy, and not quite up to the country-dance and supper with the rest."

" Do, by all means," said the master ; " I'll wait here for you."

So Tom went off to get his boots and things from the tent, to tell Arthur of the invitation, and to speak to his second in command about stopping the dancing and shutting up the close as soon as it grew dusk. Arthur promised to follow as soon as he had had a dance. So Tom handed his things over to the man in charge of the tent, and walked quietly away to the gate where the master was waiting, and the two took their way together up the Hillmorton road.

Of course they found the master's house locked up, and all the servants away in the close—about this time, no doubt, footing it away on the grass, with extreme delight to themselves, and in utter oblivion of the unfortunate bachelor their master, whose one enjoyment in the shape of meals was his " dish of tea " (as our grandmothers called it) in the evening ; and the phrase was apt in his case, for he always poured his out into the saucer before drinking. Great was the good man's horror at finding himself shut out of his own house. Had he been alone, he would have treated it as a matter of course, and would have strolled contentedly up and down his gravel walk until some one came home ; but he was hurt at the stain on his character of host, especially as the guest was a pupil. However, the guest seemed to think

it a great joke, and presently, as they poked about round
the house, mounted a wall, from which he could reach a
passage window.   The window, as it turned out, was not
bolted, so in another minute Tom was in the house and
down at the front door, which he opened from inside.
The master chuckled grimly at this burglarious entry,
and insisted on leaving the hall-door and two of the front
windows open, to frighten the truants on their return;
and then the two set about foraging for tea, in which
operation the master was much at fault, having the
faintest possible idea of where to find anything, and being,
moreover, wondrously short-sighted; but Tom, by a sort
of instinct, knew the right cupboards in the kitchen and
pantry, and soon managed to place on the snuggery table
better materials for a meal than had appeared there
probably during the reign of his tutor, who was then and
there initiated, amongst other things, into the excellence
of that mysterious condiment, a dripping-cake.   The
cake was newly baked, and all rich and flaky; Tom had
found it reposing in the cook's private cupboard, await-
ing her return; and as a warning to her they finished
it to the last crumb.   The kettle sang away merrily on
the hob of the snuggery, for, notwithstanding the time
of year, they lighted a fire, throwing both the windows
wide open at the same time; the heaps of books and
papers were pushed away to the other end of the table,
and the great solitary engraving of King's College Chapel
over the mantelpiece looked less stiff than usual, as they
settled themselves down in the twilight to the serious
drinking of tea.

After some talk on the match, and other indifferent
subjects, the conversation came naturally back to Tom's
approaching departure, over which he began again to
make his moan.

"Well, we shall all miss you quite as much as you will miss us," said the master. "You are the Nestor of the School now, are you not?"

"Yes, ever since East left," answered Tom.

"By-the-bye, have you heard from him?"

"Yes, I had a letter in February, just before he started for India to join his regiment."

"He will make a capital officer."

"Ay, won't he!" said Tom, brightening. ".No fellow could handle boys better, and I suppose soldiers are very like boys. And he'll never tell them to go where he won't go himself. No mistake about that. A braver fellow never walked."

"His year in the sixth will have taught him a good deal that will be useful to him now."

"So it will," said Tom, staring into the fire. "Poor dear Harry," he went on—"how well I remember the day we were put out of the twenty! How he rose to the situation, and burnt his cigar-cases, and gave away his pistols, and pondered on the constitutional authority of the sixth, and his new duties to the Doctor, and the fifth form, and the fags! Ay, and no fellow ever acted up to them better, though he was always a people's man—for the fags, and against constituted authorities. He couldn't help that, you know. I'm sure the Doctor must have liked him?" said Tom, looking up inquiringly.

"The Doctor sees the good in every one, and appreciates it," said the master dogmatically; "but I hope East will get a good colonel. He won't do if he can't respect those above him. How long it took him, even here, to learn the lesson of obeying!"

"Well, I wish I were alongside of him," said Tom. "If I can't be at Rugby, I want to be at work in the world, and not dawdling away three years at Oxford."

" What do you mean by 'at work in the world'?"
said the master, pausing with his lips close to his saucerful
of tea, and peering at Tom over it.

" Well, I mean real work—one's profession—whatever
one will have really to do and make one's living by.   I
want to be doing some real good, feeling that I am not
only at play in the world," answered Tom, rather puzzled
to find out himself what he really did mean.

" You are mixing up two very different things in your
head, I think, Brown," said the master, putting down
the empty saucer, " and you ought to get clear about
them.   You talk of 'working to get your living,' and
'doing some real good in the world,' in the same breath.
Now, you may be getting a very good living in a profession, and yet doing no good at all in the world,
but quite the contrary, at the same time.   Keep the
latter before you as your one object, and you will be
right, whether you make a living or not ; but if you
dwell on the other, you'll very likely drop into mere
money-making, and let the world take care of itself for
good or evil.   Don't be in a hurry about finding your
work in the world for yourself—you are not old enough
to judge for yourself yet ; but just look about you in the
place you find yourself in, and try to make things a
little better and honester there.   You'll find plenty to
keep your hand in at Oxford, or wherever else you go.
And don't be led away to think this part of the world
important and that unimportant.   Every corner of the
world is important.   No man knows whether this part
or that is most so, but every man may do some honest
work in his own corner."   And then the good man went
on to talk wisely to Tom of the sort of work which he
might take up as an undergraduate, and warned him
of the prevalent university sins, and explained to him

the many and great differences between university and school life, till the twilight changed into darkness, and they heard the truant servants stealing in by the back entrance.

" I wonder where Arthur can be," said Tom at last, looking at his watch; "why, it's nearly half-past nine already."

"Oh, he is comfortably at supper with the eleven, forgetful of his oldest friends," said the master. " Nothing has given me greater pleasure," he went on, " than your friendship for him; it has been the making of you both."

" Of me, at any rate," answered Tom; " I should never have been here now but for him. It was the luckiest chance in the world that sent him to Rugby and made him my chum."

" Why do you talk of lucky chances?" said the master. " I don't know that there are any such things in the world; at any rate, there was neither luck nor chance in that matter."

Tom looked at him inquiringly, and he went on. " Do you remember when the Doctor lectured you and East at the end of one half-year, when you were in the shell, and had been getting into all sorts of scrapes?"

" Yes, well enough," said Tom; " it was the half-year before Arthur came."

" Exactly so," answered the master. " Now, I was with him a few minutes afterwards, and he was in great distress about you two. And after some talk, we both agreed that you in particular wanted some object in the School beyond games and mischief; for it was quite clear that you never would make the regular school work your first object. And so the Doctor, at the beginning of the next half-year, looked out the best of the new boys, and separated you and East, and put the young boy into your study, in the hope that when you had somebody to lean on you, you would begin to stand a little steadier yourself, and get manliness and thoughtfulness. And I can assure you he has watched the experiment ever since with great satisfaction. Ah! not one of you boys will ever know the anxiety you have given him, or the care with which he has watched over every step in your school lives."

Up to this time Tom had never given wholly in to or understood the Doctor. At first he had thoroughly feared him. For some years, as I have tried to show, he had learnt to regard him with love and respect, and to think him a very great and wise and good man. But as regarded his own position in the School, of which he was no little proud, Tom had no idea of giving any one credit for it but himself, and, truth to tell, was a very self-conceited young gentleman on the subject. He was wont to boast that he had fought his own way fairly up the School, and had never made up to or been taken up by any big fellow or master, and that it was now quite a different place from what it was when he first came. And, indeed, though he didn't actually boast of it, yet in his secret soul he did to a great extent believe that the great reform in the School had been owing quite as much to himself as to any one else. Arthur, he acknowledged, had done him good, and taught him a good deal; so had other boys in different ways, but they had not had the same means of influence on the School in general. And as for the Doctor, why, he was a splendid master; but every one knew that masters could do very little out of school hours. In short, he felt on terms of equality with his chief, so far as the social state of the School was concerned, and thought that the Doctor would find it no easy matter to get on without him. Moreover, his School Toryism was still strong, and he looked still with some jealousy on the Doctor, as somewhat of a fanatic in the matter of change, and thought it very desirable for the School that he should have some wise person (such as himself) to look sharply after vested School-rights, and see that nothing was done to the injury of the republic without due protest.

It was a new light to him to find that, besides teaching the sixth, and governing and guiding the whole School, editing classics, and writing histories, the great head-master had found time in those busy years to watch over the career even of him, Tom Brown, and his par-ticular friends, and, no doubt, of fifty other boys at the same time, and all this without taking the least credit to himself, or seeming to know, or let any one else know, that he ever thought particularly of any boy at all.

However, the Doctor's victory was complete from that moment over Tom Brown at any rate. He gave way at all points, and the enemy marched right over him—cavalry, infantry, and artillery, and the land transport corps, and the camp followers. It had taken eight long years to do it; but now it was done thoroughly, and there wasn't a corner of him left which didn't believe in the Doctor. Had he returned to School again, and the Doctor begun the half-year by abolishing fagging, and football, and the Saturday half-holiday, or all or any of the most cherished School institutions, Tom would have supported him with the blindest faith. And so, after a half confession of his previous shortcomings, and sorrowful adieus to his tutor, from whom he received two beautifully-bound volumes of the Doctor's sermons, as a parting present, he marched down to the School-house, a hero-worshipper, who would have satisfied the soul of Thomas Carlyle himself.

There he found the eleven at high jinks after supper,
Jack Raggles shouting comic songs and performing feats
of strength, and was greeted by a chorus of mingled
remonstrance at his desertion and joy at his reappear-
ance. And falling in with the humour of the evening,
he was soon as great a boy as all the rest; and at ten
o'clock was chaired round the quadrangle, on one of the
hall benches, borne aloft by the eleven, shouting in
chorus, "For he's a jolly good fellow," while old Thomas,
in a melting mood, and the other School-house servants,
stood looking on.

And the next morning after breakfast he squared up
all the cricketing accounts, went round to his tradesmen
and other acquaintance, and said his hearty good-byes;
and by twelve o'clock was in the train, and away for
London, no longer a school-boy, and divided in his
thoughts between hero-worship, honest regrets over the
long stage of his life which was now slipping out of sight
behind him, and hopes and resolves for the next stage
upon which he was entering with all the confidence of
a young traveller.

CHAPTER IX.

FINIS.

" Strange friend, past, present, and to be;
  Loved deeplier, darklier understood;
  Behold I dream a dream of good,
And mingle all the world with thee."—TENNYSON.

IN the summer of 1842, our hero stopped once again at
the well-known station; and leaving his bag and fishing-
rod with a porter, walked slowly and sadly up towards
the town. It was now July. He had rushed away
from Oxford the moment that term was over, for a fish-

ing ramble in Scotland with two college friends, and had been for three weeks living on oatcake, mutton-hams, and whisky, in the wildest parts of Skye. They had descended one sultry evening on the little inn at Kyle Rhea ferry; and while Tom and another of the party put their tackle together and began exploring the stream for a sea-trout for supper, the third strolled into the house to arrange for their entertainment. Presently he came out in a loose blouse and slippers, a short pipe in his mouth, and an old newspaper in his hand, and threw himself on the heathery scrub which met the shingle, within easy hail of the fishermen. There he lay, the picture of free-and-easy, loafing, hand-to-mouth young England, "improving his mind," as he shouted to them, by the perusal of the fortnight-old weekly paper, soiled with the marks of toddy-glasses and tobacco-ashes, the legacy of the last traveller, which he had hunted out from the kitchen of the little hostelry, and, being a youth of a communicative turn of mind, began imparting the contents to the fishermen as he went on:

"What a bother they are making about these wretched corn-laws! Here's three or four columns full of nothing but sliding scales and fixed duties. Hang this tobacco, it's always going out! Ah, here's something better—a splendid match between Kent and England, Brown, Kent winning by three wickets. Felix fifty-six runs without a chance, and not out!"

Tom, intent on a fish which had risen at him twice, answered only with a grunt.

"Anything about the Goodwood?" called out the third man.

"Rory O'More drawn. Butterfly colt amiss," shouted the student.

"Just my luck," grumbled the inquirer, jerking his flies off the water, and throwing again with a heavy, sullen splash, and frightening Tom's fish.

"I say, can't you throw lighter over there? We ain't fishing for grampuses," shouted Tom across the stream.

"Hullo, Brown! here's something for you," called out the reading man next moment. "Why, your old master, Arnold of Rugby, is dead."

Tom's hand stopped half-way in his cast, and his line and flies went all tangling round and round his rod; you might have knocked him over with a feather. Neither of his companions took any notice of him, luckily; and with a violent effort he set to work mechanically to disentangle his line. He felt completely carried off his moral and intellectual legs, as if he had lost his standing-point in the invisible world. Besides which, the deep, loving loyalty which he felt for his old leader made the shock intensely painful. It was the first great wrench of his life, the first gap which the angel Death had made in his circle, and he felt numbed, and beaten down, and spiritless. Well, well! I believe it was good for him and for many others in like case, who had to learn by that loss that the soul of man cannot stand or lean upon any human prop, however strong, and wise, and good; but that He upon whom alone it can stand and lean will knock away all such props in His own wise and merciful way, until there is no ground or stay left but Himself, the Rock of Ages, upon whom alone a sure foundation for every soul of man is laid.

As he wearily laboured at his line, the thought struck him, "It may be all false—a mere newspaper lie." And he strode up to the recumbent smoker.

"Let me look at the paper," said he.

"Nothing else in it," answered the other, handing it

up to him listlessly. "Hullo, Brown! what's the matter, old fellow? Ain't you well?"

"Where is it?" said Tom, turning over the leaves, his hands trembling, and his eyes swimming, so that he could not read.

"What? What are you looking for?" said his friend, jumping up and looking over his shoulder.

"That—about Arnold," said Tom.

"Oh, here," said the other, putting his finger on the paragraph. Tom read it over and over again. There could be no mistake of identity, though the account was short enough.

"Thank you," said he at last, dropping the paper. "I shall go for a walk. Don't you and Herbert wait supper for me." And away he strode, up over the moor at the back of the house, to be alone, and master his grief if possible.

His friend looked after him, sympathizing and wondering, and, knocking the ashes out of his pipe, walked over to Herbert. After a short parley they walked together up to the house.

"I'm afraid that confounded newspaper has spoiled Brown's fun for this trip."

"How odd that he should be so fond of his old master," said Herbert. Yet they also were both public-school men.

The two, however, notwithstanding Tom's prohibition, waited supper for him, and had everything ready when he came back some half an hour afterwards. But he could not join in their cheerful talk, and the party was soon silent, notwithstanding the efforts of all three. One thing only had Tom resolved, and that was, that he couldn't stay in Scotland any longer: he felt an irresistible longing to get to Rugby, and then home, and soon broke it to the others, who had too much tact to oppose.

So by daylight the next morning he was marching through Ross-shire, and in the evening hit the Caledonian Canal, took the next steamer, and travelled as fast as boat and railway could carry him to the Rugby station.

As he walked up to the town, he felt shy and afraid of being seen, and took the back streets—why, he didn't know, but he followed his instinct. At the School-gates he made a dead pause; there was not a soul in the quadrangle—all was lonely, and silent, and sad. So with another effort he strode through the quadrangle, and into the School-house offices.

He found the little matron in her room in deep mourning; shook her hand, tried to talk, and moved nervously about. She was evidently thinking of the same subject as he, but he couldn't begin talking.

" Where shall I find Thomas ? " said he at last, getting desperate.

" In the servants' hall, I think, sir. But won't you take anything ? " said the matron, looking rather disappointed.

" No, thank you," said he, and strode off again to find the old verger, who was sitting in his little den, as of old, puzzling over hieroglyphics.

He looked up through his spectacles as Tom seized his hand and wrung it.

" Ah ! you've heard all about it, sir, I see," said he.

Tom nodded, and then sat down on the shoe-board, while the old man told his tale, and wiped his spectacles, and fairly flowed over with quaint, homely, honest sorrow.

By the time he had done Tom felt much better.

"Where is he buried, Thomas?" said he at last.

"Under the altar in the chapel, sir," answered Thomas. "You'd like to have the key, I dare say?"

"Thank you, Thomas—yes, I should, very much." And the old man fumbled among his bunch, and then got up, as though he would go with him; but after a few steps stopped short, and said, "Perhaps you'd like to go by yourself, sir?"

Tom nodded, and the bunch of keys were handed to him, with an injunction to be sure and lock the door after him, and bring them back before eight o'clock.

He walked quickly through the quadrangle and out into the close. The longing which had been upon him and driven him thus far, like the gad-fly in the Greek legends, giving him no rest in mind or body, seemed all of a sudden not to be satisfied, but to shrivel up and pall. "Why should I go on? It's no use," he thought, and threw himself at full length on the turf, and looked vaguely and listlessly at all the well-known objects. There were a few of the town boys playing cricket, their wicket pitched on the best piece in the middle of the big-side ground—a sin about equal to sacrilege in the eyes of a captain of the eleven. He was very nearly getting up to go and send them off. "Pshaw! they won't remember me. They've more right there than I," he muttered. And the thought that his sceptre had departed, and his mark was wearing out, came home to him for the first time, and bitterly enough. He was lying on the very spot where the fights came off—where he himself had fought six years ago his first and last battle. He conjured up the scene till he could almost hear the shouts of the ring, and East's whisper in his ear; and looking across the close to the Doctor's private door, half expected to see it open, and the tall figure in cap and gown come striding under the elm-trees towards him.

No, no; that sight could never be seen again. There was no flag flying on the round tower; the School-house windows were all shuttered up; and when the flag went up again, and the shutters came down, it would be to welcome a stranger. All that was left on earth of him whom he had honoured was lying cold and still under the chapel floor. He would go in and see the place once more, and then leave it once for all. New men and new methods might do for other people; let those who would, worship the rising star; he, at least, would be faithful to the sun which had set. And so he got up, and walked to the chapel door, and unlocked it, fancying himself the only mourner in all the broad land, and feeding on his own selfish sorrow.

He passed through the vestibule, and then paused for a moment to glance over the empty benches. His heart was still proud and high, and he walked up to the seat which he had last occupied as a sixth-form boy, and sat himself down there to collect his thoughts.

And, truth to tell, they needed collecting and setting in order not a little. The memories of eight years were all dancing through his brain, and carrying him about whither they would; while, beneath them all, his heart was throbbing with the dull sense of a loss that could never be made up to him. The rays of the evening sun came solemnly through the painted windows above his head, and fell in gorgeous colours on the opposite wall, and the perfect stillness soothed his spirit by little and little. And he turned to the pulpit, and looked at it, and then, leaning forward with his head on his hands, groaned aloud. If he could only have seen the Doctor again for one five minutes—have told him all that was in

his heart, what he owed to him, how he loved and rever-
enced him, and would, by God's help, follow his steps
in life and death—he could have borne it all without
a murmur. But that he should have gone away for
ever without knowing it all, was too much to bear.
"But am I sure that he does not know it all?" The
thought made him start. "May he not even now be
near me, in this very chapel? If he be, am I sorrow-
ing as he would have me sorrow, as I should wish to
have sorrowed when I shall meet him again?"

He raised himself up and looked round, and after a
minute rose and walked humbly down to the lowest
bench, and sat down on the very seat which he had
occupied on his first Sunday at Rugby. And then the
old memories rushed back again, but softened and subdued, and soothing him as he let himself be carried
away by them. And he looked up at the great painted
window above the altar, and remembered how, when a
little boy, he used to try not to look through it at the
elm-trees and the rooks, before the painted glass came;
and the subscription for the painted glass, and the letter
he wrote home for money to give to it. And there,
down below, was the very name of the boy who sat on
his right hand on that first day, scratched rudely in the
oak panelling.

And then came the thought of all his old school-
fellows; and form after form of boys nobler, and braver,
and purer than he rose up and seemed to rebuke him.
Could he not think of them, and what they had felt
and were feeling—they who had honoured and loved from
the first the man whom he had taken years to know
and love? Could he not think of those yet dearer to
him who was gone, who bore his name and shared his
blood, and were now without a husband or a father?

Then the grief which he began to share with others became gentle and holy, and he rose up once more, and walked up the steps to the altar, and while the tears flowed freely down his cheeks, knelt down humbly and hopefully, to lay down there his share of a burden which had proved itself too heavy for him to bear in his own strength.

Here let us leave him. Where better could we leave him than at the altar before which he had first caught a glimpse of the glory of his birthright, and felt the drawing of the bond which links all living souls together in one brotherhood—at the grave beneath the altar of him who had opened his eyes to see that glory, and softened his heart till it could feel that bond?

And let us not be hard on him, if at that moment his soul is fuller of the tomb and him who lies there than of the altar and Him of whom it speaks. Such stages have to be gone through, I believe, by all young and brave souls, who must win their way through hero-worship to the worship of Him who is the King and Lord of heroes. For it is only through our mysterious human relationships—through the love and tenderness and purity of mothers and sisters and wives, through the strength and courage and wisdom of fathers and brothers and teachers—that we can come to the knowledge of Him in whom alone the love, and the tenderness, and the purity, and the strength, and the courage, and the wisdom of all these dwell for ever and ever in perfect fullness.

THE END.

Nelson's 1/- Books.

A New Series of Shilling Books, comprising many favourite Copyright Stories, with new Illustrations and novel Cover Design. Each with four Monochrome Illustrations. The books are large and bulky, and wonderful value at the moderate price asked.

Aunt Bell. By Henley I. Arden.

Aunt Martha. By M. and E. Kirby.

Captain Polly. By Sophie Swett.

Jack and his Ostrich. By Eleanor Stredder.

Little Hazel. By the Author of "Little Snowdrop and Her Golden Casket."

The Pirate's Gold. By Gordon Stables, M.D., R.N.

The Young Emigrants. By C. T. Johnstone.

A Toast Fag. By Harold Avery.

Prince Karl. By Morice Gerard.

Rich and Poor. By C. M. Trowbridge.

The Story of the Beacon Fire. By M. E. Clements.

The Swedish Twins. By the Author of "The Babes in the Basket."

Under the Old Oaks. By the Author of "Little Hazel."

Up the Creeks. By Edward Shirley. A Tale of Adventure in West Africa.

T. NELSON AND SONS, London, Edinburgh, Dublin, and New York

Nelson's 9d. Books.

A New Series of Ninepenny Books, with Coloured Frontispiece and Vignette, attractive Cover Design. Comprises many highly popular stories at cheaper prices.

The Seymour Girls. By Mrs. Glasgow. A charming story of three girls' first efforts in housekeeping.

The Basket of Flowers.

Boy Crusaders.

Child of the Mews.

The Giants, and How to Fight Them.

A Lad of Devon.

A Little Candle.

Martha's Home.

One of the Least.

Over the Down.

The Power of Kindness.

Saved by Love.

The Story of a Lost Emerald.

Wee Doggie.

The Wreckers of Sable Island.

Nelson's 6d. Books.

A New Series of Sixpenny Books. With Coloured Frontispiece and Vignette. 96 pages.

The Carpenter's Snuff-Box.

Harry Bertram.

The Pink Sash.

A Story of Trust.

Nelson's 4d. Books.

A New Series of Fourpenny Books. With Two Illustrations. 64 pages.

The One Moss Rose.

Sowing and Reaping.

Wisdom's Ways.

Trust in God.

Faithful Nicolette.

Live to be Useful.

T. NELSON AND SONS, London, Edinburgh, Dublin, and New York.